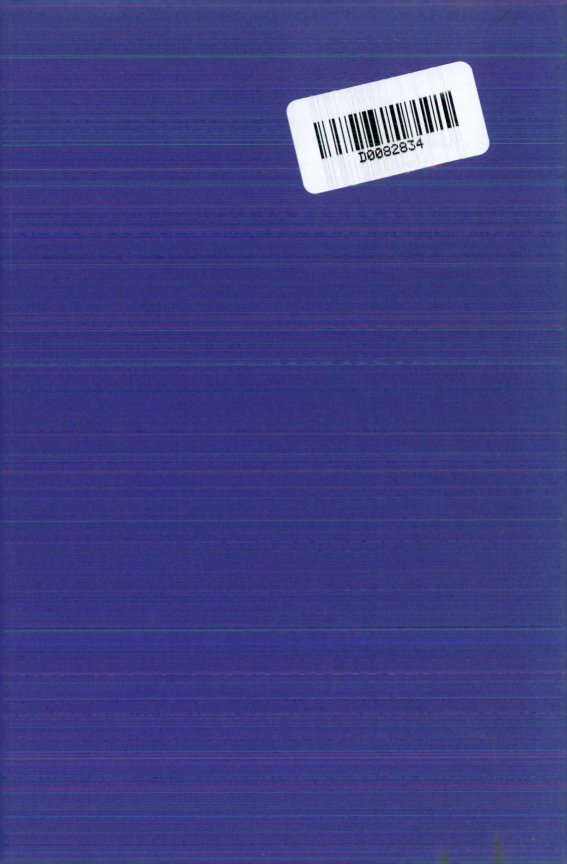

The Text of
Sidney's Arcadian World

Michael McCanles

Duke University Press   Durham and London   1989

© 1989 Duke University Press
All rights reserved
Printed in the United States of America
on acid-free paper ∞
Library of Congress Cataloging-in-Publication Data
McCanles, Michael.
The text of Sidney's arcadian world / Michael McCanles.
p. cm.
Bibliography: p.
Includes index.
ISBN 0-8223-0797-9
1. Sidney, Philip, Sir, 1554–1586. Arcadia.   2. Sidney, Philip, Sir,
1554–1586—Style.   3. Pastoral poetry, English—History and
criticism.   4. Rhetoric—1500–1800.   I. Title.
PR2342.A6M35   1989
823'.5—dc 19   88-26742

Once again for Penny

———————

Contents

———

Acknowledgments

I am grateful to the John Simon Guggenheim Memorial Foundation for a fellowship and to Marquette University for a year's sabbatical during the period in which the first version of this book was written. Parts of this study have appeared in article form: "Oracular Prediction and the Fore-Conceit of Sidney's *Arcadia*," *ELH: English Literary History* 50 (1983): 233–44; "The Rhetoric of Character Portrayal in Sidney's New *Arcadia*," *Criticism* 25, no. 2 (1983): 123–39; and "Reading Description in Sidney's New *Arcadia*: A Differential Analysis," *University of Toronto Quarterly* 53, no. 1 (1983): 36–52.

Introduction

Reading the *Arcadia*

———

Most studies devoted to any of the *Arcadia*'s three versions concern exclusively its intellectual and historical content and background.[1] Such an approach allows the student to pass quickly through the seemingly impermeable rhetorical texture of its discourse to the plane of conceptual and moral content. Having safely arrived there, one need not engage the difficult question of why Sidney deliberately heightened and extended the already dense style of the old *Arcadia* in the still denser new *Arcadia*. Such exclusive concentration on the work's content is perhaps symptomatic of a tacit agreement with critics such as Hazlitt and Virginia Woolf, who have felt no compunction about damning the *Arcadia* for its stucco-work ornamentation. Hazlitt complained that Sidney

> never lets a casual observation pass without perplexing it with an endless running commentary, he never states a feeling without so many *circumambages* [sic], without so many interlineations and parenthetical remarks on all that can be said for it, and anticipations of all that can be said against it, and he never mentions a fact without giving so many circumstances and conjuring up so many things that it is like or not like, that you lose the main clue of the story in its infinite ramifications and intersections.[2]

Virginia Woolf complained of the "unformed babble of sound" the Arcadian style soon becomes and, like Hazlitt, was impatient with prose that always "must be careful to turn away from what is actually before it."[3] In the face of such criticism Sidney's friends cede almost as much as his enemies are willing to take. Would-be defenders like E. M. W. Tillyard, R. W. Zandvoort, and Kenneth Myrick feel compelled to agree with much of the adverse criticism of the Arcadian style in the midst of attempts to deflect it.[4] And in the most serious discussion to date, Richard A. Lanham concludes that there are several Arcadian styles, the convolutions of which are often intended to be humorous.[5] Sidney himself, it would seem, agreed before the fact with his critics in finding much of the Arcadian style ludicrous and reprehensible.

The case of the *Arcadia* was not always so. This is evidenced by the many printings it ran through in the century following Sidney's death. Peter Heylyn in *Microcosmus* (1621) described it as "a book which besides its excellent language, rare contriuances, & delectable stories, hath in it all the straines of *Poesy, comprehendeth the universall art of speaking*."[6] The fact that Thomas Blount's *Academie of Eloquence* (1654) borrowed from John Hoskins's *Directions for Speech and Style*, in which the *Arcadia* was cited predominantly, led Hoyt Hudson to conclude that "Sidney's style was made an example to the generation which grew up after the last sequel was written."[7] Sir William Alexander evidenced his admiration for the *Arcadia* not only in his *Anacrisis* (1634), where he said that it "is the most excellent Work that, in my Judgment, hath been written in any Language that I understand,"[8] but also by composing a narrative to bridge the gap between the unfinished new *Arcadia* and the old *Arcadia* conclusion, in the 1613 reissue of the 1593 edition. And Richard Lovelace felt compelled to open a poem prefacing a translation of Achilles Tatius's romance *Clitophon and Leucippe* with the adjuration that the ladies "awhile lay by / Caelestial *Sydney's Arcady*."[9]

That eighteenth-century readers had nevertheless already come round to the attitude of some of their twentieth-century counterparts is suggested by Mrs. Barbauld's epigram to the effect that Sidney's *Arcadia* is a volume which "all have heard of . . . some few possess, but that nobody reads."[10] Obviously, large shifts of taste in reading and fashions of narrative style have taken place between Sidney's time and our own. The reportorial style of Defoe, Richardson's rhetoric of introspection, Fielding's style of rational common sense and moral judgment, not to mention the host of novelists both English and Continental through the nineteenth and early twentieth centuries who sought narrative methods that reflected faithfully the minutiae of physical and moral reality: all of these currents have added retroactively a thick aura of the exotic and recherché to Sidney's book absent for the first generations of its readers.

In the context of this response to the new *Arcadia* as a verbal artifact, this study takes as one of its main tasks discovering the information necessary to make the new *Arcadia* readable. Readability here does not refer to information about the biographical background of its composition, bibliographical investigations into Sidney's final intentions, the massive intellectual currents and controversies of Sidney's day, nor even the stylistic theories of composition thrust on readers and writers alike in Sidney's time by numerous textbooks and handbooks of rhetorical devices. I will in fact argue that attempts to approach the new *Arcadia* solely through the latter actually make it peculiarly inaccessible. A dominant supposition of rhetorical theory in the sixteenth century is that rhetorical figuration is a deviation from normal or ordinary syntactical and semantic modes of expression. In that perspective, the new *Arcadia* can only appear as it does to some of its modern readers, namely, an obsessive mass of rhetorical encrustation layered heavily over a plain tale.

By readability I mean the rules that govern the syntactic, semantic, and rhetorical dimensions of Sidney's text, which the reader must discover for himself in order to parse the verbal texture that mediates the *Arcadia*'s human and physical realities. Far from being an extrinsic layer of ornamentation obscuring a direct account of human actions, thoughts, motivations, and scenes, the rhetorical dimension of Sidney's text embodies its meaning. The meaning of this meaning is that the Arcadian world contains no reality that is not rhetorically structured. Sidney does not force rhetorical figuration on his characters; rather, in existing nowhere outside of the rhetorical figuration in which they constitute themselves, Sidney's characters force rhetoric on him.

In addition to its style, the *Arcadia* raises two other obstacles for the reader. The first lies in identifying which text is the "true" *Arcadia*. There are in fact three versions of the *Arcadia* to choose from:

(1) The old *Arcadia*, composed in 1580,[11] circulated in numerous manuscripts, but never published until 1912, when Albert Feuillerat brought out his four-volume edition of Sidney's prose works.

(2) The new *Arcadia*, an essentially recomposed work that retains much of the plot of the first two books of the old *Arcadia* but adds numerous characters and subplots, including a wholly new Book 3, and which breaks off in midsentence in this latter book. This work was published under Fulke Greville's editorship in 1590.[12]

(3) A composite new *Arcadia*, edited by Mary Herbert, Sidney's sister the Countess of Pembroke, which is made up of two parts: (*a*) the 1590 new *Arcadia* and (*b*) the last three books of the old *Arcadia* significantly revised in order to make them conform to changes in the 1590 edition.[13]

The old *Arcadia* of 1580 is a complete and finished production. It presents a relatively simple story involving Basilius the duke of Arcadia, his wife Gynecia, his two daughters Pamela and Philoclea, and the two heroes who woo these daughters, respectively, Musidorus and Pyrocles. Basilius ensconces himself and his family in the forests of Arcadia in order to escape dire consequences of love predicted by the Delphic oracle. Sidney pursues the adventures of these six characters through complicated and sometimes comical love intrigues, to a point where Basilius drinks a sleeping potion and is declared dead. The king of Macedonia, Euarchus, father of Pyrocles and uncle of Musidorus, arrives by chance in Arcadia to try both heroes and Gynecia for various crimes. In the end the execution of the guilty is aborted at the last minute by Basilius's revival, followed by general reconciliations all round, and the marriage of the two princesses and the two heroes.

For reasons that will be explored in this study, Sidney became dissatisfied with his first production and set about writing a radically different kind of work. This was the new *Arcadia* of 1590, which was left incomplete when Sidney went to the Netherlands as governor of Flushing, where he died in 1586 of a wound received at the battle of Zutphen. As far as these facts lead us, there would seem to be no problem in deciding which text embodies Sidney's final intentions. The first two books of the new *Arcadia* include most of the corresponding books of the old, as well as numerous new characters in subplots that precede the two heroes' arrival in Arcadia. The third book of the new *Arcadia* deals with material wholly new: the imprisonment of Pamela, Philoclea, and Pyrocles—still disguised as the amazon Zelmane—in the castle of Basilius's evil sister-in-law Cecropia; the love of Cecropia's son Amphialus for Philoclea; and the various vicissitudes suffered by the main characters inside and outside the castle during the siege. This book breaks off during the fight between Pyrocles and Anaxius, and there is no indication of how this large episode was to lead back to the material given in the last three books, 3 through 5, of the old *Arcadia*.

That the new *Arcadia* was to conclude with the old *Arcadia* ending was evidently the conviction of Sidney's sister when she spliced the last three books of the old onto the incomplete Book 3 of the new in the 1593 version. And every reader since, beginning with the countess's secretary Hugh Sanford in his preface to the 1593 version, has recognized that this conjunction is unsatisfactory. For reasons which, depending on the scholar, are partly bibliographical and partly aesthetic, the balance of present opinion is that (1) the erotic intrigue comedy of the old *Arcadia*'s last three books jars dissonantly against the thematic and characterological density of the new *Arcadia* Book 3, and (2) Sidney did not in fact intend to draw on the latter in concluding his second production.[14]

Nevertheless, the 1590 new *Arcadia* contains numerous plot elements that foreshadow the old *Arcadia* ending. The central question is whether these indicators justify our taking the 1593 composite *Arcadia* as Sidney's final version, however imperfect. I shall argue that the oracular predictions from which Basilius flees in both old and new *Arcadia*s play a decisive part in making this decision. These predictions in fact register the "fore-conceit" of the plot and in this conform exactly to Sidney's own conceptions of fore-conceit in *A Defence of Poetry*.[15] Though changed in some details to match the alterations in the new *Arcadia* main plot, the texts of the original predictions in both old and new *Arcadia*s are substantially the same, so that the oracle predicts a conclusion to the new *Arcadia* that is the same as that which rounds off the old *Arcadia*. In addition, there are several indications in the 1590 version that right up to the point where he left off composition Sidney undeviatingly retained this plan. I shall argue, then, that the 1593 composite *Arcadia* represents both in general and in many details Sidney's final intentions.[16]

For many readers and critics, however, if one grants this to be the case, there still remains the aesthetic problem of reading the composite *Arcadia*. By the time one reaches the enormous suffering and tragedy undergone by both major and minor characters in the new *Arcadia* Book 3, reversion to the comical intrigues of the old *Arcadia* seems to entail too great a shift of focus, value, and tone. That his revision entails such a decisive shift one can hardly deny. But whether or not it represents a major failure in Sidney's plan, so much so as to deny some measure of authenticity to the 1593 composite version, is intimately related to the third major obstacle I referred to above: the question of generic decorum. This is so much the case that I consider in Part Two the *Arcadia*'s generic dimension together with the matter of its final form.

If readers perceive an incompatibility in the conclusion of the old *Arcadia* tacked onto the 1590 new *Arcadia* in the 1593 composite version, it is important to note that this "incompatibility" is present throughout the 1590 text itself, which exhibits Sidney's planning from the first just such a mixture of erotic intrigue (from the old *Arcadia*) and greatly expanded epic subject matter. Complaints about the aesthetic indecorum of the composite *Arcadia* must in justice apply to the new *Arcadia* as well. My argument will be that one's stand on the matters of final text and plot implies a stand likewise on the nature, function, and significance of the mixed genres in the new *Arcadia*. The two questions can, ultimately, only be resolved together. I shall argue in Part Two that answering the central questions of Sidney's final version and the plot thereof rests on discovering the architectonic and thematic function of the new *Arcadia*'s generic components.

The way in which the genre question has often been raised, however, does not work to illuminate this reciprocity. The question usually asked is "What kind of work is the *Arcadia*?" and it is usually answered by concluding that Sidney attempted a mixed generic form, such as Guarini's *Il Pastor Fido*, which stirred up critical controversy about the violation of precise generic distinctions. From this view-point Sidney is seen attempting to harmonize various generic modes: pastoral, romance, epic, Terentian comedy, Petrarchan love lyric, to name only the most salient types.[17]

As a result, the question of genre has been identified with the quest for the *Arcadia*'s sources. Having distinguished these two problems, A. C. Hamilton points out that Sidney's debt to particular episodes from Heliodorus's *Aethiopian History*, *Amadis of Gaul*, Sannazaro's *Arcadia*, Montemayor's *Diana*, and other works is less relevant to Sidney's meaning than "the 'imitative patterns'" these works provided: "In yoking such heterogenous matter without violence, Sidney displays a more than metaphysical wit in shaping the '*Idea* or fore-conceit' of his work. The *Arcadia* is European in its origins: truly a work of comparative literature, the first in English prose."[18] My own approach to the genre question extends Hamilton's observation. The generic materials constituting the *Arcadia* focuses the reader's attention less on the kind of work it is than on the thematic significance of their joint presence within it. The central question is not so much which mixed generic models Sidney might have followed,[19] as rather what Sidney is saying about the nature of generic distinctions themselves, the contents and value systems of various genres, and the thematic consequences of joining several together. Rosalie L. Colie has argued persuasively that the practical use of generic forms in Renaissance literature went far beyond observance of various decorums regarding subject matter, diction, and theme prescribed by contemporary genre theory. Genres became themselves metaphorical "abbreviations for a 'set' on the world, as definitions of manageable boundaries."[20] As such, the generic form of a work—and this holds particularly for works like the *Arcadia* where several genres are juxtaposed—becomes itself a vehicle of meaning, a complex sign conveying its own range of values and judgments. Pursuing a line parallel to Colie's, Stephen J. Greenblatt sees the *Arcadia* exemplifying

a literature which, by exploring the problematics of literary conventions, can call into question the nature of ethical judgment. By shifting generic perspectives, Sidney exposes the limitations of modes of conduct and versions of reality. . . . the mixed mode exposes the instability and uncertainty of human judgment. . . . It forces the reader to call into the open and examine consciously those standards by which he judges experience.[21]

Sidney recomposed the old *Arcadia* to call into question some central, traditionally defined differentials for categorizing human experience: the active life versus the retired life, and the irascible faculty that spurs men on to the pursuit of honor versus the concupiscible faculty that delivers men over to eros. These differentials underlie other major Renaissance epics, including *Orlando Furioso* and *Jerusalem Delivered*, as well as a large portion of *The Faerie Queene*. We can also find them embedded in Shakespeare's *Antony and Cleopatra* and the *Henry IV* plays, where Falstaff's commitment to the flesh is played off against the heroic agenda chosen by Hotspur, and ultimately by Prince Hal himself.[22] The problem of uniting Mars and Venus, already thematized in paintings and emblems in the Renaissance,[23] is likewise Sidney's problem. And as Arthur Amos has perceived, this problem was nothing less than how to reconcile eros and civilization.[24] These differentials determine not only the inner conflicts experienced by Musidorus and Pyrocles when they abandon their heroic pursuits after entering Arcadia and becoming entangled in the coils of eros. They also govern the deliberate generic juxtapositions that Sidney created in the new *Arcadia* and which decisively set it apart from the limited concerns of the old *Arcadia*. Pyrocles and Musidorus find themselves compelled by their newly found loves to take on the roles of impassioned pastoral swains and to relinquish the heroic roles imposed by the rules of the epic romance genre reflected in the retrospective narratives added in the new *Arcadia*.[25] In this connection we discover that the fusion of heroic and pastoral genres in the later work becomes itself a vehicle of meaning.

Readers who find indecorous Sidney's apparent plan to conclude the new *Arcadia* with the old *Arcadia* ending in fact resist the large, all-controlling fore-conceit that governs his recomposition of the later work. Sidney shows himself quite aware of just this indecorum in juxtaposing the competing meanings and values of epic and pastoral, heroism and love making. The new *Arcadia* conveys essentially this message: attempts to enforce a mutual exclusion between the polar terms of such differentials as public life/private life, action/contemplation, heroism/eroticism—attempts to choose one term and exclude the other—only make inevitable Freud's "return of the repressed": the unexpected confrontation with those terms which have been rejected. And it is this confrontation, and the resolutions this confrontation brings about, that Sidney recomposed the *Arcadia* to highlight.

This study focuses on the three dimensions of the new *Arcadia* that I have already sketched in a prefatory manner: the work's style is discussed in Part One, its plot and genre in Part Two. I will show that each dimension puts the same question: how to achieve a harmonious reciprocity between the competing poles of the central differentials that govern the work as a whole. The plot unfolds these differentials where the fates of the two epic heroes and of the befuddled old king interface with each other. Musidorus and Pyrocles must confront the eros of the pastoral world as compensation for their exclusive dedication to the heroic life, while Basilius confronts the political and military conspiracy resulting from his attempt to escape in the pastoral life the fore-conceit of his own life foretold him by the oracle at Delphos. These confrontations are reflected in the mutually exclusive imperatives prescribed by the epic and pastoral genres. All three men fall desperately in love and must adapt to the roles their passions force upon them, roles strange to them and against which they are therefore all the more defenseless.

Finally, these generalizations inform perhaps most obviously the stylistic dimension of many specific passages. I refer to the stylistic practice that decisively distinguishes the new *Arcadia* from its predecessor: passages of description, dialogue, thought, and ethical analysis rendered in rhetorical patterns of antithesis. Many of the additions to and revisions of passages from the old *Arcadia* are structured in differential form. The evidence for this claim has already been brought forward by many students of the work, from Zandvoort down to the present day. Though Hazlitt thoroughly execrated such rhetorical schemes, he nevertheless correctly perceived that they act to mediate "interlineations and parenthetical remarks on all that can be said for [an emotion], and anticipations of all that can be said against." Whether in fact the Arcadian style conjures "up so many things that it is like or not like that you lose the main clue of the story," it is certainly true that the 1590 new *Arcadia* is intentionally dense with "infinite ramifications and intersections." What has uniformly been missed by Hazlitt and many others, however, is the full thematic significance of these putatively merely "stylistic" and "rhetorical" complications. I am not speaking here of those few critics who find the Arcadian style appropriate to the complexity of the work's plot situations. It is certainly true that in the *Arcadia* "substance molds the form; the event itself containing contradictory elements which express themselves in verbal opposition."[26] Such an argument is, however, not sufficient to overcome the more widely held criticism, typified by Ian Watt's comment, that the "rhetorical adornments" of the *Arcadia* "detract from the physical reality of the action itself."[27] If it is also true, as Watt goes on to say, that the style is "a finer expression of reality as [Sidney's readers] conceived it than any realistic description could be," something more than a general decorum matching style to subject needs to be uncovered.

The single most important obstacle for the modern reader is the assumption that the rhetorical figuration in the *Arcadia* is what Renaissance rhetoric called schemes of words. Such schemes, as George Puttenham describes them, are "ornaments" that are intended "to satisfie & delight th'eare onely by a goodly outward shew set vpon the matter with wordes, and speaches smothly and tunably running."[28] Conceived this way, the Arcadian style can only appear a heavy veil of highly formalized patterns that do two things: (1) deviate from a hypothetical norm of ordinary speech, and (2) obscure a described reality—character portrayal, expression of feeling, a physical scene—that might have more effectively been presented in a style conforming to this norm of ordinary speech. These two conclusions, though normally tacit in the *Arcadia* literature, usually go together. Sidney's style is thus convicted of a double sin: the obscuring of the story he wants to tell through a style that deviates from another, less figured style that would in fact illumine this story.

It is this double charge that I address in Part One of this study. I shall show that the Arcadian style in fact conforms to the Renaissance notion of rhetorical figuration as figures of thought. Figures of thought, to cite Puttenham again, convey the "sence of such wordes

& speaches inwardly working a stirre to the mynde."[29] This means, at least as regards the style of the new *Arcadia*, that the style invites the reader to discover the complex interaction among the elements of a figure, and more importantly to formulate for himself and herself the logical rules of antithesis and parallelism that govern it. In this respect, the "meaning" of a figure is discovered not in the "normal," nonfigured language of paraphrase into which the figure invites translation, but in the interplay of meanings evoked by the figure itself. In other words, Sidney requires the reader to find the meaning of his figured prose by uncovering the metatextual rules that the text posits for itself. The meaning of Sidney's rhetorical figuration lies wholly within the figures themselves.

This also means that whatever reality such figuration putatively mediates likewise lies nowhere else save in this figuration. Far from veiling behind its artificial style a fictive world of "real" characters and actions, the new *Arcadia* gives us a world in which both characters and actions are structured rhetorically, and what is not structured rhetorically is not there. A basic argument of this study is that in the fictive world of the new *Arcadia* all realities, both human and natural, are structured according to the resources of verbal figuration. Consequently, a more appropriate reading of the new *Arcadia* neatly reverses the standard method, which envisions text reflecting an extratextual reality which it mediates to the reader.

Such a reading would be appropriate to the old *Arcadia*, in which a consciously chatty narrator addresses a female audience in a narrative text that distances at once narrator, audience, and text from the characters and actions of the story. Here story and discourse[30] are ostensibly distinguishable ("I might entertain you, fair ladies, a great while, if I should make as many interruptions in the repeating [a poem Cleophila sings] as she did in the singing"),[31] and the styles of the narrative text are easily assignable to the Sidneyan narrator. The new *Arcadia*, however, radically alters the relations between its narrative texts and the characters' attitudes and actions, which these narratives recount. For one thing, Sidney assigns many of his stories —material mostly new in the new *Arcadia*—to the characters themselves. This has the effect of bringing a narrator's own psychological and ethical perspective into the reader's purview.

A more significant effect of this redistribution, however, is to fuse texts delivered by a third-person narrator with the texts assignable to the characters themselves in the story being narrated. Narrative becomes now a form of free indirect discourse, in which the narrator tells the story of certain characters in the very text—dominated by one or more set of rhetorical figures—in which these characters might have told their own stories. Since Sidney in the new *Arcadia* renders intelligible the actions of his characters by detailing the psychological and ethical structures that constitute them, he requires a narrative mode that makes these explicit. Unlike post-Renaissance narrative techniques, which overtly distinguish the narrator's own external perspective from revelations of a character's inner life, Sidney fuses both viewpoints in a single narrative text. In this way he manages to tell his characters' stories "from the inside," as it were, rendering identical the narrative text and the text of the human reality it tells of. The rhetorical figures that constitute Sidney's narrative texts constitute likewise the thoughts and actions of the characters whose stories these texts narrate. What the reader sees is, quite simply, what he or she gets. And what each gets is a fictive world the varying structures of which are all articulated in a style dominated by figures of antithesis and parallelism. Reading the new *Arcadia* thus means recuperating on the three levels of style, plot, and genre a set of rules that govern the arrangement of elements in such figures.[32]

In Part One I take up specific passages drawn mainly from the material which originates in the new *Arcadia*, that is, material which does not occur in the old *Arcadia*. These passages concern character analysis and scenic description which without exception exploit the resources of antithetical figuration. In this first part I will show that for Sidney both human and natural reality is constituted as a holistic yet dynamic interplay of multiple elements all related among themselves through patterns of mutual opposition and reciprocity. My main concern in this regard will be with the characters of the various subplots added in the new *Arcadia*, as well as characters in the main plot, namely, Pamela, Philoclea, and Gynecia.

Part Two takes up the related matters of plot and genre. Regarding the first, I shall discuss the paradoxical text of the oracular prediction, and Basilius's reactions to it. In this connection, I will show that the rules of differential relation, first discussed regarding specific passages of analysis and description in Part One, likewise apply to the main plot. It will appear that the plot is governed by a fore-conceit which is the oracular prediction itself, and which foretells that the various paradoxical events will in fact occur. It will also become apparent that the motivating force of the main plot is nothing other than Basilius's attempts to evade these predictions, evasions which succeed only in bringing the predicted events about. Consequently, the plot raises an issue structurally parallel to the ethical and psychological dialectics I discuss in Part One: the relation between free will and determinism.

The remainder of Part Two will discuss the two main heroes, Musidorus and Pyrocles. Here I am mainly concerned with the new *Arcadia*'s striking fusion of multiple genres and generic conventions. I will show, first, that Musidorus and Pyrocles as characters, like those discussed in Part One, are structured wholly according to the resources of rhetorical figuration featuring dialectical antitheses. This means that both as Sidney-the-narrator textualizes them, and as they textualize themselves in their various speeches and retrospective narratives, the two heroes have no reality save that conferred by the rhetorical figures consistent with the literary genres whose roles they successively take on. If one is to ask exactly who and what Pyrocles and Musidorus are, the answer can only be that they are the various roles, first heroic, then pastoral and Petrarchan, which they enact.

I discuss the two heroes in tandem with the matter of mixed genres in the new *Arcadia*, because it is mainly through Sidney's presentation of the heroes that he broaches the generic question for the reader. The problem of resolving the putative traditional conflict between the active and contemplative lives, between the imperatives of heroism and those of eros, is registered in the new *Arcadia* mainly as the problem of bringing into resolution the two opposed genres of epic romance and pastoral, in which these two modes of existence have traditionally been given literary form. Here also, in keeping with the pattern already displayed at the levels of style and plot, Sidney poses matters in terms of mutual oppositions and reciprocities.

The key to reading the new *Arcadia*, then, lies in discovering the logic of opposition and resolution that informs the work on all three of these levels. This logic consists of dialectical rules governing how human characters and actions are textualized according to the human resources of rhetorical figuration. What the fictive world of the new *Arcadia* is, is what the characters in that world make it. And what they make it is wholly subsumed in the texts they are capable of uttering and enacting. In this respect the style of the work, its plots and the genres it employs and exploits, are all presented to the reader as human modes of creating the self and world, outside of which there is neither self nor world. Sidney acknowledges his large debt to Renaissance humanism in the radical degree to which he finds the central ethical and political issues facing humankind intimately controlled by the verbal texts in which these issues are formulated. Consequently, it is arguable that the Arcadian style is in fact the most "realistic" imaginable. In exhibiting the fictive world of *Arcadia* as rhetorically structured, Sidney does nothing else than present that world exactly as it is.

Part One

The Meaning in the Style

$\mathbb{A}$ highly figured style such as that
of the *Arcadia* requires the reader to recognize first of all the fact of
figuration itself. This means that structures of meaning, syntax, and
sound call attention to themselves as consistently patterned. There
is, however, something circular about such recognition, because it
implies that the figured style deviates from another possible kind
of style, one nonfigured and nonpatterned. But if, as some modern stylisticians have shown, there is no such thing as a nonfigured
style, and that even the most laconic and economic expository style
exhibits figures that register these qualities, isolating a specifically
figured style becomes problematic. Such a recognition seems both to
imply and call into question a "deviationist" notion of style, such
as was dominant in Renaissance conceptions of rhetorical figuration,
and which up to the present still occur in some definitions of style in
general and of particular styles.[1]

When Abraham Fraunce in *The Arcadian Rhetorike* (1588) says that
"a figure is a certeine decking of speach, whereby the vsual and
simple fashion thereof is altered and changed to that which is more
elegant and conceipted";[2] or George Puttenham says that the figured style "may delight and allure as well the mynde as the eare of
the hearers with a certaine noueltie and strange maner of conuey-
ance, disguising it no litle from the ordinary and accustomed,"[3] both
make a common Renaissance assumption about what defines a spe-

cific style. Quintilian distinguished between a notion of figuration by which any discourse is figured and one that refers to particular figuration that calls attention to itself, involving a notion of style as deviation from "ordinary" language:

> We must interpret *schema* [i.e., "a rational change in meaning or language from the ordinary and simple form" (p. 353)] in the sense of that which is poetically or rhetorically altered from the simple and obvious method of expression. It will then be true to distinguish between the style which is devoid of figures and that which is adorned with figures.[4]

I shall take up in greater detail this anomaly in the concluding section of Part One, once I have investigated the specific information about the Arcadian style Sidney calls the reader to discover and articulate. The most important point I shall make in this connection is that Sidney does not adhere to a deviationist theory of style and in this respect deviates himself decisively from commonly accepted Renaissance rhetorical theory.

I raise this question initially, however, in order to distinguish the kinds of information which the Arcadian style elicits regarding itself. The reader may pursue two different ways of recuperating meaning. On the one hand, he can read the Arcadian style in a deviationist manner, seeking to translate a given passage back into "normal" speech in order to discover what it says. In this respect, the reader recuperates the passage by rewriting it according to the rhetorical resources at hand. The numerous monographs on the *Arcadia* I have cited and will be citing throughout generally approach the work in this way. That is, the meaning of a passage is discovered by attempting to assimilate it back to still other texts—religious, philosophical, literary—more or less contemporary with Sidney, in which the meaning of the Arcadian passage is assumed to be more intelligibly rendered. In this respect the program of historicist approaches to the *Arcadia* dovetails harmoniously with a deviationist reading of its style.[5]

On the other hand, the reader may pursue still another path in recuperating a specific passage. In a fashion partly like that required by a Ramistic analysis of a text,[6] the reader may begin by leaving the passage just as it is, in all its densely figurative glory, and proceed to construct another but different kind of text alongside the original. This second text is not a paraphrase that recuperates meaning in another form, but is instead metatextual. It concerns all the information of a semantic and logical nature that is necessary to discover the rationale underlying the specific antitheses and parallelism in the text itself. Instead of rewriting the passage as another, nonfigured text, such a reading recuperates the text by discovering how and why it is written precisely as it is written. Such passages present themselves as sets of highly compressed relations among words, phrases, and clauses, and the reader is required to discover a deep structure of logical and semantic rules that are usually only tacitly assumed and implied by the passage itself.

These passages are truly figures of thought, because they "stir the mind" in Puttenham's phrase to search out, articulate, and unfold the logical ligatures that are enfolded (literally implicit) within the passage itself. Making "sense" of such passages means not interpreting it to find out what it means, but rather discovering the dialectical rules that govern its structure. Ultimately, of course, the reader pursuing this path pursues meaning as well, since this kind of metatextual recuperation constitutes a large part of the meaning that Sidney wishes to convey in a specific passage. By refusing to by-pass the figuration of the new *Arcadia*'s style and excavating instead the dialectics that underpin the figures that constitute it, the reader comes ultimately to what the passage means. Since the dialectical rules governing the rhetorical structure of the Arcadian style govern likewise the moral, intellectual, and emotional lives of the characters in the Arcadian world, the dialectical logic of the texts' figures determines the meaning of the Arcadian world itself. Dialectical structures on the stylistic level parallel and reinforce the global dialectic between epic and pastoral that informs the work at large. Since the majority of passages featuring rhetorical schemes of antithesis and parallelism were added in the new *Arcadia*, it is reasonable to conclude that Sidney intended these to highlight such structures as part of his overall plan for recomposing his earlier work.

The arrangement of Part One will begin with set descriptions of physical scenes and characters, and proceed through passages of increasing complexity to narratives of whole episodes. Physical scenes are either static or moving. Descriptions of specific characters fall generally into the same two categories, although here more taxonomic flexibility is required. Portrayal of specific characters may be limited only to unfolding their inner moral and psychological dynamics, or such portrayals may be supplemented by descriptions of their actions, wherein actions become indices of character. A third group includes interactions among two or more characters, in which character description is embedded. Further, such interactions may develop into a complete episode, or even a series of episodes; and this development constitutes a fourth distinguishable group of passages. What follows takes up these four configurations in the indicated order.

Section 1

Descriptions of physical scenes:
The first shipwreck; Kalander's house and garden;
the equestrian Musidorus

One passage of description that is well known in the new *Arcadia* portrays the burning ship from which Pyrocles and Musidorus escape at the beginning of the story:

> . . . a ship, or rather the carcass of the ship, or rather some few bones of the carcass, hulling there, part broken, part burned, part drowned—death having used more than one dart to that destruction. About it floated great store of very rich things, and many chests which might promise no less. And amidst the precious things were a number of dead bodies which likewise did not only testify both elements' violence, but that the chief violence was grown of human inhumanity, for their bodies were full of grisly wounds, and their blood had, as it were, filled the wrinkles of the sea's visage, which, it seemed, the sea would not wash away, that it might witness it is not always his fault when we condemn his cruelty: in sum, a defeat where the conquered kept both field and spoil, a shipwrack without storm or ill-footing, and a waste of fire in the midst of water. (p. 7)[7]

First, we have the *gradatio* of "a ship, or rather the carcass of the ship, or rather some few bones of the carcass." This passage does two things at once: (1) it repeats sequentially the three stages of the ship's destruction, from whole vessel to dead vessel to disintegrated vessel; (2) this sequence reverses the order of perception, putting last what the eye would presumably see first: the "few bones of the carcass." To understand what he is seeing, the beholder must reconstruct backward from his perception, going from the bones to the carcass to the ship itself. The sequence of this passage replicates at once the progressive destruction of the ship and the reconstruction of the ship made in the viewer's mind in order to envision the implied simile comparing the gradual disintegration of the ship's hull to that of a corpse. The wreckage is thus not as static site but is organized according to causal, temporal, and metaphorical categories. To grasp what one sees here, one must first recover the various sequences and categories of statement that make what one sees intelligible.

The next part is a careful division of the ship's "bones": "part broken, part burned, part drowned." This catalogue putatively exhausts the types of destruction to be found in the wreck and traces backward the three forms of destruction that the narrative will later make overt: first by collision, then by fire, and finally by water. The efficiency of death in using his "darts" replicates the narrator's attempt to exhaust all the possible ways the ship could have been destroyed. It is typical of Sidney's descriptive practice in the new *Arcadia* that he tends toward just such exhaustion, toward making explicit and filling out the limits and boundaries of the description. There is no chiaroscuro in his descriptions, nothing only tacitly implied. Everything that is to appear in a description is verbalized and schematized, and what is not so rendered is not there.

The elaboration of the dead bodies—killed by fire, water, and themselves—continues the attempt to exhaust possibilities. Not only have men killed one another, but it is specifically noted that the sea was not totally responsible. That is, the reader is asked to pair off differentially natural versus human causes of death and to note accordingly that "human inhumanity" accounted for a preponderant number of the deaths, as distinct from the (unstated but implied) category of "natural inhumanity," that is, "the elements' violence."

The passage winds down to a paradox typical of the new *Arcadia*, by which the conquered are also the conquerors, since they "kept both field and spoil." And the shipwreck results ultimately not from natural causes ("without storm or ill-footing") but from the attacks of men upon men, attacks of self upon self repeated throughout the various plots of the new *Arcadia*, mirrored in this coalescence of opposites: "a waste of fire in the midst of water."

The scene is carefully schematized and becomes visible through the schema. The visual imagination's grasp of the physical parts of the scene cannot be divorced from the mind's perception of the logical relations of classification, and cause and effect. No element is noted that does not have a differential relation to some other part, of either a binary or ternary sort. We have, in other words, a totalized visual field in which everything that is visible is related to something else and comes into view specifically as filling out and exhausting these relations. Furthermore, categories of evaluation, whether monetary or ethical, likewise contribute to the scene's articulation, facilitating still other perceptual distinctions.[8]

Another descriptive passage evokes similar though not so complicated recognitions on the reader's part: the garden and orchard behind Kalander's house:

> The backside of the house was neither field, garden, nor orchard
> —or rather it was both field, garden, and orchard—for as soon as
> the descending of the stairs had delivered them down, they came
> into a place cunningly set with trees of the most taste-pleasing
> fruits; but scarcely they had taken that into their consideration but
> that they were suddenly stepped into a delicate green, of each side
> of the green a thicket bend, behind the thickets again new beds
> of flowers, which being under the trees, the trees were to them a
> pavilion, and they to the trees, a mosaical floor, so that it seemed
> that art therein would needs be delightful by counterfeiting his
> enemy, error, and making order in confusion. (p. 14)

The mix of thicket, flowers, and trees creates a small crisis in the text. What exactly can one call this area, where the features that distinguish field, garden, and orchard are all present so as to call for separate names and yet to cancel the demarcations drawn by these names? Kalander's garden is neither garden, field, nor orchard; and yet it is all three. The reader is invited to share in the precipitancy with which the stroller moves from one area to the next: "as soon as the descending of the stairs had delivered them down," "but scarcely they had taken that into their consideration but that they were suddenly stepped into a delicate green," "behind the thickets again new beds of flowers, which being under the trees." The text describes a perambulation that unfolds literally as a sequence of discursive segments in which the mutual exclusions separating field, garden, and orchard swiftly appear, disappear, and reappear again. The text which guides the reader's observation of this stroll can only unfold circularly the paradoxical linkage between the "neither" and the "both" of the passage's opening, which he must untangle on the metadiscursive level. In doing so he finds Kalander's garden a visual oxymoron that invites the viewer to textualize itself in just the fashion illustrated by the passage at hand. To move through the juxtaposed areas in this garden is to replicate the unfolding of a text in which the distinct names for these areas a swiftly affirmed, canceled, and then reinstated. And one can only suppose that the delight intended by this arrangement could have been nothing else than this paradoxical textualization, this frisson of delight as the stroller reaches a crisis in his own discourse and begins to wonder at each step what to call where he is at. Sidney has given us here not so much a description of Kalander's garden as a literal reproduction of the discourse through which the astonished stroller articulates for himself the piquant affirmations and denials he must deny and affirm, the boundaries he must draw in transgressing and must obliterate in drawing.[9]

A similar interplay between difference and identity occurs a little later on: "a naked Venus of white marble wherein the graver had used such cunning that the natural blue veins of the marble were framed in fit places to set forth the beautiful blue veins of her body." Here, the pun on "veins" is only the beginning of the play evoked in the reader's mind around what would have been called thirty years ago, had it occurred in Donne's poetry, a metaphysical conceit. The veins of the marble and the veins of the naked Venus intersect semantically and visually at a point where they become both. If the marmoreal medium freezes female nakedness into stone, it emanci-

21

pates it again by conferring warm blood on a figure merely pausing between movements. Once again, the discourse does not so much refer beyond itself to a nonverbal reality as replicate literally the text of the discourse in which the viewer announces to himself the swift glide of his mental glance from stone to flesh and back again. One is asked to hang fire in marveling at which is more gracefully fortuitous: the fusion of veins and veins or their sundering.[10]

A third passage, this time describing Kalander's house, exhibits physical description shading off into a mapping of the inner ethical world of its owner:

> Kalander knew that provision is the foundation of hospitality, and thrift the fuel of magnificence. The house itself was built of fair and strong stone, not affecting so much any extraordinary kind of fineness as an honourable representing of a firm stateliness; the lights, doors, and stairs rather directed to the use of the guest than to the eye of the artificer, and yet, as the one chiefly heeded, so the other not neglected; each place handsome without curiosity and homely without loathsomeness, not so dainty as not to be trode on, nor yet slubbered up with good fellowship—all more lasting than beautiful (but that the consideration of the exceeding lastingness made the eye believe it was exceeding beautiful). . . . (p. 12)

The careful balances of the house reflect the balances within its owner. The opening sentence plays "provision" off against "thrift," as well as "hospitality" against "magnificence." All four terms contain the potential for an unwholesome extreme: the devotion to thrift might possibly lead to stinting provision, which in turn would limit hospitality. At the other extreme, excess of provision for magnificence of show would in turn sin against thrift. And again, hospitality—the warmth of reception shown to guests—might very well be destroyed by the desire for magnificence—the desire to impress and awe rather than to welcome. We have instead a term of possible excess (provision) indicated as the source of a lesser show (hospitality), while in reverse we have a term of possible deficiency (thrift) indicated as a source of greater show (magnificence).

Clearly, Sidney is attempting to work out the actual balances of Kalander's household in both inner resources and outward appearance by exhibiting the complex counterforces that could send any one of these four terms off into malign extremes. The balances the text strikes are very much a dialectical function of the possible extremes they avoid. In order to see what Sidney is saying here, the reader must set up for himself the differential pairs the passage plays across: thrift/provision and hospitality/magnificence. The first two terms are related respectively as "deficient" and "sufficient," while the second two are related as "sufficient" and "excessive." When, then, Sidney makes one sufficiency the cause of the other ("provision is the foundation of hospitality") and the deficient the cause of the excessive ("thrift [is] the fuel of magnificence"), only then do we begin to realize the multiple potentialities both desirable and undesirable among which Kalander is compelled to make his choices. The paradox of thrift causing magnificence becomes intelligible only after we recognize that magnificence requires husbanding one's resources, so that thrift is in fact provision and magnificence only such when it is hospitality. Distinctions have become equivalences without ceasing to be distinctions.

Continuing, we discover that the house "affects" not so much "fineness" as "firm stateliness." This pair extends the magnificence/hospitality differential to the assertion that the house's layout is "rather directed to the use of the guest than to the eye of the artificer." The balance is struck with "and yet," when the peculiar beauties (as distinct from usefulness) of the house are introduced, also carefully defined against their possible excesses: "handsome without curiosity, and homely without loathsomeness." It is a house, as the concluding pairs of terms indicate, both beautiful and useful, and its "lastingness" in service of its usefulness becomes one of its beauties.

It is not difficult to see that Sidney depends on the reader's familiarity with the *dulce/utile* topos, which conveniently for his own purposes is traditionally framed as a differential pair. Recognizing the relevance of this topos to the passage, however, will bring the reader only partway toward understanding what the passage is getting at. He is required to recognize further that the differential relation between the beautiful and the useful is really constituted out of two other, apparently incompatible relations. On the one hand, beauty of structure may well exclude utility, and vice versa. On the other,

23

utility may as in this case create its own beauty. In the first case we have mutual exclusion; in the second, mutual implication.

And here we come upon a central piece of the information necessary for the reader's understanding what he is reading. I am referring to his recognition that the beauty/utility differential is constituted potentially of both of these relations, either of exclusion or of implication. It will be noticed that Sidney does not say that Kalander's house is useful rather than beautiful. What he does say is that the house realizes the mutual implication between beauty and utility rather than the other potentiality, namely, mutual exclusion between the two terms. The balances struck by the architecture of the building are the result of a choice not between beauty and utility, but between two relations possible within the beauty/utility differential. Thus it is "handsome without curiosity and homely without loathsomeness." "Curiosity" names the pursuit of the aesthetic to an extreme that excludes utility, while "loathsomeness" describes utility that is devoid of beauty.

Recapitulating with this information in mind, we can see how the passage has guided the reader to take cognizance of the interplay between the text on the page and that text's "countertext." A countertext consists of those terms that might have gone to make up a text alternative to the one on the page, but which it nevertheless denies and excludes.[11] Terms constituting a possible countertext would include the following: "an extraordinary kind of fineness," beauties that appeal only "to the eye of the artificer," "curiosity," "loathsomeness," "dainty," "slubbered up with good fellowship." All of these terms make explicit what in the text's "deep structure" would be the beauty/utility differential conceived only as mutually exclusive. Realizing such an exclusiveness, beauty might have yielded only extraordinary fineness, aesthetic bric-a-brac, curiosity, and daintiness; while utility would have yielded in turn loathsomeness, and marks of insensitive ownership.

The balances exhibited by the house realize the beauty/utility differential conceived rather as a mutual reciprocity, so that each of these malign extremes is tempered by its opposites. But if these balanced reciprocities exclude extremes, they also imply them. The graded sequence of choices the building's construction manifests are poised against another set of choices dialectically implied by the first, into which the first is always potentially liable to being transformed. And this process of understanding what the passage says, by glimpsing what it could otherwise have said but did not, represents a constant and recurring demand on the reader that claims the status of being a general rule for Sidney's discursive practice at large.[12] A more formal statement of this rule I shall leave until later, after more passages governed by it have been examined. But some of the applications of this rule are already clear. Most importantly, the reader is required in reading this passage to take account of all the possible choices available—in this case to the owner—in order to understand the significance of the choices that were in fact made. These choices function as paradigms or sets of alternatives, all related to one another differentially, and standing in a hierarchical relation to still other differentially structured sets of choices above and below them.

Further, it will be noted that the syntagmatic dimension of the text, the left-to-right order of the reader's processing the passage, is a sequence in which the reader incrementally collects the terms of the paradigms controlling the passage. That is, the available but excluded choices are never left out tacitly, but are excluded overtly. In fact, the passage is nothing but a sequentially unfolding traversal of the paradigms that fund the passage as a whole, requiring the reader to construct parallel to the passage the total set of available choices that the passage selects from. The passage consists of nothing but repetitions on various concrete and abstract levels of the same paradigms, which coordinate what is selected with what is rejected. Sidney "sculpts" such passages in a way comparable to Michelangelo's notion that a statue is already "in" the block of marble and is created by cutting away the extraneous material. There are no affirmations in the passage divorced from negations, no selections that are not balanced off against rejections. To paraphrase Macbeth, nothing is but by the negation of what it is not. In typically Aristotelian fashion, Sidney saw reality as realizing one-half of a dual potentiality, and this realization takes place only by actively excluding its opposite potentiality. This manner of structuring many passages in the new *Arcadia* accounts for the peculiar dynamism inherent in even

25

the most statically descriptive texts and forms an ideal set of tools for rendering physical movement, and more importantly the flux of human psychology and action.

In these passages describing the shipwreck, Kalander's garden, and the statue of Venus in that garden, as well as the house itself, I have suggested that the specific "data" of such scenes becomes organized and thus to that degree perceivable only after they are structured according to various differential categories. Among these categories, those of difference and identity, implication and exclusion predominate. In this respect the structures of these objects of perception are already imposed on them by the writer before the reader "sees" them. Or, putting my point in reverse, whatever of the physical and the concrete the reader perceives is wholly dependent on this prior differential structuring. It would seem, then, that for Sidney there is no perception prior to verbal structure. His is a kind of gestalt theory, whereby the parts of an object to be described become perceivable only after the whole is schematized and its structure—the dialectical interplay of its parts—has been articulated.

In the case of the shipwreck and even more so in that of Kalander's house, the specific qualities of the scene are themselves rendered in categories of broadly ethical import. We see little of the physical components of the shipwreck and even less of the physical sections of the house. What we are given are rather the ethical equivalents of these components. "Thrift," "hospitality," "magnificence," "loathsomeness," and the rest render not the house in its physical presence, but rather the characterological equivalents of this house, the qualities of its owner as these are presented not only to the reader but also to Musidorus, who is visiting it for the first time. We can reconstruct the physical building only by tracing backward from the ethical equivalents of its parts. Consequently, literally nothing of the house is present to us, literally nothing is seen or known or has any meaning or significance save what is filtered through the differential schema wherein the various lexematic realizations of the beauty/utility differential are textualized.

But textualized by whom? If the physical site is presented only through the categories of the verbal description itself and the logical relations these categories articulate, then the descriptive text constitutes more than the site itself. The text shows itself originating in a human viewer, who has discerned a physical structure only by first grasping its textualizable meaning as well. It is part of the house's preferred hospitality that the visitor may "read" the house in the way Musidorus does, that is, by translating architectural balances composed of building materials into the ethical balances characterizing the house's owner. Musidorus comes to understand Kalander by reading his house, which means that the text of the description —given by the omniscient narrator—replicates as free indirect discourse the text of Musidorus's own understanding of the house's meaning, and by extension of the message that Kalander wishes to convey. This passage is typical of the Arcadian style in rendering the Arcadian world as a function of how a specific character textualizes it. Such a style imitates this world, not directly, but through its imitation—exact replication, in fact—of the texts in which specific characters understand it.

In the various examples of such analyses, which I will take up in the rest of Part One, Sidney fuses third-person narrative with the text in which a character creates and acts out his or her own moral destiny, so that the rhetorical figures of dialectical opposition and reciprocity embody this destiny viewed simultaneously from without and from within. Before proceeding to these passages, I want to discuss one last scenic description, this time of something in motion. Pamela recounts to her sister, Philoclea, Musidorus's equestrian exercise, wherein Sidney allows the text of Musidorus's inner discipline expression through Pamela's descriptions of his disciplined riding.

Musidorus displays power joined with grace, and the description articulates this balance of opposites by defining it against other possible extreme and unbalanced versions of itself. Once Musidorus is given the signal to begin, he moves instantly from immobility to motion: "with a kind rather of quick gesture than show of violence" (p. 153). Even this immobility is defined against the possibility of motion amid its absence: "how at the first, standing still, with his eyes bent upon me, as though his motions were chained to my look, he so stayed till I caused Mopsa bid him do something upon his horse: which no sooner said, but," and then follows the passage just cited. Immobility is the tensive negation of motion, and nimble motion is poised against its opposite potentiality, violent action. Musidorus's fashion of sitting the horse is a combination of the horse's rapid rise and fall ("If you remember the ship we saw once when the Sea went high upon the coast of Argos"), and Musidorus's own stability ("but he, as if centaur-like he had been one piece with the horse, was no more moved than one is with the going of his own legs"). The centaur allusion is extended, and it appears that Musidorus "commanded him as his own limbs. For though he had both spurs and wand, they seemed rather marks of sovereignty than instruments of punishment." Musidorus's command of the horse, which could potentially manifest itself in the violence of punishment—reacting to the horse's recalcitrance with a violent recalcitrance of his own—is registered as the negation of all these possibilities.

The various differentials in this passage—horse/rider, nimbleness/violence, command/punishment—all record a potentially real conflict. Sidney's method here as elsewhere is to define the reciprocity of these opposites by negating their mutual exclusion. But the marvelous tensiveness of this description, its precision and therefore its vividness, results from the fact that each of these reciprocities not only negates mutual exclusion but is also poised on the edge of falling into it. Pamela goes on:

> . . . his hand and leg with most pleasing grace commanding without threatening, and rather remembering than chastising (at least, if sometimes he did, it was so stolen as neither our eyes could discern it, nor the horse with any change did complain of it), he ever going so just with the horse, either forthright, or turning, that it seemed, as he borrowed the horse's body, so he lent the horse his mind (in the turning, one might perceive the bridle-hand something gently stir, but indeed so gently as it did rather distil virtue than use violence). . . .

The discourse probes Musidorus's performance and touches it only at those points where the latter becomes verbalizable as a series of poised reciprocities. The description is consequently oddly static when compared with modern examples. In order to gain perspective on Sidney's technique for describing physical movement, I quote here a similar passage by a twentieth-century author whose descriptions of physical action have decisively formed modern tastes: Romero's bullfight from Hemingway's *The Sun Also Rises*:

> The bull did not insist under the iron. He did not really want to get at the horse. He turned and the group broke apart and Romero was taking him out with his cape. He took him out softly and smoothly, and then stopped and, standing squarely in front of the bull, offered him the cape. The bull's tail went up and he charged, and Romero moved his arms ahead of the bull, wheeling, his feet firmed. The dampened, mud-weighted cape swung open and full as a sail fills, and Romero pivoted with it just ahead of the bull. At the end of the pass they were facing each other again. Romero smiled. The bull wanted it again, and Romero's cape filled again, this time on the other side. Each time he let the bull pass so close that the man and the cape that filled and pivoted ahead of the bull were all one sharply etched mass. It was all so slow and so controlled. It was as though he were rocking the bull to sleep. He made four veronicas like that, and finished with a half-veronica that turned his back on the bull and came away toward the applause, his hand on his hip, his cape on his arm, and the bull watching his back going away.[13]

The similarity of these two passages throws into relief how Sidney's method differs decisively from Hemingway's. Hemingway wants to define the grace of the bullfight's actions, and he does this by featuring images of gentle motion and stasis. Thus, Romero "took" the bull "out softly and smoothly, and then stopped and, standing squarely in front of the bull, offered him the cape." This is followed by the bull's charge, which Romero meets "wheeling, his feet firmed." The cape billows out "open and full as a sail fills," conveying once again the smoothness and gentleness of the action. The passage in general oscillates between stasis and sharply initiated and completed action, yet Hemingway continually calls attention to the transitions between the two states: "It was all so slow and so controlled. It was as though he were rocking the bull to sleep." The conclusion of the passage leaves the bull once again motionless though poised for yet another charge.

It is often true of passages similar to this one in Hemingway that the tenseness of the actions, their potential for breaking out into sudden, uncontrolled violence, are carefully left tacit and therefore allowed to brood silently over the scene in the reader's mind. In comparison, Sidney clearly intends to bring such potentials openly into the description itself. However, the difference between the implicit and the explicit extends further than this obvious point. In the Hemingway passage the danger to the bullfighter, the difficulty of controlling an animal weighing much more than he, the conscious art mastered to the point where the art itself disappears: all these elements of a psychological and broadly ethical nature are present mainly by being only implied. A character's thought is excluded in favor of aligning the sequence of the discourse isomorphically with the sequence of the actions described. The process of the reader's reading corresponds exactly with the sequence of the fight itself. In general, the mastery of the Hemingway passage lies in the sparseness of the description itself, where the human values that inform the fight and give it significance are treated as already implicit in the actions and gestures of the bullfighter, since nothing else of his thought and motivation is specified. To know what the bull fight "means," it is necessary only to follow with scrupulous fidelity its sequence of episodes, nor (as Hemingway implies) can this significance be gathered any other way.

In turning again to Sidney's description, we are once again struck by comparison with its curiously static quality. Sidney is not interested in conveying to the reader merely the sequence of Musidorus's actions. As in his descriptions of the psycho-moral spaces of his characters, so in his descriptions of the physical spaces in which these characters move: he pursues precision of outline, the verbalization not of action simply, but of the internal substructure of stress and counterstress, movement and countermovement, the poised balances or violent oscillations between the differential poles that structure them. We are given not so much movement as an anatomy of movement, the sense not simply of what this movement looks like, but of the kinds of balances necessary within the character to achieve it. It is movement seen from the inside, as it were. And it is to be noted that Pamela's description is never of Musidorus's actions themselves, but of the verbal text in which she can imagine Musidorus himself conceiving and governing his own actions. It is, after all, a display of animal movement guided by human intelligence and skill, and therefore this movement cannot be separated from these. We see that Musidorus's actions are not random, that they have a meaning and that meaning is nothing other than the poise of stress and counterstress of which these actions are the sum. Sidney has seen that in order to make verbal description adequate to nonverbal movement he must first find that point in this movement where human discourse and therefore human thought insert themselves into it. And that is the point where the horse's actions become mastered by the internal verbal discourse of his rider. It is, in other words, precisely the potential of the animal and his movements for escaping words—the discourse of his rider whose balances are verbalized in the discourse of the narrator (Pamela-Sidney)—that the counterstress of the discourse must meet and neutralize. The text of the description replicates literally the discourse through which Musidorus controls and directs these actions.

What "moves," then, for the reader is not the horse, but his mind's eye, informed with an understanding of the dialectical structures of the differentials constituting these motions. And the discourse itself can register the movements of the horse only by passing repeatedly through the diachronic process of opposite posed against opposite, *then* of this opposition being negated, *then* of this opposition being made present as a stress through the text's verbalizing it, *then* the reader's recognition of this balance between the present and the absent which also is present. What "moves" is specifically the reader's mind through a series of recuperations similar to the one I have just recorded. Action becomes vivid, in short, by becoming abstractly intelligible.

Concluding the exercise, Musidorus is shown picking up the small ring on the ground with his staff:

> . . . wherein truly, at least my womanish eyes could not discern, but that taking his staff from his thigh, the descending it a little down, the getting of it up into the rest, the letting of the point fall, and taking the ring, was but all one motion; at least, if they were divers motions, they did so stealingly slip one into another as the latter part was ever in hand before the eye could discern the former was ended. (p. 154)

Here, as in the earlier description of Musidorus's invisible gestures in maneuvering the horse, Pamela posits disjunctions between discrete movements where the eye sees none. Sidney exploits the paradox—known from the time of Zeno—of motion and process itself: that it is at once an unbroken continuity from one point to a second, while being also a series of distinct, static demarcations. Sidney wants us to see that Musidorus's gestures are so smoothly executed that their distinct component movements are not separately articulated, but flow the one into the next. But Sidney also knows that such fluidity can only be the sum total of several distinct articulations. And so in a manner similar to that noted above but to a different purpose, unbroken movement is presented as a dialectical function of "divers motions," discrete and static in themselves. The text thus fragments Musidorus's complex gesture by spelling out its successive stages, while reconstituting its fluidity by affirming that each stage "did so stealingly slip one into another as the latter part was ever in hand before the eye could discern the former was ended." This is the problem exactly: the eye sees fluidity, while the mind understands the fact of discrete steps. Fluidity is conveyed, typically, first by adducing a series of negations of fluidity (reciting the successive stages of the action), and then by negating this negation. In this respect the discourse that segments the gesture must disown itself in order to make itself adequate for describing this action, a negation that Pamela performs as she muses on what she sees and does not see, what she can articulate in discourse and what she cannot.

Section 2

Portraits of single characters: Pamela and Philoclea; Queen Helen of Corinth; the King of Phrygia; Tydeus and Telenor; Anaxius

Whether or not Sidney was influenced by the classical "characters" of Theophrastus,[14] he usually introduces the personae of his story with an exhaustive portrait in which psychological and ethical characteristics are systematically set forth, almost without exception in differential form. The major exceptions to this practice are the two main characters, Musidorus and Pyrocles. In a manner more familiar to modern readers, the heroes of the new *Arcadia* are introduced to us gradually, through their actions, their interactions with others, and cumulative descriptions of thought and emotion.

The bulk of the new material distinguishing the new *Arcadia* from the old consists of episodes dealing with persons other than the original characters: the four lovers, and Philoclea's and Pamela's mother and father, Basilius and Gynecia. The collective meaning of these new episodes, taken in relation to the whole work, I discuss in the concluding half of this study, since they contribute to transforming the new *Arcadia* into a work wholly different from Sidney's earlier production. In this first part I examine how Sidney employs his differential schema to delineate the moral and ethical dimensions of these new characters.

Drawing on the central exclusion/implication differential illustrated in the passages of scenic description, Sidney employs a limited paradigm of logical relations among the ethical qualities of the characters he delineates. Constant, however, is his articulation of characters' traits as the dialectical interplay of various differentially related virtues and vices. In a fashion that appears at least partially indebted to Aristotle's *Nichomachean Ethics*, Sidney conceives virtues and vices as always related in various forms of mutually implicative and exclusive oppositions. Particularly relevant is Aristotle's notion that virtue and vice are not merely discrete ethical categories in polar opposition, but rather dispositions and practices aligned on a continuous spectrum of potentials.[15] It is this last feature that Sidney exploits: the notion that specific virtues and vices are related as potentials of each other. That is, a virtue is a potential for either vicious extreme of deficiency or excess. In this connection, Sidney's character portraits assume that a given virtue or vice exists and is articulatable only in relation to the other virtues and vices to which it is related as its potentials.

Sidney differs from Aristotle, however, in the specific dialectical forms in which he arranges these ethical relationships. Whereas Aristotle posits an excess/deficiency differential underlying the extremes of vice with virtue in the intermediate position, Sidney assumes a logical structure wherein mutual implication and mutual exclusion

33

between virtues and vices is based on a more general, controlling dialectical scheme, by which the relations of exclusion and implication mutually imply and exclude each other as well: a secondary level of dialectical relations governing the first. Nevertheless, other Aristotelian writings provide a model of Sidney's practice, and although these may have influenced him, they in any case make explicit the dialectical logic underlying his ethical insights. We find, for instance, in the treatise on the *Categories* the assertion, radically important to Aristotle's metaphysics as well as his ethics, that "the most distinctive mark of substance appears to be that, while remaining numerically one and the same, it is capable of admitting contrary qualities" (*C.* 5, 4a; McKeon, p. 13). Change becomes logically possible once it is understood that "it is by themselves changing that substances admit contrary qualities" (ibid.). Later in the same treatise Aristotle links the logical precondition for change with the human capacity to take on contrary ethical qualities: "But the contrary of an evil is sometimes a good, sometimes an evil. For defect, which is an evil, has excess for its contrary, this also being an evil, and the mean, which is a good, is equally the contrary of the one and of the other" (*C.* 11, 14a; McKeon, p. 33). By conflating these purely logical formulations with Aristotle's application of them to the physical world in Book 5 of the *Physics*, we discover the essential elements that fund Sidney's adaptation of Aristotle's schema in the *Ethics*. The central argument of *Physics* Book 5 is that change is always from contrary to contrary. For instance:

> Change within the same kind from a lesser to a greater or from a greater to a lesser degree is alteration: for it is motion either from a contrary or to a contrary, whether in an unqualified or in a qualified sense: for change to a lesser degree of a quality will be called change to the contrary of that quality, and change to a greater degree of a quality will be regarded as change from the contrary of that quality to the quality itself. (*C.* 1, 226b; McKeon, p. 306)

The problem of change as Aristotle inherited it from Plato, Zeno, and Heraclitus was how it was possible that any substance, whether natural or human, could change while retaining self-identity. Aristotle's solution was to posit an underlying, unchanging substance that has the potential for taking on certain qualities as well as their categorical opposites. Change then, as the passages quoted above assert, is just this movement from a quality to its opposite, a movement that nevertheless leaves the substantial identity untouched. It becomes therefore rationally intelligible that human agents may go from virtue to vice and the reverse. Because, as the *Ethics* develops at large, virtues and vices are related as logical contraries, a person's moral identity is precisely that potential for either virtue or vice that the person realizes, in opposition to those equally possible moral qualities which he or she does not.

Consequently, Sidney can be seen as either developing Aristotle's spectrum model in the *Ethics*, or deviating from it and following other Aristotelian sources in emphasizing how two ethical qualities (good or bad) both mutually negate and imply each other. In a manner similar to that dictated by the scenic descriptions I have already discussed, grasping the coherent meaning of Sidney's character portrayals requires the reader to recognize the dialectical logic by which virtues and vices that mutually exclude each other also mutually imply each other.

The strength of this scheme for Sidney's purposes is that it provided him an enormously powerful paradigm for generating widely varied combinations of ethical qualities. As Aristotle shows in the *Ethics*, we do not grasp a person's total ethical make-up until we realize that this is constituted not only from the moral qualities that positively define it but also from those that do not but might have. Characters in the Arcadian world for the most part lead complicated moral existences marked by dialectical tensions between virtues and vices, and these tensions result from the dialectical interplay between the mutual exclusions and implications defining both and relating them to one another. As Sidney saw, to communicate the totality of such moral existences, he was required to articulate the total dialectical structures that constitute them.

The following appears to be the paradigm of available dialectical relations that Sidney uses in the new *Arcadia*: (1) mutual reciprocity between opposed virtues; (2) mutual exclusion between opposed virtues; (3) mutual reciprocity between opposed vices; (4) mutual exclusion between opposed vices; (5) mutual reciprocity between opposed virtues and vices; (6) mutual exclusion between opposed virtues and vices. These six types of dialectical relationships represent an exhaustive repertoire or paradigm available, not all of which he uses. That which does not appear in the new *Arcadia* is type six: mutual exclusion between opposed virtues and vices. This type corresponds to the "normal," nondialectical assumption of mutual exclusion between good and bad qualities; and since one of Sidney's purposes is to call this nondialectical relation into question, or at least modify it in various directions, we might say that it is present throughout the new *Arcadia* as a type of relationship that is continually being negated.

Corresponding, although not isomorphically, to these available categories of opposition are several rhetorical figures recognized by the writers of contemporary handbooks. Rendering reciprocal relations of opposites is the figure *synoeciosis*, which unites contraries. Corresponding to mutual exclusion is the figure *antithesis*, likewise known as *contentio, contraposition*, and *oppositio*. *Syncrisis* is related to *synoeciosis* in that it demarcates "a comparison of contrary things, & diverse persons in one sentence" (Henry Peacham, *The Garden of Eloquence* [1593]). Relevant also to Sidney's usage is *anatanogoge*, "whereby something spoken unfavorably is in a measure counteracted, though not denied, by the addition of something favorable." [16]

Anatanogoge would correspond particularly to type five, mutual reciprocity between opposed virtues and vices, where the text figures the ways in which good and evil moral qualities imply or cause each other. In general, *synoeciosis, syncrisis,* and *anatanogoge* tend to overlap and are employed in figuring types one, three, and five. *Antithesis*, on the other hand, which figures relations of mutual exclusion, would occur in passages featuring types two, four, and six. The difference among the figures of mutual implication lies in the degree to which this implication is filled out in the text. *Syncrisis* merely compares contrary things without calling attention to a liaison between them. *Synoeciosis* does just that, while *anatanogoge* applies to more extended passages in which such a liaison is amplified and explained. Consequently, we can expect passages that consist of types one, three, and five to employ any or all of these three figures. Furthermore, the figure of mutual exclusion *antithesis* may likewise appear in passages where types of mutual implication dominate, and vice versa. However, it is generally true that one type of antithetical relation, one rhetorical figure, dominates a given character portrayal. And Sidney's descriptive practice usually involves filling out a given type by repeating it several times in different concrete versions employing one or more of the above figures of opposition.

A good example of the first type, which defines the various opposed virtues of a character as mutually reciprocal, is the introductory description of the two sisters Philoclea and Pamela:

> The elder is named Pamela, by many men not deemed inferior to her sister. For my part, when I marked them both, methought there was (if at least such perfections may receive the word of *more*) more sweetness in Philoclea, but more majesty in Pamela; methought love played in Philoclea's eyes and threatened in Pamela's; methought Philoclea's beauty only persuaded—but so persuaded as all hearts must yield, Pamela's beauty used violence—and such violence as no heart could resist. And it seems that such proportion is between their minds: Philoclea, so bashful as though her excellencies had stolen into her before she was aware, so humble, that she will put all pride out of countenance—in sum, such proceeding as will stir hope but teach hope good manners; Pamela, of high thoughts, who avoids not pride with not knowing her excellencies, but by making that one of her excellencies to be void of pride, her mother's wisdom, greatness, nobility—but, if I can guess aright, knit with a more constant temper. (p. 17)

In this passage Sidney faces a double task. He must differentiate between and relate one sister to the other, while filling out this double relation by defining in each sister the potential vices each has excluded by realizing a mutual reciprocity between potentially conflicting virtues. This dialectical interface of genial qualities both between and within Pamela and Philoclea is so intricate that Kalander cannot say which he prefers. Philoclea is sweeter than Pamela, but Pamela has a more majestic bearing. At this point we can note that Sidney at once creates his paradigmatic differential and distributes its terms along the syntagm of his text. We are, it would appear, to accept sweetness and majesty as mutually exclusive opposites. Whereas Sidney may at times employ differentials, such as that opposing beauty and utility, that have a public history and tradition behind them, ad hoc differentials occur that are limited to specific passages. This means that whatever terms Sidney treats differentially the reader is required to treat differentially also. And consequently the reader is compelled to search among the semantic markers of the two terms, that is, their meanings, for those markers Sidney is exploiting in order to set them in opposition.[17]

Having accepted the sweetness of Philoclea and the majesty of Pamela as defining characteristics that also set them in differential opposition, we are also required by the passage to understand that each of these qualities has the potential for various opposed extremes. If love "played" in Philoclea's eyes, it threatened in Pamela's. But if we associate conquering with threatening, this association is cross-biased when we discover that Philoclea's sweetness coerces, and Pamela's violence persuades the heart. The violence/persuasion differential is thus matched inversely with the majesty/sweetness differential. The interplay between both differentials yields a mutually limiting reciprocity between the terms of each. To recuperate this rather complex formulation, I would suggest that the reader is required to assemble the following information: Persuasion would normally be expected to accompany sweetness, and violence majesty. Left with these polar equivalences, the reader would see the two sisters lined up in differentially exclusive opposition to each other. But Sidney mitigates this simplistic distinction by qualifying the virtues of sweetness and majesty with terms that normally accompany each virtue's differential opposites. By transgressing the expected equivalences and asserting that Philoclea's sweetness is a kind of violence and that Pamela's majesty persuades, Sidney indicates the dialectical relations within and between both sisters at one stroke.

Each woman exhibits other though still parallel differential structures. Philoclea's humility is such that she is barely aware of her excellencies, while Pamela is quite conscious of her beauty. This self-consciousness, which might lead to pride, in turn controls and limits her pride to the exact degree that Pamela makes "that one of her excellencies to be void of pride." This last sentence is a good example of opposed virtues' limiting each other, a reciprocity that is yet poised against another possibility, that by which beauty and self-awareness might become mutually causal vices. The peculiar balance that Pamela manages to strike between her beauty and her aware-ness of it becomes intelligible only when we explore the countertext to the text which Sidney wishes us to accept. Self-consciousness of beauty may lead to pride in one direction, while a disingenuous re-fusal to acknowledge beauty in order to counter pride might covertly reintroduce it. Pamela manages, however, to hold her pride in check by turning the possible malign reciprocity between pride and beauty into a benign reciprocity. Self-consciousness extends so far as to be cognizant of its own malign potential and to create the further aware-ness that being devoid of pride can itself be a beauty.

Rhetorically, the coercion = persuasion equivalence that charac-terizes both women's beauty is a form of *syncrisis*, whereby opposites are joined together. However, when Sidney raises the possibly ma-lign relation between Pamela's beauty and her pride only to negate it, we find a version of type five—mutual reciprocity between op-posed virtues and vices—transformed into type one, whereby her pride becomes a virtue related to beauty. This initially renders the text's countertext according to the figure *anatanogoge*, but then this figure is once again displaced by *syncrisis*.

The individual reader must decide for himself or herself how much of the above metatextual information he and she must accrete in order to make sense of what the passage says. Such information as I shall make explicit in my analyses of these and similar passages in the new *Arcadia* cannot pretend to name the very words that a specific reader may arrive at. I merely want to suggest, rather, that something of this sort is in fact necessary if any meaning is to be derived at all. I would suggest that what I am doing here might be described as verbalizing, in a structuralist manner, the *langue* or grammar such passages require the reader to invent ad hoc as he comes upon them one after the other in reading Sidney's work.

A passage illustrating a similar reciprocity, this time more clearly between virtues each of which taken by itself has the potential for transforming itself into a corresponding vice, is the description of Queen Helen of Corinth's method for ruling her people:

She [used] so strange and yet so well-succeeding a temper that she
made her people by peace warlike, her courtiers by sports learned,
her ladies by love chaste; for, by continual martial exercises without blood, she made them perfect in that bloody art; her sports
were such as carried riches of knowledge upon the stream of delight; and such the behaviour both of herself and her ladies as
builded their chastity, not upon waywardness, but by choice of
worthiness: so as, it seemed that court to have been the marriage
place of love and virtue, and that herself was a Diana apparelled in
the garments of Venus. (pp. 253–54, punctuation modified)

This passage is essentially a catalogue of paired terms, each of
which could be normally expected mutually to exclude the other:
peace/war, knowledge/delight, love/chastity, Diana/Venus. Here *synoeciosis* and *syncrisis* are affirmed against a possible countertext figured as *antithesis*. All of these differentials are readily intelligible, and
Sidney seems to probe no deeper than the notion that, through whatever unusual talents and practices, Helen manages to transform differential exclusiveness into differential implication. Sidney requires
the reader to discover how the motivations of love may create rather
than negate chastity, how knowledge rather than banishing delight
invokes it, and so on. And the reader is asked to see further that, fail-
ing such mutual reciprocity, the opposed terms in these differentials
may reciprocate each other in still another way, by mutual exclusion,
so that love can never be chaste nor chastity amorous, knowledge
can never be delightful nor delight entail learning. We see that the
ultimate issue raised by this passage is not the oppositions among
these polar terms, but rather the conflict between two different ways
of understanding these oppositions. In the new *Arcadia* a central issue
is how men and women can come to understand the mutual implication and mutual exclusion between the terms and categories in
which they textualize their own ethical identities. Disaster and evil
in the new *Arcadia* are always traceable back to characters who fail
to grasp this information. Evil, in short, is the consequence of attempts to escape the dialectical reciprocity that potentially informs
all our actions, all our motivations and thoughts and judgments,
regarding both ourselves and our relations with others. If the new

Arcadia teaches anything, it is that the good life in all senses of the phrase radically depends on one's understanding the dialectical logic flowing from the differentials governing the discourse in which one textualizes one's own moral identity.

The majority of the characters and episodes added in the new *Arcadia*, within Book 2 and constituting the whole of the Book 3 fragment, are cautionary tales illustrating essentially this message.[18] Among these cases we discover another variation from the paradigm given above—type three—wherein various opposed vices generate one another.

A good example is the portrayal of the paranoiac king of Phrygia, where Pyrocles finds himself after shipwreck and separation from Musidorus:

> This country whereon he fell was Phrygia, and it was to the king thereof to whom he was sent—a prince of melancholy constitution, both of body and mind: wickedly sad, ever musing of horrible matters; suspecting, or rather condemning all men of evil, because his mind had no eye to espy goodness—and therefore accusing sycophants, of all men, did best sort to his nature—but therefore not seeming sycophants, because of no evil they said, they could bring any new or doubtful thing unto him but such as already he had been apt to determine, so as they came but as proofs of his wisdom; fearful, and never secure while the fear he had figured in his mind had any possibility of event; a toad-like retiredness and closeness of mind, nature teaching the odiousness of poison, and the danger of odiousness. (pp. 169–70, punctuation modified)

This passage is distinguished by the psychological insight with which Sidney fills out this traditional portrait of the typical tyrant.[19] All details are linked to one another in a circular causal chain, so that no element of the king's thoughts and actions is without its origin, and the sequence as a whole locks the king into a claustrophobic bind of self-confirming fears.

The origin of it all is the king's melancholy, which causes him ever to muse "of horrible matters." This in turn leads him to suspect all men, "or rather [to] condemn all men of evil." The rapidity with which suspicion is replaced by condemnation replicates the speed

41

with which suspicion leads to conviction in the king's own mind. "Condemning" becomes a rapid self-adjustment within the text, so that when Musidorus (who is telling this part of the story) said "suspecting," he had really meant to say "condemning." For the king this means that suspicion is equivalent to condemnation, the difference between them being only the moment of thought necessary to draw a boundary between the meanings of the two words before crossing it.

Sycophants who curry favor by feeding his suspicions are thus always found to have come too late with news of further dangers, since the king has already fantasized every possible danger they could invent. The devolution of the king's psychology down to the concluding sentence of the passage—"a toad-like retiredness and closeness of mind"—is thus as rapid as successive electrical circuits closing when a charge is sent through them. Melancholy leads to suspicion, suspicion to condemnation, condemnation to total isolation.

The king's predisposition to dwell in paranoiac fantasy detached from the objective truth soon enough creates actual unrest among his people: "and then thinking himself contemned, knowing no countermine against contempt, but terror, [he] began to let nothing pass which might bear the colour of a fault without sharp punishment; and when he wanted faults, excellency grew a fault; and it was sufficient to make one guilty that he had power to be guilty" (p. 170). The king is driven (or drives himself) inexorably from self-contempt to the belief that others contemn him, which in turn generates a reign of terror. Whatever appears to be a fault is punished, and even "excellency"—putatively the reverse of faultiness—becomes itself a fault. Even the power to become guilty means that guilt is realized. Appearance becomes reality, excellency a fault, self-contempt stirs the contempt of others, potential for guilt the actuality. The controlling differential in this progression is *appearance/reality,* where the appearance of a fault is taken as the sign of the reality, while the appearance of the reverse is taken as signifying a fault as well. No differential is untransgressible, all oppositions wherein he might find refuge and security are called into question. There being no difference between appearance and reality, everything threatens that appears threatening, and everything that does not appear threatening threatens also.

Sidney here as elsewhere seeks to exhaust the set of possible combinations allowed by the central differential in this passage, so that only those terms and combinations appear which this differential generates.

This exhaustiveness registers the king's imprisonment in the rhetorical figuration of his own discourse, specifically, the figure *gradatio* which leads from *antithesis* to a reversed form of *anatanogoge:* good qualities that are also evil. These rhetorical figures and their unfolding are not simply Musidorus's text imposed on the king's thoughts and actions. Rather, the king's actions flow from his own text, which is itself inscribed in these figures, and which Musidorus's description replicates. The king is thus claustrophobically trapped in the dialectical oscillations of his own text.

The King of Phrygia's vices feed on vices, just as, in reverse, virtues feed virtues in Pamela, Philoclea, and Queen Helen of Corinth. Elsewhere, Sidney registers still another of the variations available to his basic ethical paradigm: type five, in which characters who are essentially virtuous nevertheless are tainted with vices or flaws inseparable from these virtues. This differential, by which opposed virtues and vices at once exclude and cause each other, is capable of generating enormous characterological complexity. In fact, the most elaborated and possibly most fascinating character in the new *Arcadia*, Amphialus, is structured on the basis of this type. I leave a discussion of Amphialus until later, since Sidney's development of his story shows us his art at its most mature, and to that extent it is somewhat atypical of similar episodes in the rest of the work.

More typical are the two brothers, Tydeus and Telenor. These two soldiers serve the evil Plexirtus, and Sidney carefully highlights the interpenetration of their fearlessness, "goodness and justice" (p. 184) on the one hand with their injudicious assignment of their loyalties on the other. Sidney says of them (and Musidorus tells this part of the story as well) that they were "truly, no more settled in their valure than disposed to goodness and justice—if either they had lighted on a better friend, or could have learned to make friendship a child, and not the father, of virtue." But they have been brought up in loyalty to an evil master, and consequently "they willingly held out the course rather to satisfy him than all the world, and rather to be good friends than good men; so as, though they did not like the evil he did, yet they liked him that did the evil; and though not counsellors of the offence, yet protectors of the offender."

The source of the brothers' vice—their loyalty to Plexirtus despite his evil—is seen to flow from their otherwise exemplary and desirable virtues. Here a good cause has an evil result, and it would seem to be impossible to root out their flaws without rooting out their merits as well. The wedge driven between "good friends" and "good men" creates an unusual semantic situation: one where phrases are opposed that would otherwise be expected to imply each other. This reverses the crossing of differential boundaries previously observed, but the possibility for either kind of antithesis is latent in the notion of differentiality Sidney employs throughout. If exclusion implies implication, implication can imply exclusion, and so the virtues of friendship and loyalty can be misused. We see replicated in the discourse of the narrator the discriminations the two brothers must make to maintain their loyalty: they dislike the evil but not the evil doer; and though they protect the offense, they do not counsel it.

Another and more interesting instance of mingled virtue and vice is the mildly comic *miles gloriosus* Anaxius. Sidney seems to have been particularly bemused by the categorical conundrums posed by Anaxius, since he uncharacteristically accords him more than one description. We first encounter Anaxius when Pyrocles tells of the revenge sought by Anaxius against him for killing his uncle Euardes. Anaxius is immoderately proud of his own military prowess. Pyrocles says: "to [him] all men would willingly have yielded the height of praise, but that his nature was such as to bestow it upon himself before any could give it" (pp. 234–35). What intrigues the reader, and seems to have piqued Sidney and Pyrocles no less, is that Anaxius's self-conceit wholly matches the reality: "and if it be true that the giants ever made war against heaven, he had been a fit ensign-bearer for that company, for nothing seemed hard to him, though impossible, and nothing unjust, while his liking was his justice." Anaxius displays an unstable, sometimes even frivolous disposition linked to his great intrepidity: "But now that [Anaxius] understood that his uncle was slain by me, I think rather scorn that any should kill his uncle than any kindness (an unused guest to an arrogant soul) made him seek his revenge—I must confess in manner gallant enough."

Sidney has adroitly discerned the rhetorical complexities inherent in a *miles gloriosus* that, unlike Shakespeare's Falstaff and Jonson's Bobadil, is fully up to validating his own boasts. Once we understand that Shakespeare's and Jonson's characters are cowards, our attitude toward them is stabilized, because the gulf between self-vaunting and the reality behind it is never in danger of being diminished. But what are we to think of a character who mixes great prowess with the braggadocio normally expected only of a coward? When Pyrocles comes to tell of his actual confrontation with Anaxius, it is just this problem that he faces. Having kept Pyrocles waiting at the appointed place, he finally arrives. And Pyrocles says: "that I may not say too little because he is wont to say too much, [he was] like a man whose courage was apt to climb over any danger" (p. 241). Still later on the same page Pyrocles registers a similar discomfort in deciding how to textualize Anaxius when he says "he undoubtedly being of singular valour—I would to God it were not abased by his too much loftiness."

Anaxius intrigues us because he is valorous in fact and yet acts as if he were not, as if he needed to bluster to convince others that he is. Sidney does not invite us to extract from this behavior some sort of "inferiority complex" that sits down side-by-side with a real superiority. It is not Sidney's habit to hint indirectly at characterological labyrinths. His method is rather to make everything explicit and to deal with the dialectics of complicated psychologies out in the open. Instead, these passages emphasize that Anaxius lessens the glory accruing to his feats of arms by not giving others a chance to praise him first. Another reason why we are not invited to plumb Anaxius's psychology is that he is entirely too boorish to have much of one. Rather, he is a good fighter, he knows it, and he wants to make sure that others know it too: he is a victim of the need for overkill not with the sword but with words.

And what happens the moment Pyrocles and Anaxius begin their duel expands this comment for us. Before meeting Anaxius, Pyrocles had rescued the fickle Pamphilus from deadly assault by all the women he had betrayed. Now as he fights, one of these women, Dido, enters pursued by Pamphilus in turn, causing Pyrocles to break off his combat. Pyrocles finds himself in a bind, since when he leaves the fight, Anaxius calls him a coward, as do a number of rustics who happen by at the same time. Pyrocles, however, declares, "Anaxius, assure thyself I neither fear thy force nor thy opinion" (p. 242) and then spurs after Pamphilus, telling Philoclea that "the lady's misery over-balanced my reputation" (p. 243). Pyrocles' indifference to opinion defines his courage and illuminates by contrast the secret flaw in Anaxius's own prowess: his fear of others' opinions, which makes him eager to discover cowardice in others.

Sidney here articulates several points about military virtue. For one thing, courage is shown to be a matter of emotional stability and mental independence rather than merely physical capability. Anaxius thus displays a courage that, like Lord Jim's, is grounded self-reflexively on the fear of not appearing courageous. Second, Anaxius's prowess is shown finally not incompatible with his self-vaunting. The problem of interpreting Anaxius is that boasting would normally seem the compulsion of cowards. In this case the paradox would be that Anaxius's character is governed by the courage/cowardice differential, except that both seem to be present in him in an unreconciled fashion. But since Sidney has already trained us to understand that differential exclusions also imply differential implications, we need to understand in Anaxius's behavior how courage not only excludes cowardice but may imply it as well. The duel episode helps us here, since it unmasks the covert liaison between Anaxius's courage and his cowardice, between his real valor and his cowardly fear that others will not recognize it.

Section 3

Short episodes: Dido and Pamphilus; Phalantus and Artesia; Argalus and Parthenia

Sidney's narrative practice extends beyond set descriptions of characters isolated from action and plot, to include interactions among the differential patterns informing several characters. A good example of such character interaction—not sufficiently developed to merit the name of extended action—is the Dido-Pamphilus episode already alluded to. This episode represents some of the most complex dialectical analyses Sidney performs in the new *Arcadia* and for that reason alone demands attention.

Pyrocles tells Philoclea of coming upon Pamphilus tied to a tree in a forest, beset by "nine gentlewomen," who "held bodkins in their hands wherewith they continually pricked him . . . so as the poor man wept and bled, cried and prayed, while they sported themselves in his pain, and delighted in his prayers, as the arguments of their victory" (p. 236). Having unbound Pamphilus, Pyrocles soon learns from Dido, one of the lovers who have attacked him, that this assault merely extends and unmasks the sadomasochism in Pamphilus's relations with all these women. Dido's account of Pamphilus's obsessive philandering is a passage dense both in its description of Pamphilus's Don Juanism and in the teller's tortured, nuanced insight into her own complicity in his enterprises. One differential underlying this passage is the master/slave relation, not surprising given the sado-masochistic tenor of the episode's opening.

Sidney couches Dido's narration of Pamphilus's beguiling one woman after another typically as a string of linked causes and effects, emphasizing the dialectical interplay between qualities shared among several characters, and unfolding the complicity of all of them, women and lover alike. Like Donna Anna and Donna Elvira in Mozart's *Don Giovanni*, Dido and the rest of Pamphilus's lovers both desire him and desire to punish him for affronts to which they laid themselves open: "for his heart being wholly delighted in deceiving us, we could never be warned, but rather one bird caught served for a stale [decoy] to bring in more; for the more he gat, the more still he showed that he, as it were, gave away to his new mistress when he betrayed his promises to the former" (p. 238). Unpacking this statement yields the following information: each successive lover is drawn to Pamphilus by his having already possessed a previous mistress, which makes him more attractive. And then, specifically because he betrays the first in giving his affection to the second, the latter feels flattered. Of course Dido, with the benefit of hindsight, sees that these successive betrayals ought to have been rather warnings of Pamphilus's infidelity than sexual lures. He plays one woman off against another, thereby confirming the women's complicity in their own betrayal:

> But the stirring our own passions, and by the entrance of them to make himself lord of our forces—there lay his master's part of cunning, making us now jealous; now envious; now, proud of what we had, desirous of more; now giving one the triumph to see him, that was prince of many, subject to her; now with an estranged look making her fear the loss of that mind which, indeed, could never be had; never ceasing humbleness and diligence till he had embarked us in some such disadvantage as we could not return dry-shod; and then suddenly a tyrant—but a crafty tyrant. . . .

The interplay between male lover and this bevy of women is worthy of Choderlos de Laclos or Stendhal, and is exemplary of what René Girard calls triangular desire.[20] That is, Pamphilus becomes desirable to one woman because she sees another woman desire him. Each mediates the effects of her desire through him to the others, and in a sense Pamphilus is a cipher, a man devoid of desirability until a woman comes to desire him. It becomes clear that Pamphilus is motivated less by lust than by the desire for power. The women themselves are not strangers to this motivation either, since each uses her (momentary) possession of Pamphilus to dominate the others. The sequence of love affairs that Dido describes becomes a continual interchange of roles, the master becoming the slave and vice versa. Sexual possession yields to abandonment, with the whole process becoming all the more attractive to each successive mistress. Clearly, the women are themselves victims of their own masochism, and Pamphilus is merely the necessary and convenient instrument through which each woman attacks the others.

As if to confirm this next stage of realization, Dido says:

> . . . and, which is strangest, when sometimes with late repentance I think of it, I must confess even in the greatest tempest of my judgement was I never driven to think him excellent, and yet so could set my mind both to get and keep him, as though therein had lain my felicity—like them I have seen play at the ball grow

extremely earnest who should have the ball, and yet everyone knew it was but a ball.

This confirms Pamphilus's emptiness as a person, an emptiness which the women fill up with their own desire and competitiveness: they want what they see others want, thereby confirming to that extent their own emptiness. The game becomes thus a play of empty signs. Pamphilus's show of desire for one woman is enacted on a public stage, so to speak, thereby drawing the envy of another woman, who consequently desires him for this show of desire of which she allows herself to be the victim. Pamphilus's desirability thus becomes merely the function of the content and meaning that the desiring women project on to him, and once that meaning is attributed to the displayed possession of him by one woman, still another woman desires him.

Dido goes on to say that the final consequence of this multisided love affair is that all the women lost their honors "partly by our own faults, but principally by his faulty using of our faults, for never was there man that could with more scornful eyes behold her at whose feet he had lately lain." Though Pamphilus's scorn of them as their master follows his having won each of them by playing her slave, the women do not unite against him until he decides to betroth himself to one of them. And this "common injury made us all join in fellowship, who till that time had employed our endeavours one against the other" (p. 239).

These women attack in Pamphilus only what they have previously conferred on him. Each hates in him what is in herself—the need to use love as instrument of power over others—and each turns on him for being what he would never have been had not each projected it onto him: the male as empty signifier who signifies desire only because he is desired. Do they attack him because he is worthy of love and has escaped them? Or because he is unworthy of love and has imposed on them? Do they hate him because he is everything in their erotic universe, or because he is nothing?

This is one of the most complexly dialectical passages Sidney gives us in the new *Arcadia*. And it is to be noticed that the passage has few rhetorical schemes of antithesis one finds so much elsewhere in this work. Perhaps Sidney discovered that Dido's tale was unsuited to the binary rigidity of this kind of figure, because it involves too much conflict among different perspectives and motivations: the women as a group against Pamphilus, each woman against the others, Pamphilus against the women both as a group and individually, the dual perspective of each woman at the time of her infatuation as against a "present" perspective on this past, represented by Dido. In this regard the Pamphilus-Dido episode foreshadows the fall-off of antithetical figuration in the wholly new Book 3. By the time Sidney came to portray Amphialus and the human waste he unwittingly disseminates, he had perhaps seen that the complexity of human motivation, feeling, and thought could not be wholly reflected in strictly differential rhetorical figures. However, as in the other episodes I have discussed, differential structure remains as the fundamental paradigm for articulating the segments of human reality. But these articulations tend to disperse themselves through the whole text and not to condense at points of polar opposition in specific syntactical structures.

This passage represents, along with Books 2 through 5 of *The Faerie Queene* and some plays of Shakespeare (*Othello, Measure for Measure, Troilus and Cressida*), one of the most perceptive anatomies of the motives of love turned to instrument of power between the poetry of Sir Thomas Wyatt[21] and the novels of Samuel Richardson. But if Sidney in this foreshadows eighteenth- and nineteenth-century novels of love anatomized in the fashion of Richardson, de Sade, Laclos, Stendhal, and Flaubert, in still another passage added to the new *Arcadia* Sidney looks forward to the love comedy of Restoration drama. The passage I refer to is the episode of Phalantus and Artesia. Here once again we encounter two characters sharing differentially related terms that both bind them together and yet set them at enmity. This episode is recounted by Basilius to explain the tournament in which Phalantus challenges all comers to defend the beauty of his "mistress" Artesia. However silly and unperceptive Basilius appears throughout the rest of the story, the subtlety of his account of these two "lovers" does him perhaps uncharacteristic credit.

He first tells us that Phalantus pursues the heroic life as a matter of choice rather than disposition, and he can as willingly leave it as follow it. He is

esteemed . . . for his exceeding good parts, being honorably courteous and wronglessly valiant, considerately pleasant in conversation, and an excellent courtier without unfaithfulness; . . . But as it
was rather choice than nature that led him to matters of arms, so,
as soon as the spur of honour ceased, he willingly rested in peaceable delights, being beloved in all companies for his lovely qualities
and, as a man may term it, cunning [1590 reading] cheerfulness,
. . . and he, not given greatly to struggle with his own disposition, followed the gentle current of it, having a fortune sufficient
to content, and he content with a sufficient fortune. (p. 91)

This is one of the first character descriptions to appear among those
added in the new *Arcadia*, and it shows us how far Sidney had ad-
vanced in the mastery of his craft over the earlier work. Like Anaxius,
Phalantus is a well-nigh inextricable mixture of good qualities and
bad, exemplifying type five: mutual reciprocity between opposed
virtues and vices. In the opening passage quoted above, however,
this information is borne along almost incidentally on an otherwise
unqualified stream of praise. The fact that "rather choice than nature
. . . led him to matters of arms," that "he willingly rested in peaceable
delights" once "the spur of honour ceased," his "cunning cheerfulness," and even his satisfaction with his own fortune (a touchstone
of Christian stoic praise) leaves us on the whole with the impression
of a man who is not evil, but by disposition not very admirable. In
comparison with Pyrocles' enraptured exclamations of love for Philoclea, which the reader will have just witnessed, we see in Phalantus a
fatal emptiness of commitment, his easy embrace of both heroic and
amorous styles being matched by passion in neither of them.

His complacency with women, doubtless a function of his "cunning cheerfulness," leads him to play at courting the proud and
empty-headed Artesia. What happens next illustrates for Basilius the
truth of the following observation: "many times it falls out that these
young companions make themselves believe they love at the first
liking of a likely beauty, loving because they will love for want of
other business, not because they feel indeed that divine power which
makes the heart find a reason in passion." Certainly Basilius, in his
misguided passion for Pyrocles disguised as the Amazon Zelmane,

has warrant for the concluding statement. In any case, Phalantus's shallowness meets in Artesia a response matching his own behavior in earnest levity:

> So therefore, taking love upon him like a fashion, he courted this Lady Artesia, who was as fit to pay him in his own money as might be; for she, thinking she did wrong to her beauty if she were not proud of it [cf. the description of Pamela cited earlier], called her disdain of him chastity, and placed her honour in little setting by his honouring her, determining never to marry but him whom she thought worthy of her—and that was one in whom all worthiness were harboured. (pp. 91–92)

The similarities between Artesia and the women in the Dido-Pamphilus episode are obvious, though the two episodes appear in different books. For Artesia love means enacting a scenario in which she feeds her own ego by disdaining the man on whom she condescends to bestow her favors. Recognizing this, we are not unprepared for what she finally forces Phalantus to undertake in the name of her beauty and desirability.

In wooing Artesia, Phalantus "with cheerful looks would speak sorrowful words, . . . but else neither in behaviour nor action accusing in himself any great trouble in mind whether he sped or no" (pp. 92–93). On the other hand, Artesia

> made earnest benefit of his jest, forcing him in respect of his profession to do her such service as were both cumbersome and costly unto him, while he still thought he went beyond her, because his heart did not commit the idolatry. . . . she took the advantage one day upon Phalantus' unconscionable praisings of her, and certain castaway vows how much he would do for her sake, to arrest his word as soon as it was out of his mouth, and by the virtue thereof to charge him to go with her thorough all the courts of Greece, and with the challenge now made, to give her beauty the principality over all other. Phalantus was entrapped, and saw round about him but could not get out . . . but his promise had bound him prentice, and therefore it was now better with willingness to purchase thanks than with a discontented doing to have the pain and not

the reward, and therefore went on as his faith, rather than love, did lead him. (p. 93)

Frivolity and egoism enforce their rigors as well as deep passion, and we can see now what Basilius's extended and cunning portraits of Phalantus and Artesia have been preparing us for. Because Phalantus lacks any passionate devotion to either love or heroic endeavor, he unwittingly maneuvers himself into a position where he must soberly mimic both. And because Artesia cares nothing for Phalantus, she coerces him into genuine heroic endeavor for feigned love of her. Uncovered here is the comic and ironic affiliation between emptiness of mind and emotion, and chivalric enterprise. Several differentials would be adequate to this situation: passion/complacency, devotion/indifference, purposeful action/random inaction. And the episode transgresses the slash marks separating each pair of terms by showing that the dislogistic second term in each differential can generate at least a show of its eulogistic opposite: a flaccid absence of passion demanding thus a rigorous overcompensation. When in the tournament Phalantus is defeated, these two pretended lovers can as easily quarrel and part as they colluded in disingenuous courtship originally.

Sidney demonstrates here how intensity of erotic and heroic ardor —the two central values that the new *Arcadia* as a whole anatomizes—can derive as much from the absence of such passion as from its presence. Sidney was himself no stranger to the solemn rigors of courtly life and, like Jonson and Donne after him, knew well that mindless inconsequence can generate ceremonious punctilio and formal protocol in exact inverse proportion.

The story of Phalantus and Artesia contrasts with that of Argalus and Parthenia—narrated earlier in the same book—in which the normative dialectical logic binding love to heroism inverted in the later story is exemplarily set forth. This is the last two-person episode I shall deal with here.

This episode is told Musidorus by a servant of Kalander, who introduces Argalus as a collection of balances similar to those constituting Pamela and Philoclea. Though "in behaviour, some will say [he is] ever sad—surely sober and somewhat given to musing," he is "never uncourteous" (p. 27). He is rather "liberal than magnificent, though the one wanted not and the other had ever good choice of the receiver." If he possesses any flaw it lies in "the over-vehement constancy of yet spotless affection." This last qualification seems to run counter to expectation once we compare Phalantus's easy passionlessness: if the latter is a fault if not a vice, then would not constancy of affection be a virtue? The answer, invited so often by Sidney, is "yes and no." Arcadian characters are not the mere sum of their virtues and vices. Rather, each moral quality achieves significance both in the relation to the aggregate, and specifically as a function of the corresponding quality against which it is defined, and which it negates and implies. Phalantus's shallowness of desire implies an equally shallow heroism. But in Argalus "over-vehemence" of affection becomes a "spot" that in fact argues its own worth rather than the reverse. The following story demonstrates that intense passion is matched in the opposite direction by extraordinary restraint and fidelity. Consequently, whereas in Phalantus we find a malign oscillation between purposeless ease and equally purposeless action, in Argalus we discover instead a benign balance between passionate energy and rocklike fidelity and discipline.

Parthenia is likewise played off against Artesia. Where the beauty of the latter results in egoistic fatuity, in Parthenia beauty becomes the outward manifestation of quite opposite qualities:

> that which made her fairness much the fairer was that it was but a fair embassador of a most fair mind full of wit, and a wit which delighted more to judge itself than to show itself: her speech being as rare as precious, her silence without sullenness, her modesty without affectation, her shamefastness without ignorance: in sum, one, that to praise well, one must first set down with himself what it is to be excellent—for so she is. (p. 28)

The comparison with Artesia is almost point for point. If Artesia's beauty is emptyheaded, in Parthenia beauty manifests a fair mind. Though her inner wit is mated with a self-awareness similar to Artesia's, unlike the latter's ostentatious airs, "her silence" is "without sullenness, her modesty without affectation."

The interplay among these qualities in the love between Argalus and Parthenia gives Sidney a chance to work out an extraordinarily rich texture of dialectical relations. Parthenia's mother intends that she marry a predictably undesirable suitor, and her attempts to coerce Parthenia, as well as the tasks she sets Argalus in order to discourage him, only confirm the love between them: "But the more she assaulted, the more she taught Parthenia to defend; and the more Parthenia defended, the more she made her mother obstinate in the assault" (p. 29). She sends Argalus on "as many dangerous enterprises as ever the evil stepmother Juno recommended to the famous Hercules. But the more his virtue was tried, the more pure it grew, while all the things she did to overthrow him did set him up upon the height of honour." The upshot of these actions, which serve only to incre.. e the affection they intend to destroy, is that the mother's candidate in revenge disfigures Parthenia's face with poison.

This act initiates the second movement of the lovers' travail. Argalus's love for Parthenia is not diminished by her disfigurement, while the greatness of her love for him is such that she does not want to burden him with an ugly wife:

> . . . she took as strange a course in affection; for where she desired to enjoy him more than to live, yet did she overthrow both her own desire and his, and in no sort would yield to marry him— with a strange encounter of love's affects and effects, that he by an affection sprung from excessive beauty should delight in horrible foulness, and she, of a vehement desire to have him, should kindly build a resolution never to have him—for truth is that so in her heart she loved him as she could not find in her heart he should be tied to what was unworthy of his presence. (p. 31)

Sidney goes out of his way here to couch causes and effects in paradoxical and differential form. Parthenia's love leads to consequences wholly different from what one would expect. Instead of entailing the continued desire to marry the man she loves, this love quenches desire in order to fulfill itself. The effect and significances of such paradoxes always depend on their violating the nondialectical assumption that human motivations and moral qualities can generate only actions and qualities that are univocally derivable from them as like from like. And if one did not make such an assumption, there would be no significance in detailing otherwise. But it is dialectic's disruption of univocal determinacy that opens up the discursive space of the new *Arcadia* for its radically complex anatomy and taxonomy of human moral reality. Rather than being fixed and substantial identities, men and women for Sidney seem bundles of potentials, any one of which may come to the fore and set in motion a malign or benign dialectical chain of events or internal motivations and emotions. It is thus stating the obvious that the narrator comments on Parthenia's "strange course in affection," and on the "strange encounter of love's affects and effects" between the two lovers. What is "strange" about these is precisely the dialectical logic that causes, on Argalus's part, a love born out of beauty to continue in its absence, and on Parthenia's, a desire born out of love to elicit its own frustration. We might be tempted to dismiss Sidney's attempts to move us with this tale had he conceived erotic fidelity as a simple monolithic structure of unchanging ethical qualities. But the case here is quite different. Their love is appealing and rhetorically successful through a stability achieved amid competing motivations and pressures coming both from outside of them and from within. Both lovers, confronted with Parthenia's disfigurement, are required to respond with inner strengths before uncalled-upon, and to evoke potentials already latent in their love, exhibiting a fidelity that survives not despite but through taking account of the dialectical shifts imposed upon it.

The love of Argalus and Parthenia is the only example in the new *Arcadia* of erotic passion that achieves harmonious consummation and stability—and it is doomed to destruction by Amphialus's onslaughts in Book 3. Her disfigurement having been cured, Parthenia searches out Argalus and joyfully allows herself to marry him. When Basilius's messenger arrives at their castle, he finds

> a happy couple, he joying in her, she joying in herself, but in herself because she enjoyed him; both increasing their riches by giving to each other; each making one life double because they made a double life one, where desire never wanted satisfaction, nor satisfaction never bred satiety; he ruling because she would obey—or rather, because she would obey, she therein ruling. (pp. 371–72, punctuation modified)

Without analyzing in depth the complex harmonies between husband and wife, desire and desired, ruler and ruled, we can observe here how Sidney appropriates a standard topic of traditional erotic discourse and gives it inner life. I am referring to the notion of two hearts and minds in one body extensively developed from Plato's *Symposium* down to Ficino's commentary on this dialogue. He anatomizes the distinct stages of this reciprocity, noting how each polar term calls up rather than excludes its opposite. Sidney fills out and exhausts the psychological and emotional space in which these reciprocities operate. The notion of one soul in two bodies can mean something, Sidney seems to say, only as a series of circular bestowals moving from the self outward and back again. As in many other passages in the new *Arcadia*, each stage while distinct from the others is redolent with an inner energy that derives it from the preceding one and transforms it into the next.

When the messenger gives the missive to Argalus, her sense of the impending disruption of these reciprocities Parthenia textualizes as a set of differential reciprocities as well:

> . . . though she knew not what to fear, yet she feared because she knew not; but she rose and went aside while he delivered his letters and message. Yet, a far off, she looked now at the messenger, and then at her husband—the same fear which made her loath to have cause of fear, yet making her seek cause to nourish her fear. . . . (p. 372)

The dialectics of Parthenia's foreboding—her oscillation between fear of nothing and consequently her greater fear—are here articulated precisely. And we are suddenly struck by a sharp sense of how the wholly organic and self-supporting field of reciprocation in which plays their mutual love can become a nightmarish prison in which intensity of love creates intense fear for its loss. I have up to this point, although without making the point explicitly, been arguing that Sidney is a master of psychological analysis. I would suggest further that nothing in the new *Arcadia*, save perhaps the full-scale anatomy of the self-tortured Amphialus, approaches these passages for keen delineation of the pulse and fluctuation of psychological movement. Such psychological portraits are not essentially different from descriptions of physical movement, like Musidorus's equestrian exercise analyzed earlier. In both cases, Sidney renders the dynamic fluidity of movement more vivid by segmenting this fluidity into its distinct parts, each segment becoming distinctly meaningful only through its dialectical generation by and of still others.

Section 4

Extended episodes: Dethronement of the King of Phrygia; Andromana, Plangus, and the King of Iberia; Amphialus and Cecropia

The next group of passages is distinguished from the previous because it involves extended episodes wherein two or more characters work out their dialectical interrelations. In these passages differential structure generates not merely limited set pieces but the various extended plots of the new *Arcadia* and, ultimately, the meaning of the work as a whole. I have as yet ignored the central plot, that involving the two lovers, the two daughters of Basilius and his wife Gynecia, the plot to which the old *Arcadia* was limited and which retains its central and framing status in the new *Arcadia*. I leave this dimension of the work to Part Two, since reading and interpreting it involves the problematic relationship between the two works. Consequently, in this section I draw my examples from the characters and subplots that are wholly original with the later work.

An exemplary passage to begin with extends from and carries forward the description of the King of Phrygia, which I have already discussed above. Pyrocles, having been separated from Musidorus during a shipwreck, is imprisoned by the king and is about to be executed. Musidorus searches him out and offers himself in Pyrocles' place. Pyrocles in turn disguises himself and comes to rescue Musidorus just as he mounts the scaffold. What happens next gives us a paradigm for understanding Sidney's differential fashioning of larger narrative units. The passage opens with Musidorus about to be killed and concludes with him declared king of Phrygia. Musidorus, who is telling the story to Pamela, says at the conclusion that "fortune I think [smiled] at her work therein, that a scaffold of execution should grow a scaffold of coronation" (p. 174). Clearly, Sidney anatomizes here nothing other than the revolution of Fortune's wheel.

As the two princes fight for their lives against the soldiers of the king, one of the soldiers retires from the scaffold, leading a second "to pick a thank of the king" by striking "him upon the face, reviling him that so accompanied he would run away from so few." The first in turn "thrust him through—which with his death was straight revenged by a brother of his, and that again requited by a fellow of the other's" (p. 173). This leads to a riot among the soldiers themselves, which alarms the people who, "used to fears but not used to be bold in them . . . began to cry 'Treason!'" (p. 174). The king consequently flees, which causes the instantaneous rumor that the king has been killed, "wherewith certain young men of the bravest minds cried with loud voice, 'Liberty!'; and encouraging the other citizens to follow them, set upon the guard and soldiers as chief instruments of tyranny." The princes soon aid them. "But some of the wisest, seeing that a popular licence is indeed the many-headed tyranny, prevailed with the rest to make Musidorus their chief."

Sidney has figured this comic-opera revolution as a *gradatio* in which the individual stages become links in a chain of undeviating causes and effects. Each moment is demarcated from the preceding one while with equal clarity linked with it. Important for our purposes is this sequence's exploration of the transitional middle ground separating and linking the two opposed stages of Musidorus's predicament. If it is possible for a man to evolve from criminal to king in a matter of minutes, then, Sidney would seem to say, this is how it happens. Other passages I discuss in this section indicate that the rhetorical figure *gradatio* is Sidney's main device for filling out the semantic space between differentially defined moments in a plot. In the characterological set pieces I have already cited, the reader is asked to construct paradigmatic sets of differentially opposed terms in order to recuperate the rapidly unfolding sequences of these terms. Extended plot seems similarly to be for Sidney nothing but the causal sequence linking one term or stage to an opposed term or stage farther up or down the line. Consequently, he needed a schema for articulating this causal sequence, one which would allow the two polar *termini* to be linked in a step-by-step fashion. Each step may itself be constituted differentially, in which case we have links that are themselves bipolar: the first pole linked either differentially or by equivalence to the preceding one, and the second pole linked to the first pole of the next link in the same way.

A similar episode, exhibiting this latter and more complicated kind of linkage, narrates the devious process by which the evil Andromana seduces and enslaves the King of Iberia. Andromana first has an affair with the king's son, Plangus. The king discovers this affair and falls in love with Andromana himself. Andromana takes advantage of a time when Plangus has left the country and ensconces herself in the king's bed. Sidney strings out the process of seduction by featuring Andromana's continual oscillations between offering herself to the king and then drawing back from him. This oscillation is figured in typically dialectical fashion: She never allowed

> his fear to fall to a despair, nor his hope to hasten to an assurance. She was content he should think that she loved him, and a certain stolen look should sometimes (as though it were against her will) bewray it—but if thereupon he grew bold, he straight was encountered with a mask of virtue. (p. 217)

> . . . she did not only use so the spur that his desire ran on, but so the bit that it ran on even in such career as she would have it. . . .

The king finds himself torn between encouragement and frustration, each generating the other in turn. This circular sequence finally opens out toward a linear conclusion, when the king insists on marrying Andromana to resolve this frustration.

The next section of this episode details Andromana's carefully orchestrated plan to call her husband's ire down on Plangus and have him banished. Imitating the story of Phaedra and Hippolytus, Andromana attempts to seduce Plangus, now her stepson, who repulses her and causes her to plan revenge. Sidney (and also Pamela, whose story this is) now give us a complex account of Andromana's projection of her own thoughts onto Plangus, but in reverse. For instance, she projects her own desire for Plangus onto him, but in displaced form as his condemnation of this desire:

> But she who, besides she was grown a mother and a stepmother, did read in his eyes her own fault, and made his conscience her guiltiness, thought still that his presence carried her condemnation, so much the more as that she, unchastely attempting his wonted fancies, found, for the reverence of his father's bed, a bitter refusal; which breeding rather spite than shame in her (or if it were a shame, a shame not of the fault, but of the repulse), she did not only (as hating him) thirst for a revenge, but (as fearing harm from him) endeavoured to do harm unto him. (pp. 217–18)

The syntax of this passage fairly creaks under the weight of the qualifications Pamela finds she must articulate to do justice to the serpentine movement of Andromana's thoughts. Here, rhetorical figuration gives way to an elaborate Jamesian hypotaxis, though differential structures continue to dominate. As Pamela recreates these, Andromana must take account not only of her own desires and fears but of the thoughts and actions she projects onto Plangus. Like the nesting structure that characterizes Musidorus's narrative of his wooing Pamela (discussed in Part Two), this passage likewise encapsulates a series of embeddings: Pamela imagines Andromana's text, which consists of the latter's own proleptic recreation of Plangus's reactions to her plans and her reactions to these in turn. What is guilt in her —as if the deed were already done—becomes outraged conscience in him. The bitterness of his refusal deriving from this outrage becomes shame in her, which in turn is subdivided into differentially opposed causes: moral shame for the fault and immoral shame for the rejection. Driven by the latter, Andromana is torn between hatred resulting from her frustrated desire for Plangus and fear of him, which leads to her plans to kill him.

Read both as Pamela's ex post facto narration of Andromana's reflections, and as the text of these reflections in which Andromana projects action and possible reaction into the future before the fact, this passage takes on stereo-optic, perspectival depth conjured by our seeing the same text from two different viewpoints. Like the King of

Phrygia, Andromana is constrained by the text in which she plans her actions and foresees their consequences, thereby turning this text into a self-fulfilling prophecy. Consequently, Pamela is enabled to narrate after the fact the story of Andromana's rush toward the reactions she most fears, because Andromana has already "narrated" her own story before the fact, binding herself within a chain of actions and reactions of her own making. Pamela's speculations on Andromana's speculations on Plangus's thoughts and motivations fuse the standpoints of third-person and first-person narratives, so that the text on the page becomes an imitation of a character's actions which were already in the past written in that character's text. The circularity of this relationship is paradigmatic of Sidney's narrative practice outlined earlier: the Arcadian world is constituted from nothing other than the texts it contains, because narration and description reproduce the human texts in which the acts and scenes narrated and described originated.

Both desire and fear become dialectically entwined in her attempts to call down the king's wrath on his son:

> Therefore did she try the uttermost of her wicked wit how to overthrow him in the foundation of his strength, which was in the favour of his father; which because she saw strong both in nature and desert, it required the more cunning how to undermine it. And therefore shunning the ordinary trade of hireling sychophants, she made her praises of him to be accusations, and her advancing him to be his ruin. (p. 218)

What then follows is an extended passage detailing how Andromana's praise of Plangus's excellent qualities actually portray him as a threat to his father's throne:

> . . . for first with words nearer admiration than liking she would extol his excellencies (the goodliness of his shape, the power of his wit, the valiantness of his courage, the fortunateness of his successes) so as the father might find in her a singular love towards him—nay, she shunned not to kindle some few sparks of jealousy in him.

In this passage Andromana uses the same strategy for condemning Plangus as she used in winning his father to marriage: moving in one direction by initially going in the opposite one. Here, Andromana banks on the dual potential of virtues for becoming their opposite vices. By praising Plangus's excellencies as virtues, she invites the king—already susceptible to such reverse pressures—to reinterpret them as the latter. There is not a little of Iago and Othello in Andromana's equivocal feelings for Plangus and in the king's reactions to her temptations.

Having planted in the king's mind the conviction that she means no harm to his son, she then proceeds "to praise him with no less vehemency of affection, but with much more cunning of malice." She now calls to the king's attention

> the liberty of his mind, the high-flying of his thoughts, the fitness in him to bear rule, the singular love the subjects bare him; that it was doubtful whether his wit were greater in winning their favours, or his courage in employing their favours; that he was not born to live a subject-life, each action of his bearing in it majesty, such a kingly entertainment, such a kingly magnificence, such a kingly heart for enterprises: especially remembering those virtues which in a successor are no more honoured by the subjects than suspected of the princes. (punctuation modified)

We may pass over without comment Andromana's perversity in verbalizing, for the purpose of destroying him, the very qualities she finds attractive in Plangus, and note only that this passage further unfolds the mixture of desire and hatred Andromana feels. Less obvious is that Pamela here continues to pass unobtrusively from a narrator's perspective, giving Andromana's words as wholly indirect or paraphrased discourse, to replicating these words themselves as free indirect discourse. Pamela begins to use the actual words that Andromana might have used herself, particularly the reiterated adjective "kingly."[22] Andromana exploits the semantic indeterminacy in the adjective as it passes back and forth between being merely metaphorical and therefore a figure of praise, and being a symptom of Plangus's putative monarchal ambitions.

Then would she, by putting off objections, bring in objections to her husband's head, already infected with suspicion. "Nay," would she say "I dare take it upon my death that he is no such son as many, of like might, have been, who loved greatness so well as to build their greatness upon their father's ruin. Indeed, ambition, like love, can abide no lingering, and ever urgeth on his own successes, hating nothing but what may stop them. But the gods forbid we should ever once dream of any such thing in him! who perhaps might be content that you and the world should know what he can do, but the more power he hath to hurt, the more admirable is his praise that he will not hurt." (pp. 218–19)

The cunning and complexity of this passage are almost beyond disentangling. We have, first of all, Andromana's climaxing her praise of Plangus's virtues with the insistence that such virtues are themselves the very factors limiting their own perversion. We may well remember similar statements occurring elsewhere about Pamela and Queen Helen of Corinth. But Sidney never lets us forget—and indeed Andromana keeps ever before her husband's mind—that such strong virtues imply their concomitant vices. Of course, by denying that such is possible in Plangus's case, Andromana only plants the suspicion ever more deeply.

When we find, then, that "all Plangus' actions began to be translated into the language of suspicion," we discover that Andromana usurps the Sidneyan narrative practice. By speaking, as it were, the text of Plangus's goodness, Andromana continually implies that there is still another text, a countertext in which the benign potential of this goodness is translated into potential for evil. A devilish thing about Andromana's discourse is that from a certain perspective it is not inaccurate. Not that Plangus is really plotting against his father, as she wants him to believe. Rather, she is correct in pointing out that every virtue she names could lead, within the dialectical logic that structures human moral qualities, to its related vice. The slide of this reversal takes place wholly within the semantic dimension of Andromana's text—which is overt—and its interplay with its own countertext in the king's mind, which we must infer. Given the potential of human moral qualities to turn into their own opposites, every textual selection carries within itself the possibility of displacement by what is rejected. Therefore, to textualize Plangus's virtues as Andromana does is to cause both king and reader to recognize how they could be textualized in the opposite manner.

Nothing we have seen so far in the new *Arcadia* exhibits Sidney playing so much the virtuoso with the dialectics underlying his ethical vision. More than any other character in the work, Andromana is a master of this vision; nothing that Sidney knows about the dialectical potential of human moral qualities is unknown to her. But clearly such knowledge is like chaff before the fires of anger, desire, hatred, and fear. Whatever the new *Arcadia* tells of the ethical knowledge necessary to avoid the dialectical shifts and slides of one's moral identity, if an Andromana is conceivable and possible, then nothing and no one are safe. For this reason Sidney explores the perversions latent within the most sophisticated understanding of human moral potentials that he was able to achieve.

As fine as is Sidney's portrayal of Andromana's labyrinthine evil, this episode yet pales before the highwater mark of Sidney's art in the new *Arcadia*: the story of Amphialus, his vicious mother Cecropia, and his tormented love for Philoclea. Largely ignored in the critical literature on the work, and when mentioned usually dismissed with scant attention, Amphialus represents a qualitative leap in Sidney's capacities as narrator and delineator of character. If a central issue in the new *Arcadia* is the profoundly Renaissance conundrum of the secret liaison between love and war, tenderness and cruelty, then Amphialus becomes the character in the *Arcadia* where this conundrum is most fully portrayed. His emotions and thoughts, motivations and actions, indeed his very words, are imprisoned within the rhetorical figuration that constitutes the Renaissance understanding of human love. Caught between enslavement to love and the need to dominate, between tenderness and violent rapacity generated by this tenderness, Amphialus goes beyond any other Renaissance version of this self-division, such as Ariosto's Orlando and Spenser's Artegall, and becomes the most precisely drawn example of love's pains before Shakespeare's Othello. Amphialus is par excellence the character in the new *Arcadia* enslaved to the dialectical determinism inflicted on those whose inner lives are textualized according to strictly enforced differentials. However, quite unlike other characters in the work similarly enslaved, Amphialus is endowed with a full and intense consciousness of these paradoxes.[23]

Virtues and vices are so mixed in him that Sidney in effect abandons the rhetorical figurations of *gradatio, syncrisis,* and *anatanogoge* that have served so well in drawing other characters. As in the portrayal of Andromana but to a more developed extent, differentiality remains the deep structure funding Amphialus's character. And as in that episode, Sidney discovers that back-and-forth, pro-et-contra oscillation of paradoxes is too limited for expressing the enormous dynamic rush of Amphialus's thoughts and passions. The style that Sidney invents for Amphialus exhibits instead a flexibility and sinuous sensitivity to the curves of the human psyche that prefigures Richardson and the "great tradition" of the English novel extending through Jane Austen to Henry James.

Though the whole of the Book 3 fragment is given over to Amphialus's story, we first meet him in Book 1, where his early history is told to Musidorus by Queen Helen of Corinth. We discover that he is the son of a brother of Basilius, which makes him a cousin of his beloved Philoclea. His mother Cecropia, until Basilius married Gynecia late in life and had two daughters (Pamela and Philoclea), conceived high hopes of inheriting the throne of Arcadia. With the birth of two female heirs, however, Cecropia is reduced to plotting darkly against them, and it is on her orders that they, along with Pyrocles still disguised as an amazon, are kidnapped and imprisoned in her castle. It is indeed the conflicted relationships Amphialus bears to his mother and to the imprisoned Philoclea that bring his tragedy to crisis. He is, as Book 3 develops at length, compelled against his will to acquiesce in her imprisonment while as a consequence suffering immense inner anguish.

In the story which Queen Helen tells we first come upon the dominant motif of Amphialus's life: a destiny which dooms him to kill or injure those whom he loves and values. In this episode Amphialus has been asked by his friend Philoxenus to woo Queen Helen as proxy for himself. Predictably, Helen falls in love with Amphialus instead, causing Philoxenus to challenge his friend in jealous anger and leading Amphialus to kill him. No sooner does Amphialus pause to look dismayed at his friend's body, but Philoxenus's father, who raised Amphialus as an orphan, comes upon the scene and dies from the shock. Amphialus in an agony of self-hatred turns on Helen, blaming her for the whole affair, and vows never to see her again (pp. 60ff.). When Musidorus hears this story told by Helen herself, she has long been searching throughout Greece for Amphialus, and as the final pages of the new *Arcadia* tell us, she is destined to find him again only after he has been (apparently) mortally wounded first by Musidorus in battle and then by himself, having finally understood his complicity with the tortures undergone by Philoclea at his mother's hands.

We see him next in Book 2, this time through the eyes of the jealous Pyrocles. Pamela and Philoclea have been bathing naked in the river Ladon, and Pyrocles, who for all anybody knows is in fact a woman, finds himself rapturously indulging his voyeurism. He soon realizes, however, that this delicious scene has not been for his eyes only. He discovers Amphialus innocently wandering the same woods, and, as becomes apparent later on, he has suffered irremediable damage to his heart at the sight of the enticing Philoclea. Despite matching Pyrocles' jealous wrath with apologies and courteous refusals, Amphialus finds himself reluctantly defending himself from the enraged amazon. Attempting to fight only on the defensive, Amphialus nevertheless is wounded by Pyrocles but for all that cannot find it in himself to relinquish his courtesy: " 'I would,' " answered Amphialus, 'I had many more such hurts to meet and know that worthy Prince [Pyrocles, with whose vengeance the disguised Pyrocles has threatened him], whose virtue I love and admire, though my good destiny hath not been to see his person' " (p. 197).

In both of these episodes Sidney prepares us for the still later episode in which Amphialus will play a major part. Our impression is summed up in what Pyrocles himself thinks when he first sees him: "for, she [Pyrocles] thought, in her life she had never seen a man of more goodly presence, in whom strong making took not away delicacy, nor beauty fierceness—being indeed such a right manlike man as nature, often erring, yet shows she would fain make" (p. 195).

When, finally, Amphialus discovers that his mother has taken Philoclea and her sister hostages to coerce Basilius's yielding his throne to her son, we are prepared to witness an intense struggle between the twin drives of his passion: desire to keep Philoclea imprisoned and win her love, and his anguished awareness of the psychological wounds he inflicts on her by doing so. The first issues in demonic rage on the battlefield, and the second in continual inner laceration.

Amphialus's initial dialogue with Cecropia adumbrates all these inner divisions. His mother, being unencumbered by love of anyone except her son—and that seems mainly the projection onto him of her own self-aggrandizement—cares nothing for Philoclea. When Amphialus remonstrates with her for keeping Philoclea prisoner, Cecropia answers "with a feigned gravity" (p. 320) that she will then send Philoclea away. This evokes in him the other consequence of his passion, namely, his desire to keep her captive, which in turn allies him with the purposes of his mother. Loving her, he wants her love in return, which means that he does indeed take the role of enslaved lover, as Cecropia says. Because he is torn between his love for Philoclea and the injury he does her in allowing his mother to keep her captive, his love for her will issue in contradictory results. As Cecropia remarks, with not a little of Iago's nasty humor, "pretty intricate follies."[24] She here and throughout has little patience with Amphialus's inner torments and divisions, thinking it would be simpler merely to align himself with her own desire for revenge and power.

Cecropia's viciousness represents a side of Amphialus intimately linked with his love for Philoclea: his life's plague of causing pain and death to those he loves. In this scene with Cecropia his very reasons for objecting to her imprisoning Philoclea—his love for her—causes him in the end to acquiesce in her actions. He will throughout Book 3 be forced by this love to violate this love. That he has sufficient self-awareness and sensitivity to recognize all this only increases his anguish.

Sidney uses Amphialus's long conversation with Philoclea, which follows immediately after (pp. 322–24), to sharpen further the contradiction between his loving and hurting her. He begins by protesting his enslavement to her, to which she answers by pointing out the numerous anomalies involved in his being her slave while he holds her captive. She develops this paradox at length, arguing that if he really wishes her well, he should release her. Thus Philoclea presents Amphialus with the same dilemma as had Cecropia a little earlier: if he loves her enough to let her go, then he should do so; but if he doesn't free her, then he doesn't love her.

Amphialus's torture is carefully laid out for the reader:

> But Amphialus was like the poor woman, who loving a tame doe she had above all earthly things, having long played withal and made it feed at her hand and lap, is constrained at length by famine (all her flock being spent, and she fallen into extreme poverty) to kill the dear [*sic* Feuillerat] to sustain her life: many a pitiful look doth she cast upon it, and many a time doth she draw back her hand before she can give the stroke—for even so, Amphialus by a hunger-starved affection was compelled to offer this injury, and yet the same affection made him with a tormenting grief think unkindness in himself that he could find in his heart any way to restrain her freedom. But at length, neither able to grant nor deny, he thus answered her. . . . (p. 323)

He protests that he would never willingly harm her if he had free choice but insists that he is enslaved to the "tyrant, love." This in turn leads to his spinning out the dialectical logic by which he is driven to injure the one he loves and she becomes the author of her own imprisonment:

> What then shall I say, but that I who am ready to lie under your feet; to venture, nay, to lose my life at your least commandment, I am not the stay of your freedom, but love—love, which ties you in your own knots. It is you yourself that imprison yourself! It is your beauty which makes these castle walls embrace you! It is your own eyes, which reflect upon themselves this injury!

The only way Philoclea can redeem herself from imprisonment is by returning Amphialus's love, and since she is already pledged to Pyrocles, she refuses.

Amphialus's passionate and enraged course impels him toward injuring more than Philoclea. In a passage already discussed, Argalus leaves his wife Parthenia at Basilius's request and dies in single combat with Amphialus. A passage typical of Sidney's nuanced presentation of Amphialus gives his written reply to Argalus's challenge:

> "Much more famous Argalus, I, whom never threatenings could make afraid, am now terrified by your noble courtesy, for well I know from what height of virtue it doth proceed, and what cause I have to doubt such virtue bent to my ruin. But love, which justifieth the unjustice you lay unto me, doth also animate me against all dangers, since I come full of him, by whom yourself have been (if I be not deceived) sometimes conquered. I will therefore attend your appearance in the isle carrying this advantage with me, that, as it shall be a singular honour if I get the victory, so there can be no dishonour in being overcome by Argalus." (p. 374)

Amphialus knows the story of Argalus and Parthenia and is fully aware that in fighting him he assaults a love he can feel more than ordinary sympathy with. As the fight proceeds, it increasingly appears that Argalus is overmatched, a fact that makes Amphialus all the more reluctant to continue:

> But his [Argalus's] mind was evil waited on by his lamed force, so as he received still more and more wounds, which made all his armour seem to blush that it had defended his master no better. But Amphialus perceiving it, and weighing the small hatefulness of their quarrel with the worthiness of the knight, desired him to take pity of himself. (p. 376)

Argalus refuses this appeal and instead puts all his remaining strength into a final assault, thereby compelling Amphialus to answer him in kind. As he is about to kill Argalus, Parthenia, whose forebodings have led her to the battlefield, rushes between the two knights and parts them. Her appeal to Amphialus is cunningly calculated by both her and Sidney to strike deeply into the heart of his own exacerbated torment:

> "My Lord," said she, "it is said you love. In the power of that love, I beseech you to leave off this combat. As even your heart may find comfort in his affection, even for her sake I crave it. Or if you be

mortally determined, be so pitiful unto me, as first to kill me, that I may not see the death of Argalus." (p. 377)

Her final appeal foreshadows yet another slaughter lying behind the present one to be forced on the unwilling Amphialus: he will likewise kill Parthenia when she challenges him muffled in armor. In the present fight Amphialus tries his uttermost to end it. Yet Argalus is moved by the same motives as Amphialus, and in the following passage Sidney replicates in more than usually tangled prose the dialectical causality which links the two knights together in the midst of their fight:

But Amphialus, not only conjured by that which held the monarchy of his mind, but even in his noble heart melting with compassion at so passionate a sight, desired him [Argalus] to withhold his hands, for that he should strike one who sought his favour and would not make resistance—a notable example of the wonderful effects of virtue, where the conqueror sought for friendship of the conquered, and the conquered would not pardon the conqueror, both indeed being of that mind to love each other for accepting but not for giving mercy, and neither affected to overlive a dishonour; so that Argalus not so much striving with Amphialus (for if he had had him in the like sort, in like sort he would have dealt with him, as labouring against his own power which he chiefly despised) set himself forward, stretching his strength to the uttermost. (p. 377)

This final effort, however, destroys Argalus: "the fire of that strife, blown with his inward rage, boiled out his blood in such abundance" that he soon bleeds to death in Parthenia's arms.

Sidney could hardly develop further the complex dialectics by which the virtues of chivalry and courtesy shared by both knights only results in increased enmity, with self-destruction on the one side and on the other increased self-recrimination. Sidney has clearly gone beyond the buoyant portrayals of knightly combat featured in other Renaissance romance epics, such as those of Ariosto, Tasso, and Spenser. We are by this point in our reading, however, not unprepared for the perspective he takes on the code of chivalry. Far from repudiating it, he makes us feel that Amphialus's adherence to it is one of his saving virtues. But he is not ignorant either of the real anguish forced on those who feel they must obey such imperatives, nor of the heart-rending slaughter of others and the rending of one's own moral sensibilities which such obedience entails. The play of differentials in this passage, by which the motives of chivalry and honor enforce violations of the very uprightness of mind and heart that cherishes them, reaches a high seriousness and tragedy wholly absent from similarly structured passages which the reader has encountered earlier. For, as his final destiny informs us, Amphialus is ultimately devoted to nothing else than his own death, and, unwittingly, the deaths of as many as become entangled in this destiny. As Sidney shows us in Book 3, dialectic is the name not only of psychological and moral double binds; it is also the name of human tragedy.

It shows, then, even more the tremendous leap in character portrayal Sidney has made when he comes to write Book 3, that he should increase our sense of this tragedy with another portrayal that for its dark comedy is like nothing in English letters since Chaucer's Pardoner. I am referring to Amphialus's mother, Cecropia, whose single-minded malice, buoyant and sinister by turns, forms the perfect foil against which Amphialus plays out his doom.

Cecropia is truly unique among the characters of this work, and Sidney's art in delineating her has been uniformly missed. She is much more than a stereotyped villain, a mouthpiece for immoralism and atheism against which Pamela may score points in the famous debate between the two. Her Iago-like impatience with the moral and psychological complexities of those around her and her capacity to mimic such complexities when they suit her purposes show just how much Sidney was willing to risk of the central values of his work in laying them open to her droll and vicious parodies.

We see Cecropia at her best in the two scenes with Philoclea and Pamela, respectively. Realizing that her son is disastrously hamstrung by his love for Philoclea, she soon recognizes that she must find some way to satisfy his passion. Her first recourse is to prevail upon Philoclea to reciprocate Amphialus's suit. She begins by praising Philoclea's physical beauty, which, she informs her, will not always maintain itself against the onslaught of time (p. 330). She next, in a parody of Amphialus's own desperate address to Philoclea, says to her:

". . . you misconster everything that only for your sake is attempted: you think you are offended, and are indeed defended; you esteem yourself a prisoner, and are in truth a mistress; you fear hate, and shall find love. And truly, I had a thing to say to you— but it is no matter. Since I find you are so obstinately melancholy as that you woo his fellowship, I will spare my pains and hold my peace"—and so stayed indeed, thinking Philoclea would have had a female inquisitiveness of the matter. (p. 330)

This last comment by the narrator gives us a clue at once to Cecropia's cunning and her stupidity: she cannot conceive that other women may be prompted by motives other than her own. This is shown when she next seeks to tempt Philoclea with the same commodities she finds attractive: power and pleasure:

". . . imagine, that I . . . am come to lead you not only to your desired and imagined happiness, but to a true and essential happiness; not only to liberty, but to liberty with commandment. The way I will show you, which, if it be not the gate builded hitherto in your private choice, yet shall it be a door to bring you through a garden of pleasures as sweet as this life can bring forth—nay, rather, which makes this life to be a life." (p. 331)

When Philoclea, unwilling to admit her love for Pyrocles, says that she has taken a vow of virginity, Cecropia finds it in herself to exhort participation in Nature's bounty, and to expound the joys of small children:

" 'A vow,' quoth you? No, no, my dear niece, Nature, when you were first born, vowed you a woman; and as she made you child of a mother, so, to do your best to be mother of a child, she gave you beauty to move love, she gave you wit to know love, she gave you an excellent body to reward love—which kind of liberal rewarding is crowned with unspeakable felicity; for this, as it bindeth the receiver, so it makes happy the bestower: this doth not impoverish, but enrich the giver. Oh, the sweet name of a mother! Oh, the comfort of comforts! to see your children grow up, in whom you are as it were eternized. If you could conceive what a heart-tickling joy it is to see your own little ones with awful love come running to your lap, and like little models of yourself still carry you about them, you would think unkindness in your own thoughts that ever they did rebel against the mean unto it." (p. 332)

This is high comedy, which Sidney pushes to even greater heights when Cecropia laments the loneliness of widowhood and remembers with maudlin fondness her dead husband and her own married life. The reader will not have forgotten that the main emotion she felt when her husband died was chagrin that he had not yet succeeded in dethroning Basilius:

> "O widow-nights, bear witness with me of the difference! How often, alas, do I embrace the orphan side of my bed, which was wont to be imprinted by the body of my dear husband, and with tears acknowledge that I now enjoy such a liberty as the banished man hath, who may, if he list, wander over the world but is forever restrained from his most delightful home; that I have now such a liberty as the seeled dove hath, which, being first deprived of eyes, is then by the falconer cast off? For believe me, niece, believe me, man's experience is woman's best eyesight. Have you ever seen a pure rose-water kept in a crystal glass? How fine it looks! How sweet it smells, while that beautiful glass imprisons it! Break the prison, and let the water take his own course: doth it not embrace dust, and lose all his former sweetness and fairness! Truly, so are we, if we have not the stay—rather than the restraint —of crystalline marriage. (p. 333)

Sidney has here created a masterpiece of mimicry. We hear Cecropia's voice turn from fulsomeness to slyness and back again. The notion of this deadly woman going on in the fashion of the Nurse in *Romeo and Juliet* about the joys of matrimony and children strikes such a note of precisely mingled comedy and sinister threat as will not be sounded again until Dickens. We hear the trick of her voice in the carefully distinguished rhythms and vocabulary of various sections of her speech. This is something readers have generally ignored in the new *Arcadia*, used as they are to viewing it as uniformly and tediously ornamented from first to last as a rococo room in a late Renaissance Italian palazzo.

Her appeal to Philoclea not to be over-finicky about the particular door she takes out of her prison manifests at once her casual cruelty, her insensitivity to love, and her genuine perplexity that anyone should balk at such an offer. And this is perhaps the most deliciously comic feature of this passage: her offers of the powers and pleasures to be had from a marriage of convenience and her praise of seizing the joys offered by a beautiful body are not merely cunning speeches. They in fact represent her honest belief that women are incapable of seeing sex and power in any other light. She is genuinely perplexed by Philoclea, Pamela, and her son alike. She has little use for or patience with complicated scruple, and her resigned but petulant comment on the dialectical tangles of Amphialus's erotic problems —"pretty intricate follies"—is rather a breath of fresh air in a work otherwise crowded with characters devoted to nursing their Jamesian sensibilities.

There is then throughout Sidney's portrayal of Cecropia a muted, bitter humor at her expense. Here she is, with a clear plan in mind that requires for its success nothing but the casual destruction of a couple of women, and she finds herself caught in a dense network of emotions and values that she cannot begin to comprehend. Hers is a perpetual state of exasperation at the moral and psychological complexity of the world she lives in. She must perforce obliquely do obeisance to this complexity and take it into account, if only because her own son is one of its prime victims. Cecropia cannot but think that she lives in a world of fools, who refuse to see straight on the simple brutal facts of life. Given Sidney's dedication to creating in the new *Arcadia* a fictive universe of dialectically entangled values and emotions, it is a stroke of comic genius to have invented a Cecropia whose tunnel-vision—the product of her unquestioning, serene ego-ism—can encompass nothing of this universe, and must react to it only with uninterrupted bafflement.

But her puzzlement likewise signals an essential blindness in her cunning and worldly wisdom. For Cecropia's evil is fatally flawed to the exact degree that she cannot understand how anyone can act any differently than herself. Consequently her remarkable capacity to mimic in turn the phrases of fulsome compliment, generous offers of position and power, old wives' prattle in praise of marriage and domestic bliss, and finally her teary lament for her dead husband: all of these masquerades finally prevent her from recognizing her incapacity to see past her own rough-and-ready dedication to supreme power with no strings attached. Such obtuseness can fathom neither the loves of her prisoners and of her own son, nor their remarkable capacity to endure. Wrapped in her smug evil, she becomes at once threateningly sinister and oddly petty.

The complex interplay of Cecropia's and Amphialus's visions of his situation reaches a climax after Amphialus has slain the grief-obsessed Parthenia. In an agony of self-recrimination Amphialus throws himself into melancholy contemplation of his whole misfortune-laden life. When his mother comes to stir him to action, he spills all his anguished meditations out before her. Cecropia's response turns out to be the perfect banal complement to Amphialus's anguish. She cannot, in effect, understand why he refuses to take by force what every woman fully intends to yield anyway, whatever her protestations to the contrary. Citing classical authorities for this piece of advice, she points out that Theseus, Hercules, and Paris all discovered that "she, who could never like him for serviceableness, ever after loved him for violence" (p. 402). It is difficult to know whether we are to laugh or weep at this exchange. Although we sense the immense gulf of incomprehension that separates mother's and son's grasp of his passion, or Philoclea's own beauty and endurance, and indeed of the whole universe of tangled motives that the new *Arcadia* is rife with, we still recognize Amphialus's secret complicity in Cecropia's dedication to rough-and-ready sex. Two differential reciprocities between love and violence meet and clash here, and we cannot recognize their incommensurability without also taking account of their mutual implication. For Cecropia, love *is* war, and that's the way women like it. For Amphialus, love generates violence despite itself. And whether we view it through the eyes of either, the fact remains that violence is inflicted on the loved one not despite this love but because of it. However we react to this exchange, then, our emotions are complicated even further in recognizing that Amphialus in loving Philoclea cannot escape that dimension of this love that is embodied in his mother's cruelty.

The logic of this secret complicity Sidney traces out with unerring accuracy. Having been mortally wounded by Musidorus disguised as the Black Knight, Amphialus returns to the castle to learn finally of the tortures to which Cecropia has subjected Philoclea without his knowledge. He rises from his bed and rushes toward his mother on the parapet of the castle, who stepping backward in fear of his rage falls off the wall and is killed. The death of Cecropia becomes then the logical foreshadowing of Amphialus's own death. He traces out yet once again the sequence of unmitigated disasters of which throughout his life he has been the unwitting cause and attempts to kill himself. He slips because of his weakness, only to discover in his clothes the case of knives which Philoclea brought with her to the castle, and with these stabs himself. Sidney's words rendering the sight presented to the servants when they discover him sum up cogently Amphialus's tragedy: They "came in, and there found him swimming in his own blood—there giving a pitiful spectacle, where the conquest was the conqueror's overthrow, and self-ruin the only triumph of a battle fought between him and himself" (p. 442).

This is the last we see of Amphialus. Queen Helen of Corinth, having finally located him, enters the castle and carries him away to try to heal him. Whether Amphialus was to survive these final assaults on himself or was to die is something we shall never know, since his destiny was finally closed up in the author's own death.[25] In him, in any case, we witness the farthest reach of insight and character portrayal to which Sidney's differential structuring of the new *Arcadia* led him. The inner divisions which Amphialus suffers from first to last extend to self-destruction all the other differential portrayals that Sidney added to the earlier work in writing the later one. Amphialus consequently stands alone in the new *Arcadia* as a singular embodiment of the differential structure of human identity that radically informs every detail of the work. For only in him are we allowed to observe the full range of the dire potentialities of this structure pursuing themselves to the final conclusions they always portend in other characters but which, save here, are never realized. In Amphialus alone we understand what Sidney finally understood when he became dissatisfied with the original *Arcadia* and came to write the new: that the ethical dialectics inseparable from human moral identity can lead to human tragedy and self-destruction.

Section 5

Expansions of the old *Arcadia*:
Gynecia; Philoclea

All of the passages discussed so far occur only in the new *Arcadia*.
As such, they register one of the major *desiderata* Sidney evidently
wished to fill when he left behind the old *Arcadia*: exploring the
possibilities of structuring the whole range of fictional discourse—
scenic description, character portrayal, narration—according to the
resources of differential rhetorical figuration. Among the characters
of the old *Arcadia*, however, there are two whose earlier portrayals
contain the seeds of this sort of figuration, though greatly expanded
in the new: Gynecia and Philoclea. These two characters undergo
psychological and moral traumas generally similar to those explored
in the subplots of the new *Arcadia*, and I shall conclude my consideration of specific passages in this first part by citing Sidney's greatly
expanded treatment of these two erotically obsessed women.

In Gynecia, Sidney chooses to work out the most dire complexities
of erotic passion that we observe in the main plot. Doubly jealous of
her husband and her daughter, Gynecia is wracked with guilt to the
point where she has a prophetic dream in which she sees her husband dead. Awakening only to discover that Pyrocles has stolen some
distance away with Philoclea, she runs after them, meditating as she
goes on the disastrous emotional transformations she has undergone:

> But the great and wretched Lady Gynecia, possessed with those
> devils of love and jealousy, did rid herself from her tedious hus-
> band; and taking nobody with her, going toward them [Philoclea
> and Pyrocles], "O jealousy," said she, "the frenzy of wise folks, the
> well-wishing spite and unkind carefulness, the self-punishment for
> other's fault and self-misery in other's happiness; the cousin of
> envy, daughter of love, and mother of hate, how couldst thou so
> quietly get thee a seat in the unquiet heart of Gynecia—Gynecia,"
> said she sighing, "thought wise, and once virtuous? Alas, it is thy
> breeder's power which plants thee there; it is the inflaming agony
> of affection that works the chilling access of thy fever, in such sort
> that nature gives place. The growing of my daughter seems the

decay of my self; the blessings of a mother turn to the curses of a competitor, and the fair face of Philoclea appears more horrible in my sight then the image of death." (pp. 278–79)

Gynecia perceives as clearly as Amphialus her own condition and is among the few Arcadian characters (including the two heroes) who suffer not only the dialectics controlling the texts of their moral and psychological identities but a conscious understanding of these texts as well. The types of differential transgressions Gynecia catalogues here are by now familiar to the reader, and there is no need once again to recuperate the kind of information they imply. The intensity of Gynecia's passion and jealousy, the inner division of her motives, and the self-destructiveness with which she eagerly embraces punishment after having (as she supposes) killed her husband: all of these elements link her with the erotically disoriented women in the subplots of the new *Arcadia*: Erona,[26] Andromana, even Helen of Corinth. One may also see in her an avatar of Amphialus. For this reason her portrayal offers us structurally nothing that we have not already examined.

However, the case of Philoclea is something different, since it is the most extended example in the *Arcadia* of Sidney's demarcating a character's identity through its capacity for continuous dialectical transformation. This is done in Philoclea's anguished meditation on her growing love for Zelmane-Pyrocles. Sidney expands this meditation greatly from its original form in the old *Arcadia* and in doing so once again confirms his general intent in the new *Arcadia* to explore the dialectical conditions of human wholeness, that is, the harmonious and discordant dialectics that constitute this wholeness. In Philoclea's case Sidney portrays the development of female eroticism from sexual innocence through latent homosexuality to heterosexual love.

In a passage the new *Arcadia* shares with the old, Sidney commences by pointing out the instability inherent in Philoclea's sexual innocence:

The sweet-minded Philoclea was in their degree of well doing to whom the not knowing of evil serveth for a ground of virtue, and hold their inward powers in better form with an unspotted simplicity than many, who rather cunningly seek to know what goodness is than willingly take into themselves the following of it. But as that sweet and simple breath of heavenly goodness is the easier to be altered because it hath not passed through the worldly wickedness, nor feelingly found the evil that evil carries with it, so now the Lady Philoclea, whose eyes and sense had received nothing but according as the natural course of each thing required (which from the tender youth had obediently lived under her parents' behests without framing out of her own will the forechoosing of anything), when now she came to appoint (wherein her judgement was to be practised in knowing faultiness by his first tokens), she was like a young fawn, who coming in the wind of the hunters, doth not know whether it be a thing or no to be eschewed—whereof at this time she began to get a costly experience. (pp. 143–44)

Unlike her mother's erotic transformation, Philoclea's will take place in a manner more or less unconscious, and the narrator depends on the reader's sexual sophistication to recognize the causal links through which each stage grows out of the one previous and entails the next. The reader must supply the information to make this sequence intelligible, because Philoclea, like Pyrocles and Musidorus earlier as well as some of the subsidiary characters, unwittingly becomes enslaved to the entailments of her own text, and understanding what has happened to her comes only as the final step in this entailment.

Philoclea's progress is broken by the narrator into four stages. The first stage carefully articulates Zelmane-Pyrocles' friendliness toward Philoclea and the initial emotions this friendliness awakens in her. Since the amazon was noble, Philoclea paid "her" "a kind of heedful attention" (p. 144). The loneliness of the lodges created also "a willingness of conversation," while Zelmane-Pyrocles' "wit and behaviour" create "a liking and silent admiration." All of these causes yield in Philoclea "a most friendly affection." As a consequence Philoclea's mind "would receive no message from her senses without that affection were the interpreter."

This initial stage gives way to the second by a typical Sidneyan *chiasmus:* "matters being so turned in her that, where at first, liking her manners did breed goodwill, now goodwill became the chief cause of liking her manners, so that within a while Zelmane was not prized for her demeanour but the demeanour was prized because it was Zelmane's." Cause and effect have switched places, and the affection resulting from Pyrocles' attractiveness increases that attractiveness. This second stage is narcissistic, and Philoclea begins to imitate Zelmane (pp. 144–45). These imitations are not limited to demeanor and gestures but extend to gazing at Zelmane in exactly the same way that "she" gazes at her: "so that, as Zelmane did often eye her, she would often eye Zelmane; and as Zelmane's eyes would deliver a submissive but vehement desire in their look, she, though as yet she had not the desire in her, yet should her eyes answer in like-piercing kindness of a look" (p. 145). This allusion to the myth of Narcissus will be developed when Philoclea becomes increasingly conscious of the frustration she must suffer in striving to consummate her love for another woman, that is, another self.

The stage of latent homosexuality is the third. Here imitation brought on by an as yet innocent affection leads to the desire for the ultimate imitation: the obliteration of any difference between lover and beloved. Within stage three Philoclea makes her first acquaintance with passionate desire: through imitating Zelmane's outward appearance she is brought to imitate the emotions behind it:

> . . . till at the last, poor soul, ere she were aware, she accepted not only the band, but the service; not only the sign, but the passion signified. For whether it were that her wit in continuance did find, that Zelmane's friendship was full of impatient desire, having the more than ordinary limits, and therefore she was content to second Zelmane, though herself knew not the limits, or that in truth true love, well considered, have an infective power, at last she fell in acquaintance with loves harbinger, wishing.

It should be apparent that each of these stages is really composed of gradual transformations that link the end of a previous stage to the beginning of the next. Recapitulating the sequence so far—attraction creates liking, liking creates attraction, attraction leads to imitation including imitation of the lover's love—we can see that Sidney envisions each stage as a relay joining the previous moment to the one following. However, there is a paradox in all this. Though every stage in this sequence is univocally implied by what precedes it, the total process leads nowhere else but from one term to its differential opposite: this passage transgresses the differential that sets off sexual innocence from sexual knowledge or experience. Nevertheless, this sequence becomes a *gradatio* charting the paradoxical entailment that links Philoclea's sexual innocence with its potential for erotic passion.

Stage four, issuing from the conclusion of stage three, places squarely before Philoclea the apparently insurmountable problem raised by her falling in love with another woman:

> First she would wish that they two might live all their lives together like two of Diana's nymphs. But that wish she thought not sufficient, because she knew there would be more nymphs besides them who also would have their part in Zelmane. Then would she wish that she were her sister, that such a natural band might make her more special to her. But against that, she considered that though being her sister, if she happened to be married, she should be robbed of her. Then, grown bolder, she would wish either herself or Zelmane a man, that there might succeed a blessed marriage betwixt them. (punctuation modified)

The terminus of this sequence is Philoclea's final discovering the nature of love and her complete enslavement to it: "the sweet Philoclea, while she might prevent it she did not feel it, now she felt it when it was past preventing . . . for now indeed love pulled off his mask, and showed his face unto her, and told her plainly that she was his prisoner" (p. 146).

After a long meditation on her lost innocence Philoclea finally confronts the most agonizing aspect of her passion: the impossibility of consummating it: "Oh, then, oh ten times unhappy that I am, since where in all other hope kindleth love, in me despair should be the bellows of my affection! and of all despairs, the most miserable, which is drawn from impossibility" (p. 149). Seeing that her mother loves Zelmane as well, she reasons that such love cannot be without some hope of fulfillment, however impossible it may be for Philoclea to imagine it. This, in addition to Zelmane's manifest love for herself, implies something about love that she is ignorant of, and Philoclea is thus left in a kind of sexual limbo.

The new *Arcadia* version goes beyond its old *Arcadia* counterpart primarily in this extended exploration of female sexuality as it moves from what Sidney presents as an incomplete homosexual eroticism toward heterosexual love. In all this, however, one discovers perhaps another purpose: a kind of teasing prurience that appeals to the reader's delight in watching the gradual evolution of sexual consciousness in an innocent young person who has as yet little or no knowledge of the sexual act itself. In exhibiting to the sexually knowledgeable reader the inexpert gropings of a young woman moving in a direction which she does not understand and the reader does, Sidney also shows us that the rules governing the successive differentials unfolding these feelings are the rules of human sexual passion itself. For the reader to recuperate this passage, she must bring these rules to mind and recognize how much Philoclea's sexual awakening depends on her growing ability to "write" a text the rules of which she is ignorant. We have here a kind of ribald version of Chomsky's notion that young children absorb and synthesize competence in the grammar of their own language while exercising only a performative role as language users. In Philoclea we have a young woman who step by step learns to speak a *parole* the *langue* of which she is ignorant. Of course, she will "know all" by the end—that is, by the time Pyrocles unfolds himself to her and they betroth themselves to each other. But if my description is correct, then Philoclea enacts just the kind of recuperations the reader is required continually to make in order to understand what the new *Arcadia* says and means. Like Philoclea, the reader discovers the rules governing the text she is reading only after one has proceeded some of the way into it. The text's unfolding, like the unfolding of Philoclea's sexual passion, is not only a "horizontal" process, teleologically aimed at a final terminus in the syntagmatic dimension. It is in addition a "vertical" process as well, where at each succeeding stage of the process a new aspect of the whole synchronic, paradigmatic set of units and rules governing the disposition of these units is called upon.

The reader's interest in this passage is thus encouraged to be partly sexual and partly semiotic, in that her attention is directed to an anatomy of the semiotic process through which a full-scale text of sexual consciousness is gradually constituted. It is a matter of ontogeny once more recapitulating phylogeny, when we witness the evolution of the public text of sexual sophistication being traced out yet once again in the private world of Philoclea's developing desires. It is as if Sidney had set himself this standard problem for the writer of fiction: how to make plausible the final discovery of sexuality on the part of a young woman who begins with nothing but unconscious and therefore unsemioticized emotions, and who must guide herself along the path of the development of these emotions without any external help, or very little. His answer is to give us a "definition of love" that terminates a process of textual evolution structured by *chiasmus* and *gradatio*. The sophisticated reader is reminded that sexual self-consciousness both results from and yet contains as a kind of Hegelian *aufhebung* all the previous stages in its own development: sexual maturity both concludes this development and includes the consciousness of this development. Philoclea undergoes the first and finally arrives at the second, while the reader, having previously enacted Philoclea's process, recapitulates it, but now as a gradual recuperation of the rules that govern the unfolding text of sexual sophistication itself.

Section 6

Style, paradox, free indirect discourse, and the dialectical rules of the new *Arcadia*

I have shown in the preceding sections that a reader traversing the text of the *Arcadia* must confront certain questions ab ovo. First among these questions, and in a sense the source of all the rest, is the nature of the antithetical rhetorical figuration constituting the work's discourse. The Arcadian style does not point beyond itself to a meaning couched in the neutral, nonfigured language of thematic paraphrase. On the contrary, the Arcadian style calls attention to and thematizes several aspects of the style itself—aspects at once rhetorical, logical, psychological, and thematic—that turn the reader's regard toward the intelligible, significant structures of the style and the rules that govern it. My general method in this study has been so far to disclose first what is problematical about the Arcadian text, and then to pursue those theoretical dimensions of the text that resolve these problems. For this reason I have postponed global questions of the *Arcadia*'s thematic content and the significance of the Arcadian style for this content until Part Two of this study, in order to isolate those aspects of this style which must be understood in order to take on thematic significance.

The passages I have discussed in Part One indicate that the reader is invited to take cognizance of several distinct dimensions of the Arcadian style: (1) the logical dimension of antithetical figuration, which calls for understanding the logical rules that make paradox possible, that is, those rules that paradox violates; (2) the relation between this antithetical figuration and the world of natural and human phenomena this figuration organizes. On this topic my main argument is that the *Arcadia* gives us no "external" world existing outside of the figuration in which it is constituted. (3) This nonmimetic, essentially structuralist thesis is balanced by another, which concerns the relation of the Arcadian style to the characters who are the origins and sources of the Arcadian text itself: the Sidneyan third-person narrator, the third-person narrators who are also characters in the story, and the relation of these two narrative texts to the first-person texts submerged in these. My argument on this score is that the *Arcadia* imitates, in the mode of free indirect discourse, the texts in which the individual characters in the story textually organize their own moral identities; and that the Arcadian world, both human and natural, is constituted in these texts. In short, the three, usually separate dimensions of third-person narrative, characterological psychology, and external world (which also includes human agents) fuse in the single text of the Arcadian world. (4) Finally, the rules that govern this text, and which recuperate and make sense of the paradoxes that constitute it, are the rules of dialectical logic, some form of which the reader must grasp in order to understand individual passages and, as I argue in Part Two, the global meaning of the whole work.

If I appear to say that a central aspect of Sidney's new *Arcadia* concerns the "theory" of the book itself, this appearance is accurate.

Every literary work of major significance contains an element of the self-reflexive and to that extent is "about" the theory of writing and reading itself. This is not to say that this circular looping back of regard exhausts the meaning of the new *Arcadia*, any more than it does that of Dante's *Commedia* or Milton's *Paradise Lost*, which are also highly self-reflexive works. Rather, understanding what these works have to say to us, whatever that might be, requires a prior understanding of the rules that govern the texts themselves, the text's "grammar," which not only enables it to say this or that but enables it to say anything at all. Since I contend that the new *Arcadia* is not merely written according to certain dialectical rules governing its global structures and its style but that in addition these rules are what the work is about, it is necessary in concluding Part One and as a preface to Part Two to make these rules explicit. What follows in this concluding section is fuller exploration of the theoretical aspects of the Arcadian style which have arisen ad hoc in my preceding analyses. These explorations have two purposes: to complete these analyses by clarifying the theoretical formulations underlying them, and in doing this also to make clearer the concrete thematic import of these passages. Here, meaning and theory of meaning are finally inseparable, since the first involves fictional characters and reader alike in exploring the second.

In this section I will take up in the following order these topics, already discussed incompletely in the preceding sections: (1) The Arcadian style as derivation of, rather than deviation from, rhetorical figuration available in the grammatical resources of Sidney's native English language; (2) Arcadian paradox as irreducible to nonparadoxical paraphrase and recuperation; (3) the dialectical rules that govern the Arcadian text; (4) finally, Sidney's use of free indirect discourse to link his fictive characters to the Arcadian world they live in and textually constitute.

In my introductory summary of comment critical of the Arcadian style, I pointed out that one obstacle to understanding this style lies in seeing it as a complex overlay of rhetorical figuration imposed on an otherwise relatively straightforward story. This assumption implies still another of broader import, namely, that a specific style is distinguished by various verbal figures that deviate from "normal" speech patterns. The first assumption works to drive a wedge between the verbal text and a supposed core of conceptual or empirical reality lying behind or beneath this text, while the notion of style as deviation from normal word patterns splits style along another axis into two kinds of verbal patterning. These two assumptions lead together to the conclusion that there is a "normal" style that efficiently mediates meaning, as distinct from a non-normal, figured style that only serves to obscure meaning.

Significantly enough, we can discover this notion of style in the analysis of Richard A. Lanham, who has had most to say about the Arcadian style. In his monograph "The Old Arcadia" Lanham finds Sidney in writing the old *Arcadia* first "wholly intoxicated with language, then sobered after his overindulgence."[27] He sees evidence in *A Defence of Poetry* of a "disenchantment with his own prose style [which] may have caused Sidney to leave the New *Arcadia* incomplete" (p. 344). But since Sidney went on after the *Defence* to be "if anything more ornate, more methodically ornate, in the New than in the Old," Lanham concludes that Sidney intended the rhetorical ornateness of the new *Arcadia* to be read comically and ironically by the reader:

> This explanation agrees with the evidence we have found in the Old *Arcadia* that Sidney often uses an elaborate style for comic purposes. According to this view, Sidney was from the first aware of the dangers of excess. Like anyone sensitive to language in that time, he enjoyed playing with it, perhaps even too much, at too great length, so that an apology was necessary. But he was never swept entirely off his feet by a tidal wave of fashion. He preserved his sense of proportion, even when his characters did not. (ibid.)

In this perspective, taking the Arcadian style seriously is to lose one's sense of proportion. As I suggested in my introduction, Lanham's argument implies that Sidney himself found the *Arcadian* style reprehensible and laughable, therein preserving a sense of humor that was to desert William Hazlitt and Virginia Woolf later on.

Lanham does not argue here specifically a deviationist notion of style. What he gives us, however, is a recuperation of the Arcadian style that requires the reader to envision it as rhetorically over-ornate, and within the context of my own analysis this assertion implies just the kinds of discountings and paraphrases that a deviationist argument would require. I cite Lanham's discussion of the Arcadian style, however, only as a preface to taking up two of his later treatments of rhetoric from which I draw support for my own position: *Style: An Anti-Textbook* and *The Motives of Eloquence: Literary Rhetoric in the Renaissance*.[28] In the first he announces a view of stylistic complexity that confronts head-on the deviationist cult of efficient, styleless prose featured in college composition courses. And in the second he formulates a theory of Renaissance literary rhetorical practice that to my mind describes Sidney's practice in the new *Arcadia*.

In *Style: An Anti-Textbook* Lanham wittily unmasks prose that seeks to be styleless, efficient, and clear for what it often is: simply uncouth and enslaved to its own forms of—often opaque—figuration. For Lanham, styles that are artfully "opaque" direct the reader specifically to what they want to say: "The opaque segment of the spectrum [of available styles], by compelling this attention to surface, guides with more accuracy to the passage's center. Only attention to the stylistic surface yields the meaning it adumbrates—a meaning not beneath it but on it" (p. 53). And in what appears (in the context of his monograph on the old *Arcadia*) to be a total about-face regarding such texts as the new *Arcadia*, Lanham extends this argument:

> From one point of view, then, there is no such thing as excessive ornament in prose. We can never be, as the hero of an Elizabethan romance complains, poisoned with roses, unless the poisoning constitutes the main business at hand. The denser the ornament, the more manner becomes matter, style subject, words things. Within such an aesthetic, Swift's cozy "proper words in proper places" becomes meaningless. All words are proper words, and proper places are the places the opaque stylist carves out as proper. (p. 63)

In keeping with this perspective Lanham in *The Motives of Eloquence* distinguishes in western writing two notions of textuality: that which refers past itself to a transtextual reality, and that which calls attention to itself, which resists allowing the reader to go beyond it (pp. 18–19). Commenting on the centrality of mimetic (i.e., referential) notions of textuality in western thinking, Lanham argues:

Our sketch of the rhetorical ideal suggests that this exclusive focus is incomplete. What of the reality imitated? Posit a rhetorical, rather than a serious, reality, and mimesis is reversed 180 degrees. If reality is rhetorical, dramatic, then "serious" literature is no longer serious, realistic literature no longer realistic.

Despite apparent inconsistencies Lanham's position in his study of Sidney may be in essence consistent with that in his later two books. His distinction between "serious" and rhetorical (i.e., "playful") writing still maintains, though in disguised and ambiguous form, a commitment to the deviationist distinction between text and world. Of interest in the context of my own argument, however, is his willingness to grant rhetorically dense styles not only a functional role in communication (in *Style: An Anti-Textbook*), but a mimetic role as well (in *The Motives of Eloquence*). The Arcadian style, in fact, fulfills both functions. In guiding the reader through its rhetorical figures to recuperate the logical and semantic rules that govern them, the Arcadian style in addition presents itself as nothing other than a mimesis of the rhetorically structured ethical realities it deals with.

Some contemporary theories of style recognize that rhetorical figuration can be conceived as either deviating from or deriving from the "normal" patterns available to the resources of a language. Pierre Guiraud, a proponent of style-as-deviation, sums up the central argument of this position when he says that

> the "effect of style" produced on the reader would depend on a "surprise," or on an "unfulfilled expectation" (or eventually on a fulfilled expectation). Now how can surprise or expectation be defined if not in terms of probability? And how can probability be defined if not in terms of statistics? And how can one evaluate, if not in reference to a series of events which are external and anterior to the message? Clearly, reference to the code can only be rejected by substituting for it a criterion which exists only in relation to the code.[29]

By code, Guiraud means the repertoire of phonological, semantic, and syntactical combinations available to a specific natural language. The reader becomes conscious of the "effect of style" when he discovers that combinations normal to that language are in some way deviated from. Consequently, he concludes that the peculiar characteristics that delineate and define the style of a work or an author must be the sum total of such deviations.

A main argument against style as deviation concentrates on the difficulties entailed in deciding what constitutes "normal" language usage. It is at least intuitively obvious that many distinctive styles are characterized by total conformity to the constraints of a natural language grammar—that is, they do not violate these constraints —while remaining nevertheless distinctive. Consequently, Roland Barthes insists that the notion of "normal" style is quite arbitrary:

> The opposition Norm/Deviation implies a vision which is eventually moral (under the guise of a logic of *endoxa*): there is a reduction from the systematic to the sociological (the code is what is statistically determined by the greatest number of users), and from the sociological to the normal, where social discourse begins.[30]

If the characteristics of a specific style can be defined only against putatively normal or statistically usual speech patterns, then such a definition ends up assuming what it must demonstrate. That is, the normal turns out to be whatever is absent from the style to be described, which means that categories of stylistic description must construct first of all categories of normality in order to be descriptively significant.[31]

That in fact Guiraud is partly right is, however, likewise intuitively obvious. It would be impossible for me to embark on the analyses of Part One if I could not isolate recurrent rhetorical figures that cause these passages to be foregrounded and claim my attention. Foregrounding implies stylistic features that call attention to themselves and implies further that certain other possible features are either not present in the text, or are thematically unimportant. In other words, recognition of some sort of foregrounding is necessary for stylistic features to be apparent to the reader. The question then is, against what background are such characteristics foregrounded?

Nils Erik Enkvist's distinction between two ways of approaching deviance offers the beginning of an answer:

We may proceed in two ways. Either we derive the deviant text from an already existing grammar of non-deviant language, noting what rules we have to change in the process of derivation, or we write a complete new grammar for the deviant text and then proceed to compare the deviant grammar with the normal—always assuming that the two grammars are sufficiently akin to permit such comparison.[32]

The second alternative views the stylistic system of a work or an author as an autonomous structure with its own rules that deviate from those of the natural language grammar, and it corresponds to Guiraud's position summarized above. The first alternative envisions style as derived from this grammar but governed by an additional set of rules that do not cancel the first but rather build on them. In this perspective, the rhetorical figuration we find in the new *Arcadia* is foregrounded not in opposition to putatively normal word patterning, but in opposition to (in being derived from) a global repertoire of available rhetorical schemes, such as those catalogued in Renaissance rhetorical handbooks. Such handbooks define a system of possible figures, many of which (though not all) are merely specific word patterns and usages made available by the natural language itself. Such a system is a repertoire of figures derived from the language, despite the commonplace in both classical and Renaissance rhetoric that these figures are recognizable as violations of normal word patterning. It is, for instance, possible to label practically any locution and classify it as a specific figure. And this fact suggests once again that repertoires of rhetorical figures are not so much deviations *tout court*, as rather secondary systems that formulate additional rules of combination that exploit available natural language locutions rather than run counter to them.[33]

Another point relevant to the Arcadian style concerns the causes of stylistic foregrounding itself. This is the fact that stylistic features are foregrounded not through linguistic criteria alone, but preeminently through thematic motivation. In this connection M. A. K. Halliday derives stylistic foregrounding not negatively from deviation but positively from relevance to meaning:

Foregrounding, as I understand it, is prominence that is motivated. It is not difficult to find patterns of prominence in a poem or prose text, regularities in the sounds or words or structures that stand out in some way, or may be brought out by careful reading; and one may often be led in this way towards a new insight, through finding that such prominence contributes to the writer's total meaning. But unless it does, it will seem to lack motivation; a feature that is brought into prominence will be "foregrounded" only if it relates to the meaning of the text as a whole. This relationship is a functional one: if a particular feature of the language contributes, by its prominence, to the total meaning of the work, it does so by virtue of and through the medium of its own value in the language—through the linguistic function from which its meaning is derived.[34]

In other words, Guiraud's "effect of style" as Halliday would reinterpret it necessarily takes into consideration the thematic import of certain stylistic features. Whereas the deviationist model assumes a unilateral input from style into meaning, whereby meaning derives from a reader's prior discovery of regular stylistic deviations, Halliday's remarks uncover the dependency of style's visibility on its functional subordination to textual meaning. In short, a style is recognizable only if it has or supports meaning.

And this conclusion leads directly back to my argument regarding the radical significance of the differential figures constituting so many passages of description and narration in the new *Arcadia*. The deviationist notion of style that some readers and students of the work take for granted envisions its style as essentially superfluous because lacking thematic motivation, and therefore irrelevant to the meaning of the work. However, as I have shown, there is literally no meaning in the passages I have discussed that does not derive from the specific figurative articulations that constitute them. Following Halliday's analysis, I would conclude that differential figuration statistically dominates such passages because motivated by the differential structures of meaning Sidney wants to communicate. And to miss either—to ride through and past the Arcadian style in order to "get at" finally the Arcadian meaning—is to miss both.

I have shown that there is in the new *Arcadia* no scene, action, thought, or emotion that exists outside of or beyond the rhetorical figuration in which these are constituted. Sidney shows us not so much that human and natural reality in the work are in fact nothing but texts, as rather that nothing of these realities become available to our perception and understanding except through the discursive and rhetorical structures in which their components are articulated and combined. The living dynamism of such realities becomes one with the dialectical interplay across the semantic differentials that generate the text of the new *Arcadia* itself, and what is not so constituted quite literally does not exist for the reader. There are in the text no discursive, descriptive, or narrative "free variants"; that is, no terms or statements are included that could have been left out or been otherwise than what they are. All these elements are motivated, in other words, by still other elements. Each is only recuperable as a moment of paradigmatic selection, which selection has a consequence either immediate or delayed in the syntagm of the text, which in turn opens up another moment of choice. There is no "slot" in the text that is not a moment of choice, so that every element is marked as the result of that choice.

It is quite possible to discover in the ambiance of rhetorical formulation in Sidney's own time distinctions between style as deviation and style as derivation that correspond to those made in modern stylistics. Lanham's arguing a constitutive function for rhetoric in some Renaissance literary productions implies such a distinction without actually stating it. More to the point is Rosemond Tuve's insistence in *Elizabethan and Metaphysical Imagery* that Renaissance poetic does "not identify *end* with *content* and *means* with *form*." [35] On the contrary,

> Figurative language, ornament, is conceived of as one of the modes through which a purpose operates, but so, too, are any overt statements the poet makes of his "idea"; so, too, is the matter or argument whose invention probably led him to the conceiving of his purpose. A poem's content is not its end; it is the first choice of instrument made by the poet. One might boil down the poem's statements-and-images into a paraphrase, a sort of core or structure, but that paraphrase would not state the meaning of the poem

until one included in one's statement what the poet was using that structure *for*. Ideas stated and texture of ornament had precisely the same relevance to the end of the poem—the relevancy of instrument. The meaning of the poem is what-its-ideas-in-that-form-do. (pp. 110–11)

The end or purpose is of course the rhetorical end of communication and/or persuasion. So far in this discussion I have subsumed the question of ultimate purpose of the new *Arcadia* to matters of local stylistic effect on the reader. At this level I have been concerned mainly with uncovering the kinds of mental acts and their content which the reader must become conscious of in order to recuperate and interpret what lies under his eye. In Part Two of this study I take up the larger questions that Tuve's statement raises, to which the passages already discussed are subordinated. For my present purposes, however, I want to point out that Tuve's notion that *inventio* applies to selections of both subject and style reinforces my contention that in the new *Arcadia* the two are necessarily chosen together. And if this is the case, it is impossible to read the new *Arcadia* on the assumption that the style merely mediates a fictive world that lies behind and independent of it.

Supporting both my argument and Tuve's is a passage from Puttenham's *Arte of English Poesie* that exemplarily crosses the bridge from style as deviation to style as derivation:

Figuratiue speech is a noueltie of language euidently (and yet not absurdly) estranged from the ordinarie habite and manner of our dayly talke and writing and figure it selfe is a certaine liuely or good grace set vpon wordes, speaches and sentences to some purpose and not in vaine, giuing them ornament or efficacie by many maner of alternations in shape, in sounde, and also in sence, sometime by way of surplusage, sometime by defect, sometime by disorder, or mutation & also by putting into our speaches more pithe and substance, subtilitie, quicknesse, efficacie or moderation, in this or that sort tuning and tempring them, by amplification, abridgement, opening, closing, enforcing, meekening or other wise disposing them to the best purpose: . . .[36]

Though the passage begins by reiterating a deviationist perspective on figuration as "estranged from the ordinarie habite and manner of our dayly talke and writing," it soon comes round to the positive notion that ornament gives speech "efficacie . . . to the best purpose." The opposition this passage finally settles for is not between normal and deviant locutions, but between speech that does not operate effectively and that which does. Like Tuve and Halliday, Puttenham clearly understands that rhetorical ornament is functional. And in seeing so much, Puttenham likewise sees that such ornament functions to embody meaning and purpose by calling attention to itself in this capacity. What such speech deviates from is not "normal" speech so much as ineffective speech. And as such he leaves the way open to such writers as Sidney to conceive rhetorical figuration as the exploitation of locutions available already in the natural language of English, rather than merely as deviations from it.

Consequently, it is appropriate to understand the complex logical information that differential figuration in the new *Arcadia* elicits from the reader as a matter of invention and not merely of elocution. But I would want to go further and argue that the Arcadian style registers the subject matter which is selected and arranged according to its suitability for fitting into such figuration. To this degree Sidney would agree with Halliday's assertion that style "constitutes a norm, a world-view, a structuring of experience that is significant because there is no *a priori* reason why the experience should have been structured in this way rather than in another."[37] Sidney does not force antithetical figuration on his story; rather, it is his story that forces such figuration on him.

If this is the case, then it is possible to find in Renaissance rhetoric justification likewise for my notion that the passages discussed in this part are intended to elicit from the reader the metatext of rules that govern them. Referring once again to Puttenham, we can discover in his distinction between *energeia* generated by figures of thought and the *enargeia* by figures of words a conception that fits Sidney's apparent purpose reasonably well. Rhetorical ornaments are

> of two sortes, one to satisfie & delight th'eare onely by a goodly outward shew set vpon the matter with wordes, and speaches smothly

and tunably running: another by certaine intendments or sence of such wordes & speaches inwardly working a stirre to the mynde: that first qualitie the Greeks called *Enargia,* of this word *argos,* because it geueth a glorious lustre and light. The latter they called *Energia* or *ergon,* because it wrought with a strong and vertuous operation. (pp. 142–43)

Several points ought to be made in this connection, one of which concerns figures of thought that cause "a stirre to the mynde." In my analyses in this first part, I have shown how passages of dense differential figuration operate to stir the reader's mind, and to a quite specific end: to make explicit the often tacit and impacted information of logical and semantic articulation that these passages encapsulate. To the degree that such passages fall within the genre of "paradox" as the Renaissance understood it, it was generally accepted that they were intended to operate on the reader in just this way. For instance, Charles Estienne prefaces his translation of Ortensio Lando's *Paradossi* (1553) with the following remark:

For this reason I have offered in this book the debate between various propositions that the ancients have wished to call Paradoxes: that is, contrary to the general opinion of men: in order that through these discourses the opposite truth might become clearer and more apparent: and also to excite debate about matters which require you diligently and laboriously to search out reasons, proofs, authorities, histories, and memoirs quite diverse and obscure.[38]

Estienne's notion of paradox, like that of Donne, is that "by a show of deceit [it] force(s) the reader to uncover the truth. The true nature of the paradox is revealed when the reader overturns it. . . . And further, the paradoxes do not really have a nature at all; they are nothings. They exist only within the antithetical action of the reader."[39] Clearly, not all of this conception applies to the new *Arcadia.* What applies preeminently, however, is the idea that paradoxes are intended to elicit from the reader further thought in the interest of unraveling them. In this connection Rosalie L. Colie extends the function of the Renaissance paradox to a positive purpose:

Paradoxes are profoundly self-critical: whether rhetorical, logical, or epistemological, they comment on their own method and their own technique. The rhetorical paradox criticizes the limitations and rigidity of argumentation; the logical paradox criticizes the limitations and rigidity of logic; the epistemological paradox calls into question the process of human thought, as well as the categories thought out (by human thought) to express human thought.[40]

The specifically thematic function of such paradoxes in the new *Arcadia* I take up in Part Two. I have already demonstrated, however, the extent to which some of the reader's assumptions about logical opposition and equivalence are at least modified if not called into question when he is confronted with interpreting the passages I have analyzed. The dialectical relation between mutual implication and mutual exclusion that informs so many of these passages calls upon him to recognize the complex potentialities built into the dynamic ethical structure of the human psyche. So far I have been concerned mainly to make this kind of information explicit, and to argue further that this is how the new *Arcadia* demands to be read.

Another conclusion can be drawn from linking Puttenham on *energeia* and *enargeia* with the rhetorical figuration of the new *Arcadia*. This concerns the question of just how much its differential figuration can be classified as figures of words rather than figures of thought. It should be obvious by now that deviationist readings of the new *Arcadia* assume that its rhetorical figuration must be understood as figures of words only. Regarding differential figuration in particular, it would appear that one has to assume rather a spectrum linking both types of figuration at the extremes and enclosing several types between them.

In what remains after many years still the best study of this question, John E. Hollingsworth in *Antithesis in the Attic Orators from Antiphon to Isaeus* argues that a sharp and mutually exclusive distinction between differential schemes of words and schemes of thought is an unreal one.[41] Anaximenes was the first to distinguish figures that concern words only, thought only, and both. But for Hollingsworth there is no differential figure of words that is not also to some extent a figure of thought:

> The underlying fallacy is evident. There is no distinction between word and thought: a word is the embodiment and expression of thought. Nor can we with impunity dissociate the thought element as expressed in verb, noun, or attributive, and classify an antithesis as one of Word or of Thought. In "Let the rich give to the poor," there is not only a real opposition of thought between *rich* and *poor* but the idea of *giving* on the part of the rich necessarily implies its mental counterpart—that of *receiving* on the part of the poor. It is thus a virtual active-passive antithesis . . . so inseparably in all such cases are words and ideas bound up together. (p. 13)

It is significant that Hollingsworth demonstrates his conclusion by making explicit the metatextual formulations the reader of such an antithesis must discover, in a manner essentially identical with that I have found required by the Arcadian style. That is, the mere mental processing of this statement about rich and poor requires one to go beyond the figure of words and reconstruct the model ("active/passive") that governs it.

Nevertheless, it is certainly true that there are degrees to which the reader may be stirred by such figures. In comparing the euphuistic style of Lyly, for instance, with that of the *Arcadia*, one becomes immediately aware that Lyly's antitheses evoke much less interest because they stir much less thought. An explanation of the spectrum stretching between differential figures of thought and differential figures of words that we often find in Lyly is given by Hollingsworth in the best statement about the differential style I have encountered:

> As antithetic writing became more systematic, it was natural that every word be made to count either for symmetry or cogency of expression, or should be made as unobtrusive as possible. Hence arose parison, paronomasia, homoeoteleuton, etc. Repetition and the use of synonyms aided the process, synonymous expression marking a more highly developed and artistic form of antithetical writing. By these means the coordinate clauses were elaborated to

the utmost degree of artistic symmetry and pleasing euphony. . . .
(p. 35)

The most important sentence in this passage is the first one. Hollings-worth perceives that cataloguing and systemizing the verbal means for constructing antithetical figures generates a kind of hypertrophic urge to coerce the total structure of the phrases, clauses, and sentences of a passage into antithetical form. The realm of purely verbal figures comes into play to the exact degree that this urge is surrendered to. And it is exactly this kind of hypertrophy of differential figuration, one which subordinates or drives out all elements that do not subserve this form, that we discover in a typical passage from Lyly's *Euphues*:

> Seeing thou wilt not buy counsel at the first hand good cheap, thou shalt buy repentance at the second hand at such an unreasonable rate that thou wilt curse thy hard pennyworth and ban thy hard heart. Ah, Euphues, little dost thou know that if thy wealth waste thy wit will give but small warmth, and if thy wit inclines to wilfulness that thy wealth will do thee no great good. If the one had been employed to thrift, the other to learning, it had been hard to conjecture whether thou shouldest have been more fortunate by riches or happy by wisdom, whether more esteemed in the commonweal for wealth to maintain war or for counsel to conclude peace.[42]

Such figuration becomes quickly wearisome the moment the reader discovers that the parallels, balances, symmetries, and oppositions in this passage are mechanically generated by the writer's intention to tie up one side of a differential by always making explicit the other. "Good cheap" demands "an unreasonable rate," while the waste of wealth and the small warmth yielded by wit is matched in a *chiasmus* by willful wit and useless wealth. The alternative proper use of both distributes the happiness/fortunate differential to riches and wisdom, respectively, leading to a further, parallel distribution of the war/peace differential.

Such a passage works on the reader in a manner just the opposite to that characteristic of the Arcadian style. Lyly's statement here, and indeed throughout *Euphues*, assumes simple, sharp, and uncomplex exclusions between opposed alternatives, and these are registered rhetorically in a style wherein each unit or segment is uniformly answered by its corresponding parallel or antithesis. The reader quickly exhausts what the statement is saying, because the statement itself quickly exhausts the possible relations among its constituent components. Having made his point early on, Lyly can only beat it to death by mechanically generating parallels and oppositions whose raison d'être is nothing but the urge to complete the verbal patterning as such. Such writing may fulfill Puttenham's notion of *enargeia*—figuration that "geueth a glorious lustre and light"—but it works rather to close down the reader's thought than to stir it.

Morris Croll long ago pointed out that whereas such figures play in the styles of Isocrates and Cicero a minor role subordinated to the comprehensive period, they often make up the totality of Lyly's sentences.[43] The fact that Lyly's style is dominated by differential figuration conceived as figures of words is illuminated by George Williamson's observation that verbal structures tend to eschew figures of words to the degree that they subserve figures of thought.[44] One of Williamson's central points in *The Senecan Amble* is that styles must be defined not simply by the types of rhetorical and grammatical schemes they feature, but according to how they are used. Although it is quite possible to find in the new *Arcadia* passages that superficially resemble euphuism, it is clear that they do not function in the same way. In *Euphues* there is a kind of inverse economy, wherein hypertrophy of differential figuration results in a rapid entropy of the information conveyed. But Sidney uses such figuration to just the opposite purpose and effect. If as John Hoskins says these figures are intended "to stir admiration in the hearer and make them think it a strange harmony which must be expressed in such discords,"[45] then it is clear that Sidney's use of them stirs such wonder and thought, and that Lyly's does not.

The major difference between these two uses of antitheses lies in the kind of information they are intended to convey. One can conceive paradox as a word game whereby the reader is invited to "unparadox" what are only apparent contradictions and discover the quite nonparadoxical and noncontradictory truth the paradox conceals. Jonathan Culler describes the first type of paradox, and how it operates on the reader:

> With ordinary prose statements one can register immediate dissent or agreement, but with paradoxes interpretation is a quest for possible grounds of truth. The correct interpretation of the contradictory terms is presumed to be that which makes the paradox acceptable, and the process of understanding is a search for meaning which would make it so. This process, however, is also one that exposes the tenuousness and fragility of paradox itself. If to interpret a paradox is to resolve or reduce the contradiction, then it is also to expose that contradiction as artifice, wit.[46]

In the passage quoted above from *Euphues* we find paradox used in a way that invites just such an interpretation, and consequently just such discounting of the paradoxical figures themselves. Once one discovers, for instance, the fact that all the wealth in the world will not make up for stupidity, or that the education of wit that wealth can buy will yield felicitous uses for both, the wealth/wit differential dissolves, and we are left with the proverbial and the trite.

On the other hand, paradox can be understood as rendering a truth that is truly paradoxical, a tangle of unresolvable oppositions and contradictions. In the passage describing Kalander's house, or in the extended portrayal of how Amphialus's love for Philoclea propels him continually into actions that harm her, we are not able to expose "the tenuousness and fragility of the paradox itself," "to resolve or reduce the contradiction." Kalander's thrift leads to magnificence by a complex process of cause and effect which the reader must recuperate. But in recuperating this passage, the reader is required to understand the dialectical cross-currents wherein thrift may in fact lead to the opposite of magnificence, but if it does not, this is because "thrift" names a conscious, sophisticated disposition of resources that has true magnificence as its goal. Likewise, given Philoclea's imprisonment, the reader cannot explain away the paradoxical consequences of Amphialus's love for her, because Amphialus himself cannot do so. To love Philoclea is to desire to possess her, and such a desire works to confirm her imprisonment in the name of love.

Culler's mistake lies in arguing that explaining a paradoxical statement must necessarily mean explaining it away. For him such explanation takes the form of a nonparadoxical interpretive text in which the paradox is analyzed and reduced to a kind of verbal wit, a play on double meanings. Viewed this way, the Arcadian style becomes exactly what a deviationist reading makes of it: an overelaboration of otherwise fragile paradoxes easily reduced to nonparadoxical meanings, and therefore thematically unmotivated. I have tried to demonstrate, however, that the paradoxes in the new *Arcadia* demand and yield to another notion of interpretation altogether. Rather than inviting the reader to reduce itself to a nonparadoxical interpretive text, the Arcadian style requires him to discover why and how the scenic and human realities the style mediates demand such figuration. "Interpretation" means discovery not of meaning, but rather of the rules that govern and structure these realities in such a way that opposites exclude and yet also imply opposites.

Ultimately, the two kinds of information that paradox conveys depend on whether the reader is open to understanding paradoxical opposition as grounded on the dual potentialities latent in reality and language alike. The reductive interpretation that Culler describes and which Lyly invites is based on the assumption that ultimately there can be no truth that does not conform to the law of noncontradiction. And from this perspective, opposites can only exclude and never imply or cause each other. That is why, then, euphuistic paradox is reducible to nonparadoxical meaning and the Arcadian style is not. As long as paradoxical figuration is written and read on the assumption that such paradoxes can mediate only static relations of mutual exclusion, any attempts in such paradoxes to obscure this fact can only direct the reader, as Culler says, to unmask this pretension, and to dissolve paradoxical predication into simple opposition. But if, as Sidney clearly does, one assumes that human moral nature is constituted from a dynamic interplay of mutual exclusions and mutual implications, and are thus radically dialectical, paradoxical figuration that renders this dialectic cannot be discounted.

I have used "dialectic" in the analyses of Part One to mean both a discursive practice and rules governing this practice, the knowledge of which allows the reader to understand it. More particularly, the dialectics of Sidney's text invite the reader to assimilate the mutual implication between opposed terms, and the secondary, more abstract relationship of mutual implication and mutual exclusion between the relations of implication and exclusion themselves. I limit theoretical discussion here to what Sidney's text seems to require, and what follows makes explicit and rationalizes Aristotle's analysis of the human person's dual potentiality for taking on opposed ethical qualities, as Sidney modified this analysis and embodied it in the three dimensions in the new *Arcadia* of character, plot, and genre.

All the texts I have examined so far are founded on a central lexical opposition: beauty and utility in Kalander's house; beauty and pride in Pamela; love and chastity, and pleasure and labor in Queen Helen's agenda for her court; courage and cowardice in Anaxius, virtue and friendship in Tydeus and Telenor, love and destruction in Amphialus; sexual innocence and sophistication in Philoclea. Such lexical oppositions obey the universal constraint on the semantic well-formedness of any text: the law of noncontradiction. Such a text must select terms central to its argument whose semantic markers are mutually compatible and reject terms that are the contraries or contradictories of the first. The fact that in these texts the dominant antithetical terms coexist and even reinforce each other creates anomalies for the reader and invites him and her to discover the rules that make such coexistence possible. These rules are, collectively, the dialectical component, which extends this account of well-formed (i.e., noncontradictory) discourse by including the notion that those terms that a text rejects it likewise implies. This is because the lexicon that funds a text includes terms that are defined doubly by other terms in the same lexicon: those terms that give its meaning (i.e., its semantic markers); and those terms differentially paired off with its semantic markers as their contraries. The selection/rejection process that occurs in the writing and reading of a text assumes differential relations among the terms of the text's funding lexicon, which relations are logically structured according to both mutual exclusion (i.e., noncontradiction) and mutual implication. Because all terms in a lexicon are defined by their exclusion of the terms opposed to them, mutual exclusion between terms must also imply mutual implication between them.[47]

At the discursive level the well-formed text enacts a parallel dialectic, excluding countertexts composed of the terms it has rejected, and therefore implying such countertexts as well. Texts fall into two classes: those that exclude their own countertexts and those that admit them (becoming thereby paradoxical), with a sliding scale of inversely proportional exclusion and inclusion between these two extremes. The first kind of text is nondialectical. It rejects its counter-text(s) on the assumption that differentiality can mean only mutual exclusion. The second kind of text is a dialectical text. It admits into itself its own countertexts and forces on the reader an understanding of how mutual exclusion between differentially opposed terms—and the texts composed from these—both excludes and implies mutual implication between these terms and texts. Nondialectical texts in the first class reject one of the semantic conditions of their own meaning —mutual implication between opposed terms—whereas texts of the second sort admit this condition and exploit it.

In general, Sidney assigns blameworthy or incompletely evolved characters nondialectical texts and sympathetic and complete characters dialectical texts. Latter characters include Kalander, Pamela, Argalus and Parthenia, and Queen Helen of Corinth. In these cases the countertextual linkages among opposed virtues are realized, while the potential implication of opposed vices is overtly confronted and thereby excluded. The majority of characters in the new *Arcadia*, however, including the two heroes, Philoclea, Gynecia, Basilius, Amphialus, and most of the personae in the Book 2 retrospective narratives, become problematic (and therefore interesting) because the texts of their respective moral identities excludes one or another ethical quality that it also implies. Their ethical make-ups are unstable, since what they exclude they find they must also unwittingly and unwillingly confront. Pyrocles' and Musidorus's roles of martial heroism both exclude and imply the roles of pastoral lovers. Philoclea's sexual innocence excludes and implies sexual sophistication; Gynecia's and Basilius's resistance to lust leaves them vulnerable to it; Plangus's virtues are subject to dialectical reversal in Andromana's retextualization of them; the King of Phrygia's fear of usurpation creates the conditions of usurpation. Characters in this latter class, unlike those in the first, find themselves entangled in plots wherein the ethical qualities excluded by their nondialectical textual identities return to confront them. And these plots collectively make up most of Sidney's additions to the new *Arcadia*.

When therefore I refer in this study to the "rules of dialectic," I mean the following sequence of generalizations governing the text of the new *Arcadia*, which I also treat as the essential information the reader must elicit from the text (whether or not in this precise form) in order to read it:

(A) A necessary condition of well-formed discourse is that it rejects inclusion of central terms that feature mutually incompatible markers.

(B) A second necessary condition of well-formed discourse consequent on rule (A) is that it implies terms (and countertexts constructible out of them) that it must reject on the basis of rule (A).

(C) Consequently, the rule (A) that makes well-formed discourse possible implies rule (B) that makes well-formed discourse impossible, namely, the dialectical implication/exclusion that binds mutual exclusion and mutual implication logically together.

(D) In obeying rule (A), well-formed discourse implicitly seeks to escape regulation by rule (C); that is, in identifying discursive well-formedness only with semantic exclusiveness, such a discursive practice rejects rule (B), namely, the mutual implication binding together terms that mutually exclude each other.

(E) But in seeking to escape regulation by rule (C), well-formed discourse falls under regulation of rule (C). This is because rule (A) at once negates and implies rule (B).

(F) Well-formed discourse is thus inherently dialectical, since it implies conditions that mutually negate each other—rules (A), (B), and (D)—that also mutually imply each other—rules (C) and (E). "Textual well-formedness" or "textual wholeness," particularly as Sidney's new *Arcadia* exemplifies it, means the acceptance of the full dialectical conditions of discourse, since rejection of dialectic is tantamount to coming under its regulation (rule E).

The new *Arcadia* thus builds a massive and detailed critique of nondialectical (and non-Aristotelian) models of human ethical structure by exploring the failures of these models to account fully and adequately for the dialectics inherent in them. Such dialectics, to the extent they are rejected, remain present and subversive, unerringly directing characters toward the destiny they most completely reject. But if the nature of human ethical identity is problematic for Sidney, and before him for Aristotle, then the prior matter that had to be dealt with was the logic—which I have called "dialectical"—that makes sense of this problem. Without such a logical explanation, human beings must perforce remain at best irresolvable paradoxes and at the worst simply mysteries. Merely to talk about them, to utter and write discourse in which the paradoxical structures of human ethical qualities are given clear exposition and clarification, is to write discourse in which paradox is the governing rhetorical figure.

For this reason Sidney exploited the match-up between the resources of differential figuration and the range of dialectical moral structures he wanted to articulate. And it is also for this reason that I have argued the impossibility of sundering the stylistic and conceptual dimensions of the Arcadian text. We discover in the new *Arcadia* the figure *synoeciosis,* which joins contrary terms; *antithesis,* which opposes them; *syncrisis,* which compares contrary things; and *anatanagoge,* which asserts the good aspects of a bad quality and vice versa. The new *Arcadia* shows the reader that these labels not only name available figures of opposition; they also name the central spectrum of ethical structures of which human beings are capable. Consequently, we can see that for Sidney, drawing from Aristotelian logical and ethical thought on the one hand, and from the classical/ Renaissance tradition of rhetorical figures on the other, the world of the new *Arcadia* is one in which human moral character exists precisely to the degree that it is textualizable in rhetorical figuration. Indeed, as Sidney shows us, human moral identity consists entirely of the rhetorical figures by which men and women choose to be constrained in writing the text of this identity.

In fusing the ethical realities of his fictive characters with the rhetorically figured texts in which they are textualized—in presenting his characters enacting the texts which they "write" for themselves —Sidney derives precedent from ideas current in Renaissance literary theory. He combines the notion that fictive mimesis imitates not only the actions of people but their words as well, with the idea that human ethical reality is radically constituted by the texts in which men and women articulate this reality.

In the first regard, Sidney exploits a distinction between descriptive and mimetic narrative modes first formulated by Plato, repeated by Aristotle, and well known to Renaissance literary criticism. In *Republic* 3, Plato distinguishes in the opening passages of the *Iliad* between sections where "the poet himself is the speaker and does not even attempt to suggest to us that anyone but himself is speaking," and other sections where the actual words of characters are given (392d–394c).[48] Aristotle in the *Poetics* (chapter 3) similarly distinguishes telling a story "either by speaking part of the time in character, as Homer does, or by speaking in one's own person without any change."[49] Aristotle's distinction is reproduced by Jacopo Mazzoni in his *Defense of the Comedy of Dante* (1587),[50] as well as by Lodovico Castelvetro, though with an interesting addition:

> In actuality, he [Castelvetro] simplified the complexity in the way that was standard or soon to become standard by recognizing three main kinds of poetic imitation: a first direct kind, in which the poet or assumed narrator speaks throughout in his own person; an oblique kind, in which the action is presented in indirect discourse; and a second direct kind, in which the poet presents speeches of his characters verbatim. This second direct kind of imitation Castelvetro called similitudinary.[51]

Castelvetro's oblique kind of narration, presented in direct discourse, is particularly relevant to Sidney's practice, since it falls between the other two modes of narration and description in the narrator's own voice, and direct imitation of the discourse of a specific character. As such, the oblique mode points to a form of free indirect discourse that manages to combine the other two, direct modes, by embedding elements of a character's speech within the text of the narrator.

In my foregoing discussion I have shown that the reader's recuperating the semantic and logical information governing the style is never separate from his recuperating the ethical information in the portraits of specific characters. To discover the logical sense of a complex set of rhetorical figures requires likewise discovering the ethical articulations predicated of this character. In both cases, the reader is required to create, in however ad hoc and implicit a manner, a metatext in which he formulates the rules of dialectical implication/

exclusion that make sense at once of statement and significance, of rhetorical figure and of ethical purport. For this reason I have argued that the ethical structures of his characters are conformed to the kinds of articulation allowable to differential rhetorical figures.

In such passages Sidney describes a character in a text that is also a *mimesis* or verbal replication of the actual text in which that character articulates himself and herself, such a text which such characters might use given sufficient introspection and insight to describe themselves.[52] In the new *Arcadia* such texts become third-person narrations and envision a character from the outside. Were a character actually to describe himself or herself, the text would be direct discourse, a literal, quoted replication of the person's own words. But Sidney gives us a third thing, which in twentieth-century discourse analysis is called free indirect discourse: the presence in descriptive discourse by an outside observer of elements of the actual text that the character might use to articulate himself.[53] Free indirect discourse combines third-person description and narration with mimetic replication of first-person speech, so that we read both simultaneously.

The reader is led to recognize free indirect discourse by various grammatical and thematic markers. Among the latter is the presence of words and phrases that reproduce the viewpoint not of the narrator but of the person being described. In the passages analyzed we are often given an indirect representation of the thoughts, perspectives, and judgments of the character, but translated into the grammatical modes required by third-person narration. The balances of Kalander's house, Pamela's awareness that her beauty may be enhanced by her refusal of pride in that beauty, the serpentine progress of the King of Phrygia's suspicions, and in its most extended form, the narration of Andromana's corrupting the King of Iberia: in all these cases the reader is presented with these characters' actions by an outside observer, and in this respect the text clearly falls into the category of third-person narrative and description. But what is described must be understood as the observer's perceptions and judgments of motivations and thoughts which can only be contacted from a perspective within that character. The narrator thus takes both of the positions enumerated by Plato and Aristotle: he or she at once speaks in his or her own voice and obliquely replicates the voice of the character being described. Far from being an account limited to what the observer can see from his external viewpoint, all of these passages articulate in differential figuration the stress and counterstress of thought and emotion, motivation and desire that sum up a character's inner moral life. Consequently, we are required to see such figuration not simply imposed on this moral life by the speaker's own text. To the degree that the dialectics of moral action are embodied in antithetical figuration, it is accurate to say that there is no difference between the two. What the narrator speaks is what the character enacts; and what the character enacts is the text of rhetorical figuration reproduced, as free indirect discourse, by the narrator.[54]

And this conclusion leads to the argument that I shall set forth in Part Two: that the global structure and concerns of the new *Arcadia* registered in its main plot and in the interplay of its generic materials and allusions replicates the textualization of reality I have illustrated in local passages and predicates this textualization of the Arcadian fictive world at large. If individual characters structure their moral identities according to the resources of rhetorical figuration, one can look in turn for the interaction among several characters to be the confrontation between competing texts of the self, or the cooperation in the writing of a single text. Such cooperations can be seen in the story of Argalus and Parthenia, where the benign liaison of opposites underlying the moral characters of both enables them to spin out a tale of love dominated by specific examples of the figure *syncrisis*. In an ironic mode we discover a malign version of the same cooperation in the stories of Artaxia and Phalantus, and of Pamphilus and his many lovers. Here we witness cooperation in the construction of a meretricious erotic text full of egoism, frivolity, anger, and destructiveness. In both stories Sidney gives us characters entrapped in the cooperative texts they write and speak precisely because of their egoistic blindness. In another direction we have the competing texts of martial honor enacted by Pyrocles and Anaxius, respectively. Though funded by the same terms and differentials, both texts join and distinguish two opposed implications of the central term "courage" itself: Pyrocles, who understands courage to be ability to ignore, slurs on his courage; and Anaxius whose courage includes the fear of not being thought courageous.

In general, then, the Arcadian world conforms to Nancy Struever's contention:

Humanists assume that the model for the structure of history is the structure of discourse. Both consciously and unconsciously they resume the Aristotelian position that man is a political animal by virtue of his capacity for discourse; for the Humanists rhetoric is essentially conflict or dialogue, politics is dialogue of expressions of power, and history is the articulation of this power dialogue. In this respect, they see no tension between the historian's engagement as rhetorician and his commitment to truth, since the forms of rhetorical argument—definition, equation, analogy, parallelism, antithesis—inform the political life they wish to describe; both rhetorician and politician must master the same structure and method.[55]

The liaison between differential figuration and a dialectical schema of moral behavior according to which Sidney textualizes many of his individual characters yields in the global concerns of the new *Arcadia* plot and generic mixture to other problems in structuring the total span of one's life. On the one hand Sidney deals with the interplay of free will and determinism. When Basilius receives what is in effect a recipe, the fore-conceit of his own life set forth by the Delphic oracle, he is faced with the decision either to reject or accept this recipe. By rejecting it and exercising his free will in opposition to oracular determinism, Basilius finally discovers that he cooperates with it. On the other hand, the two heroes Musidorus and Pyrocles obey the rules dictating a life of strenuous heroism derived from several literary genres: the classical and hellenistic models of Homer, Xenophon, and Heliodorus; and medieval and Renaissance romances purveying the matters of Arthur and Charlemagne. These heroes, like Basilius, fall victims to texts that they cannot read correctly, and they suffer accordingly. Like Basilius who rejects the paradoxical textualizing of his own life and that of his family in the Delphic oracle, the two heroes interpret the text of the romantic epic to exclude the domain of eros. All three men become victims of an incapacity to deal with the dialectical realities mediated by the texts they follow (in Basilius's case, inadvertently). And all three men, like the reader, are required to learn the dialectical rules that govern these texts in order to interpret them and consequently themselves.

Part Two

The Dialectics of Plot and Genre

In Part One I discuss passages selected from the material Sidney added to the old *Arcadia* when he came to compose the new. I seek there to illuminate the kinds of information the reader requires in traversing Sidney's new text in order to make it readable. I limit my discussion mainly to passages constituting the various subplots in the new *Arcadia*, partly because they illustrate this information most fully, and partly because they constitute much of Sidney's attempt to expand the significance of the old *Arcadia* main plot. The dialectical rules of discourse and human ethical psychology that these new passages collectively establish govern the actions of the main characters as well. The nature of textualization in the new *Arcadia*, the semantic differentials that fund that textualization, and the dialectical rules governing these differentials —all illustrated collectively by this added material—illuminate the significance of the main plot.

Part Two discusses the following three issues raised by the main plot: (1) the dimension of individual ethical psychology: the transformation of Musidorus and Pyrocles from epic heroes into pastoral lovers; (2) the dimension of plot: the significance of the Delphic oracle as the "fore-conceit" regulating the whole work, and Basilius's attempts to avoid its predictions; (3) the dimension of genre: the conflict between the motives, values, and meanings of the pastoral and the epic. In this last connection I also discuss Sidney's plan in recomposing the relatively simple pastoral comedy of the old *Arcadia* as the complex, mixed-genre romance epic of the new *Arcadia*.

Sidney always develops these dimensions in the verbal discourse through which each character mediates his and her own thoughts and situation to the self and others. We shall consider, for example, the continual crisis raised in the text by the gender distinction of personal pronouns whenever the text speaks of Pyrocles-Zelmane. Is he to be referred to as "he" or "she"? In another direction, there is the elaborate textual game in which Musidorus disguised as the shepherd Dorus tells Pamela the story of his previous heroic adventures in third-person narrative. In addition, the debate between Musidorus and Pyrocles on the relative merits of the heroic and erotic vocations—taken over from the old *Arcadia*—gains new significance in the context of the generic crisis created in the new *Arcadia* by its juxtaposing the opposed values of the epic and pastoral genres.

In the generic dimension, Sidney's plan seems in general to stipulate conditions for resolving this opposition. Musidorus and Pyrocles initially are treated (and treat themselves) as characters pursuing the actions appropriate to traditional romance epic. They overtly textualize themselves as wandering heroes performing various salvific tasks, prior to their "fall" into the embrace of erotic passion in the pastoral world of Arcadia.[1] They register this fall by revising their self-textualization and taking on the roles and accompanying texts dictated by their newly discovered pastoral and erotic identities.

Finally, in the dimension of plot we shall see that it is the dialectical text of the oracle itself—its predicting apparently contradictory actions in the future—that generates the main action of the *Arcadia* and drives it forward to a resolution of its paradoxical conundrums in the concluding books, that is, the concluding books of the old *Arcadia* appended to the new *Arcadia* in the 1593 version. In attempting to escape the oracle's paradoxical predictions, Basilius succeeds only in initiating chains of actions that fulfill them. And we can recover from this central instance a more general rule applying to many of the other characters: namely, that attempts to escape dialectical regulation of the differential elements constituting one's ethical and psychological identity can result in becoming governed by dialectical regulation despite oneself (cf. rule E, Part One, section 6, above).

Section 1

Musidorus and Pyrocles as heroic lovers

Departing from his practice of set character descriptions discussed in Part One, Sidney expands the characters of the two heroes, Musidorus and Pyrocles, from the two-dimensional portraits delineated in the sections devoted to their early epic activities, to encompass the complex introspection induced by erotic passion. Sidney lays out the transformations these characters undergo along the differential axis separating and joining the two genres of epic and pastoral, with all their antithetical values, motivations, and actions. Both heroes find themselves compelled to reject the roles dictated by their dwelling in the world of romance epic and to take on those imposed by the genre of erotic pastoral. Consequently, we can expect Sidney's exposition of their characters to unfold as a series of inner monologues and dialogues in which the conventional gestures, emotions, and discourse of the erotic pastoral provide the dominant mode of self-realization.

We are given initially a set description of Musidorus by an Arcadian noble after the shepherds have saved him from the burning wreck and brought him to Kalander:

> [Musidorus has] a mind of most excellent composition, a piercing wit quite void of ostentation, high-erected thoughts seated in a heart of courtesy, an eloquence as sweet in the uttering as slow to come to the uttering, a behaviour so noble as gave a majesty to adversity—and all in a man whose age could not be above one and twenty years. (p. 14)

The descriptions of Pamela, Philoclea, and Queen Helen of Corinth examined in Part One have made familiar this way of sculpting character. Musidorus is constituted from a series of reciprocally balanced qualities, which are also negations of various unrealized though possibly malign characteristics. Thus his "piercing wit," which might manifest itself in "ostentation," is yet "quite void" of it, while his "erected thoughts" leading potentially to condescension are yet "seated in a heart of courtesy." Like all other characters portrayed sympathetically in the new *Arcadia*, the balance in Musidorus of vari-

113

ous virtues among themselves escape their undesirable corresponding potentials.

If this description appears somewhat facile, that is because Musidorus's inner consciousness has yet to evolve under the rigors of erotic passion. Sidney develops this one-sidedness in Musidorus's self-conception when he pits him as a cool, righteous advocate of the strenuous heroic life against his friend Pyrocles, who having fallen in love displays a penchant for pastoral retiredness. Musidorus's commitment to epic heroism reveals him ripe for comic reversal when he too succumbs to his passion for Pamela. It is of course not accidental that Musidorus in this debate should resurrect every classical and Renaissance cliché Sidney can lay his hands on, to advocate the supreme value of active endeavor in pursuit of public good.[2]

Musidorus is in firm command of his argument, unlike Pyrocles, who already exhibits the (equally stereotyped) instability of mental and physical control conventionally associated with being in love. Pyrocles having delivered himself of lengthy praise of the Arcadian landscape and his desire for a life of ease, the narrative gives us a running list of the arguments Musidorus has poised ready to pour out to his friend:

> For having in the beginning of Pyrocles' speech which defended his solitariness framed in his mind a reply against it in the praise of honourable action (in showing that such a kind of contemplation is but a glorious title to idleness; that in action a man did not only better himself but benefit others; that the gods would not have delivered a soul into the body which hath arms and legs, only instruments of doing, but that it were intended the mind should employ them; and that the mind should best know his own good or evil by practice—which knowledge was the only way to increase the one and correct the other; besides many other arguments which the plentifulness of the matter yielded to the sharpness of his wit). . . . (p. 52)

This passage is suspended on the verge of a main clause putatively detailing Musidorus's actual utterance, and remains suspended for good. Seeing that Pyrocles' "humour" makes him impervious to such arguments, he pretends to join him in praising Arcadia and asserts that Pyrocles is only exercising his wit to show that it can display "itself in any subject." He finally suggests that Pyrocles is actually beginning to sound like "one of these fantastical mind-infected people that children and musicians call lovers!" Musidorus, of course, cannot believe this of his partner in the top of all enterprise; but when Pyrocles does in fact admit to this malady, Musidorus is horrified: " 'Now the eternal Gods forbid,' mainly cried out Musidorus, 'that ever my ear should be poisoned with so evil news of you! Oh, let me never know that any base affection should get any lordship in your thoughts.' " (p. 53)

Musidorus's uncritical commitment to epic heroism has been textualized as a cascade of topics tumbling easily to the tip of his tongue, a list without order and so obvious (to him) in their sovereign persuasiveness as to require no development.[3] We can then understand his recoiling in horror from his friend's enslavement to all the values which negate his own. This passage, as well as the later one when Musidorus discovers to his further horror Pyrocles disguised as a woman, are not debates in any real sense, because Musidorus cannot grasp or admit any arguments that might reasonably conflict with his own. Sidney shows in *Astrophil and Stella* that he is no stranger to the total incommensurability between the arguments of reason and the motives of passion. For Pyrocles as for Astrophil, reason fails to subjugate passion not because the latter has any arguments of its own to answer those of reason, but simply because passion ignores reason totally and does not engage it at all. For Musidorus, the same is true in reverse. It is important to take note of this imperviousness of each hero to the other's *rationale*, because it is initially through these debates that Sidney poses the central problem of the epic versus the pastoral genres. The question here is not merely a matter of theoretical poetics, but quite concretely the opposition which divides two modes of human existence that Sidney seeks to bring together.

Musidorus takes up the debate again when he confronts the transvestite Pyrocles, and arguments that had hung fire earlier are now poured out to rescue his friend from abomination. Pyrocles is reminded that "the reasonable part of our soul is to have absolute commandment" (p. 70); that "forsooth, love—love, a passion, and the basest and fruitlessest of all passions" (p. 71); that one can only expect a host of unquiet emotions to follow upon it; and that, finally,

> this effeminate love of a woman doth so womanize a man that, if you yield to it, it will not only make you an Amazon, but a launder, a distaff-spinner, or whatsoever other vile occupation their idle heads can imagine and their weak hands perform. (p. 72)

Musidorus is of course proved right in one thing: Pyrocles has been transformed, as far as is possible, into a woman. It is easily predictable from the dialectics of the subplots examined in Part One that Musidorus's rigid rejection of erotic passion can prelude nothing else than his falling victim to it.[4] Cupid's inevitable revenge comes pat a little later on, when Pyrocles encounters Musidorus disguised as a shepherd and lamenting in verse his own enslavement to passion. Thrust across the differential gap separating reason from passion (and epic from pastoral), Musidorus in the role of shepherd can only look across back to his former identity and lament:

> "Alas," said Musidorus, "what shall I say, who am loath to say, and yet fain would have said? I find indeed that all is but lip-wisdom which wants experience. I now (woe is me!) do try [i.e., experience] what love can do. O Zelmane, who will resist it must either have no wit, or put out his eyes. Can any man resist his creation? Certainly, by love, we are made, and to love we are made." (p. 106)

Musidorus, now in the role of the lovesick shepherd Dorus, can only find his previous role of romance hero as unintelligible as he had previously found erotic passion itself.

> And therefore a little to punish him, "Why, how now, dear cousin!" said she [Pyrocles]. "You that were last day so high in the pulpit against lovers, are you now become so mean an auditor? Remember that love is a passion, and that a worthy man's reason must ever have the masterhood." "I recant, I recant!" cried Musidorus; and withal falling down prostrate, "O thou celestial or infernal spirit of love, or what other heavenly or hellish title thou list to have—for effects of both I find in myself, have compassion of me, and let thy

glory be as great in pardoning them that be submitted to thee, as in conquering those that were rebellious."

Sidney lets us and Musidorus taste again the old arguments against love, but now from the perspective of a man victimized by passion.

There is, however, a real sense in which neither Pyrocles nor Musidorus have changed. If passion amid the fields, woods, and flocks had previously appeared to them wholly incompatible with the heroic life, they remain convinced of its incompatibility. The fact that they find themselves thrown violently from one mode of human existence into its opposite confirms for them the mutual exclusion between the two. If, as Musidorus has previously argued, the heroic man cannot yield himself to love, then the lover must relinquish all hopes of attaining heroic action. But if the genres of epic and pastoral are to be reconciled, along with their opposed values, motivations, and agendas, then both heroes must come to understand that the differentials distinguishing them connote mutual implication as well as mutual exclusion. It was largely to give himself the narrative scope for demonstrating this radical vision that Sidney recomposed the pastoral old *Arcadia* as the new *Arcadia* wherein both modes are given full development.[5]

Having once embraced the shepherd's life, Musidorus next encounters the problem of how to woo the aristocratic Pamela. Needless to say, the very disguises Musidorus and Pyrocles take on to subvert Basilius's cloistering of his daughters from all suitors become as much obstacles to as instruments for this subversion. Not only does Musidorus find himself hindered by Pamela's aristocratic disdain of shepherds in general, but he also must wriggle free from two other clogs on his enterprise: his apprenticeship under the base and pretentious Dametas, to whom Basilius has given the guardianship of Pamela; and the watchfulness of Dametas's uncomely daughter Mopsa. To overcome these obstacles Musidorus discovers in himself resources as yet untapped by the demands of the heroic life. He must become an actor, a story teller, and even a Roman comedy intriguer, all the while fulfilling the traditional demands on literary shepherds: he must tend sheep and from time to time recite pastoral eclogues.

The next stage of Musidorus's development coincides with a decisive turn in his wooing Pamela. This takes place at the beginning of Book 3 of the new *Arcadia* (and therefore is material wholly new). At this point Musidorus has sent Pamela a letter declaring his true identity and his love for her. She in turn has communicated to him her growing love for him. The result is two consecutive differentially structured sequences: the first culminates in Musidorus's stealing a kiss from Pamela, and the second details the sequence of his emotions resulting from her angry reaction. These passages mark out a significant stage in Musidorus's development as a character, namely, his enslavement to oscillations typical of the characters in the retrospective narratives.

Sidney is careful to segment both processes into relatively small units in order to highlight the causes and entailments that lead from one stage to the next. In the first passage Pamela's disclosure of her affection makes Musidorus "like one frozen with extremity of cold overhastily brought to a great fire—rather oppressed than relieved with such a lightening of felicity" (p. 308). But having now been brought from one extreme to the other, he cannot be satisfied with "mediocrity" but must give way totally to his desire. "[Not] content to give desire a kingdom but that it must be an unlimited monarchy," Musidorus finds himself standing on ground "over-high in happiness and slippery through affection," so much so that "he could not hold himself from falling into such an error, which with sighs blew all comfort out of his breast and washed away all cheerfulness of his cheer with tears." Pamela's "favour" encourages hope, which in turn encourages desire, and desire considers nothing but opportunity. The upshot is that when Mopsa leaves them alone, occasion elicits desire, which does not stay to "ask reason's leave" (p. 309) but instead drives Musidorus to take Pamela in his arms and kiss her.

There is perhaps something comic in this rather extended anatomy that leads laboriously from Pamela's telling Musidorus she loves him to his kissing her. But this very care to segment the sequence into the smallest delimitable stages exhibits once again how much Sidney's discursive practice abhors a vacuum. Each segment of the sequence displaces the previous one, only to entail and be displaced by the one that follows the second one in turn.[6] These segments are presented in this fashion as all pieces of some yet-to-be disclosed totality, the completion of which drives the whole process of entailment/displacement forward. It is as if the total experience of love must include nothing less than ecstasy, hope, desire, and consummation as well as all their opposites. If Musidorus is to experience the first set of emotions, Sidney seems to be saying, it is only at the risk of the second. If Sidney seeks to define in the new *Arcadia* a holistic resolution of the radically competing segments of human experience—heroism and love, action and contemplation, public endeavor and private retirement—then this resolution demands not a harmonious structure into which are admitted only terms that logically and univocally imply each other. On the contrary, this structure of human experience must necessarily include in addition the differentially implied terms, the countertext to the text of this experience.

It would appear, then, that for Sidney human wholeness rests on men's and women's fathoming in the antithetically figured texts of their own human identities the dialectical countertexts to these texts, wherein are inscribed all those terms differentially implied by them and yet rejected. To avoid enslavement to dialectical reversal, Sidney's characters must first comprehend the potential for such reversal built into the discursive structures of their ethical constitutions.

The second passage, following hard on the first, exhibits Musidorus's despair after Pamela's angry reaction to his stolen kiss. This passage completes the circle initiated in the first passage from love and hope to despair, and back to hope again:

> for finding himself not only unhappy, but unhappy after being fallen from all happiness, and to be fallen from all happiness not by any misconceiving but by his own fault, and his fault to be done to no other but to Pamela, he did not tender his own estate, but despised it, greedily drawing into his mind all conceits which might more and more torment him. (p. 309)

Seeking perversely to torture himself, Musidorus submits his anguish to the inner dynamic of *gradatio* and *anatanogoge,* and encourages it to run by metonymic extension to the point of greatest suffering. The predicate of each previous phrase becomes the subject of the next, and each phrase is calculated to make him feel worse.

In what immediately follows—Musidorus's verse letter to Pamela —Sidney gives us a comically emotional version of the compositional process visible in the new *Arcadia* at large:

> This word was not significant, that word was too plain: this would not be conceived, the other would be ill-conceived. Here, sorrow was not enough expressed; there, he seemed too much for his own sake to be sorry. This sentence rather showed art than passion; that sentence, rather foolishly passionate than forcibly moving. At last, marring with mending, and putting out better than he left, he made an end of it—and being ended, was divers times ready to tear it; till his reason assuring him, the more he studied, the worse it grew, he folded it up, devoutly invoking good acceptation unto it. . . . (p. 310)

Each choice Musidorus agonizes over derives from a limited paradigm of possible rhetorical effects: significant/plain, well-conceived/ill-conceived; not enough sorrow/too much sorrow; art/passion; foolishly passionate/forcibly moving. Musidorus attempts to cancel his violent oscillation between antithetical extremes by arriving at the perfectly balanced letter to Pamela. And as we might expect, every locution he considers appears to him under the sign of its undesirable opposite version.

Musidorus's inability to abide in a "mediocre" state between excessive hope and despair repeats the generic problem which the composite intertextuality of the new *Arcadia* enacts as a whole: the problem of striking a balanced fusion between the claims and values of opposing modes of human existence. Affirming exclusively only the text of his epic, heroic identity and negating consequently its countertext—the text of the erotic pastoral—Musidorus like so many of the subsidiary characters discussed in Part One is forced to confront it.[7]

Pyrocles undergoes a similar, dialectically determined reversal. Once we grant Musidorus's earlier arguments that falling in love transgresses not only the epic/pastoral differential but the male/female differential as well, Pyrocles' love for Philoclea appropriately dictates his relinquishing his male role of epic hero for the effeminate role of pastoral lover.[8] When, however, Pyrocles tells Musidorus that despite his woman's clothes "there is nothing I desire more than fully to prove myself a man in this enterprise" (p. 74), this transformation falls short of completion. Both heroes find themselves poised painfully in a kind of neutral space, somehow both heroes and lovers, and yet not quite wholly either. During the rebellion of the peasants that concludes Book 2, as well as the siege of Cecropia's castle that takes up Book 3, both men are required to reassert their epic identities. But if they do so, it is only while continuing to be masked in their roles of amazon and shepherd, respectively. Musidorus several times comes to battle disguised as a knight, while Pyrocles' amazonian role allows a more direct show of the martial arts. My point is that their being both heroes and lovers and yet wholly neither is quite the reverse of the ideal balance and fusion between the two modes of existence that Sidney envisions. On the contrary, Musidorus's and Pyrocles' oscillating uneasily between their two roles demonstrates that they conceive these roles as mutually exclusive. Continuing to envision the epic/pastoral and male/female differentials only under the sign of mutual exclusion, Musidorus and Pyrocles are compelled to alternate between the opposed terms of these differentials, until they can recognize how both opposites imply each other.

If Pyrocles hopes "fully to prove myself a man in this enterprise," then he must overcome the very obstacles his amazonian disguise was originally donned to circumvent. Like Musidorus in wooing Pamela, Pyrocles must contrive to maintain his disguise to everyone else while conveying to Philoclea that he is not as he appears. Unlike his friend, however, Pyrocles endures plot complications of farcical complexity. The senile Basilius, having banished love from his daughters, finds himself hopelessly enamored of the comely amazon and risks replicating his daughter's brush with homosexuality. In addition, his much younger wife Gynecia manages to pierce Pyrocles' disguise and falls equally hopelessly in love with him as well. Pyrocles thus confronts a kind of objective correlative to his divided identity when he finds himself dogged continually by a man who takes him for a woman and a woman who takes him for a man. If this were not enough, he must also covertly aid in allaying the emotional and moral crisis undergone by Philoclea herself when she finds herself falling in love with Pyrocles while still believing that he is a she.

Sidney develops this comic love tangle fully and with relish, and loses no opportunity to display the inner conflicts Pyrocles must endure as a consequence of his divided identity. Pyrocles' transformation and its significance draws a connection between the dialectical reversals and upheavals suffered by the other three characters, and the problem of genre posed by transgression of the epic/pastoral differential. This double connection is made in Pyrocles' account to Musidorus of how he fell in love with Philoclea.

This account is, as we might expect, structured as an extended *gradatio* through which Pyrocles finds himself moving, as Musidorus will later, from his role of epic hero to that of pastoral lover. He begins by telling Musidorus of the picture Kalander has shown him of Philoclea along with her mother and father. This picture was painted after Basilius decided to remove both daughters to his forest lodge in order to sequester them from suitors and makes plain to the viewer Philoclea's sorrow. Pyrocles says:

> "Yet alas, so sweet was it unto me that I could not be contented till Kalander had made it more and more strong with his declaration; which the more I questioned, the more pity I conceived of her unworthy fortune; and when with pity once my heart was made tender, according to the aptness of the humour, it received quickly a cruel impression of that wonderful passion which to be defined is impossible, because no words reach to the strange nature of it. They only know it which inwardly feel it; it is called love." (p. 78)

Pyrocles confesses that he was as yet ignorant of the true meaning of his emotions, "thinking it only such a wonted kind of desire to see rare sights, and my pity to be no other but the fruits of a gentle nature." The more he argues with himself the more thoughts of Philoclea increase, leading him to desire to see her in person "to be judge, forsooth! of the painter's cunning" (p. 79). This admirable desire to extend his education, however, leads down paths as yet unfamiliar to him:

> "But when within short time I came to the degree of uncertain wishes, and that the wishes grew to unquiet longings; when I could fix my thoughts upon nothing but that, within little varying, they should end with Philoclea; . . . then indeed, then I did yield to

the burthen, finding myself prisoner before I had leisure to arm myself. . . ."

The concluding passage allows us to see over Pyrocles' head that something more will be required than merely "arming himself" in the manner of a hero dedicated to epic action. Pyrocles describes here his unwitting transgression of the epic/pastoral differential, experienced concretely in the ebb and flow of his own unwontedly complicated emotions. Pyrocles' ignorance, like Musidorus's, is indigenous to the whole conception of the heroic life that they have up to this point taken for granted. Assuming that the heroic life can be maintained only by excluding eros, Pyrocles is unprepared for the secret liaison of mutual implication which binds both opposed states across the differential gap that separates them. To dedicate oneself wholly to heroic action without understanding how it implies pastoral eroticism is to prime oneself for nothing other than traversing eventually the rhetorical *gradatio* in which is textualized this implication.[9]

Having recounted to Musidorus his unforeseen entanglement with the mother and father as well as with the daughter, Pyrocles is returned by the narrator to the lodge, where Sidney recounts with comic dialectical precision this entanglement:

> Zelmane returned to the Lodge, where inflamed by Philoclea, watched by Gynecia, and tired by Basilius, she was like a horse desirous to run and miserably spurred, but so short-reined as he cannot stir forward. Zelmane sought occasion to speak with Philoclea, Basilius with Zelmane, and Gynecia hindered them all. If Philoclea happened to sigh (and sigh she did often), as if that sigh were to be waited on, Zelmane sighed also—whereto Basilius and Gynecia soon made up four parts of sorrow. Their affection increased their conversation, and their conversation increased their affection. The respect borne bred due ceremonies, but the affection shined so through them that the ceremonies seemed not ceremonious. Zelmane's eyes were like children afore sweetmeat, eager, but fearful of their ill-pleasing governors; time in one instant seeming both short and long unto them—short in the pleasingness of such presence, long, in the stay of their desires. (p. 89; punctuation modified)

Here, the rhetorical figures of *zeugma* and *chiasmus* govern them all. All are spurred by their desires, and yet the desire of each hinders the other three. Affection increases conversation and conversation affection. Affection also increases the ceremoniousness of their inter- actions, while the power of affection destroys the disguises that cere- mony is intended to maintain. Gynecia, we eventually discover, is motivated not to unmask Pyrocles because she recognizes that doing so would move Basilius to send him away. Consequently, she must acquiesce in Pyrocles' remaining a woman to her husband's eyes, thereby assuring that he will continue to be her own rival and con- sequently hinder her access to Pyrocles. Gynecia thus finds herself in a double bind similar to that which constrains Pyrocles himself, one made all the more painful by the added fact that by keeping Pyrocles near her Gynecia risks losing him to her own daughter. Pyrocles is faced—impossibly—with playing simultaneously the roles of suffering lover and disdainful mistress, all the while taking care not to provoke Gynecia's erotic anguish to the point where she will betray him. It is, indeed, as the old *Arcadia* tells us, precisely Pyro- cles' secret sharing with Gynecia in their common predicament that brings matters to a crisis. In order to satisfy Gynecia, Pyrocles in that version agrees to a tryst in a cave, thereby setting up the substitution of Basilius for himself (whom he also sends to the cave hoping to meet his beloved Zelmane), and Gynecia's administering the sleep- ing draught to her husband. These matters, however, I shall take up later when I come to consider the relations between the new *Arcadia* fragment and the final three books of the old *Arcadia*.

The portrayals of the six characters of the main plot, drawn mainly from the old *Arcadia* but significantly altered and developed in the new *Arcadia*, all exhibit some significant parallels. In each case is real- ized a potential dimension of the character's conception of himself or herself which is consciously rejected and repressed, or otherwise allowed no overt development. Erotic enslavement to an unattain- able mistress reverses Musidorus's and Pyrocles' heroic freedom in their previous adventures. Basilius's senile infatuation with the ama- zon Zelmane matches dialectically his equally ill-considered rejection of the erotic misadventures augured by the oracle. Gynecia's virtue is, as she admits, peculiarly vulnerable to turning itself inside out as a virulent form of jealousy and near homicide. And Philoclea's passionate ignorance is, appropriately enough, the result by *chiasmus* of her ignorance of passion. Only Pamela remains untouched by eros until well into Book 2, mainly by reason of her reserved nature and her inability to think of Prince Musidorus as anything but a lowly shepherd. Her resistance to love—the only resistance found among this sextet of players at the Arcadian game—is of course consonant with her majestical aloofness described by Kalander to the unwary Musidorus early in the story. In this respect she undergoes no dialectical reversal, nor does Sidney's portrayal of her steadfastness under the traumatic tortures inflicted on her in Book 3 of the new *Arcadia* suggest that he had finally intended to relax her stringent treatment of Musidorus, which continues well after she admits to Philoclea that she loves him.

Section 2

The oracular fulfillment of
the main plot

Little attention has been given the decisive significance of the oracular predictions that drive Basilius and his family from regal responsibility into the forests of Arcadia.[10] The most obvious aspects of this prediction are also the most significant. In essence, the prediction affirms that paradoxical events will take place, that both alternatives of contradictory possibilities can coexist: Basilius's elder daughter will be stolen but not lost; his younger daughter will enjoy a love that is both natural and unnatural; all four lovers will have to explain how they have contributed to Basilius's death when Basilius himself will be present and alive; and Basilius will commit adultery with his own wife. As the plot of the old *Arcadia* shows, these predictions are self-fulfilling, since they imply in disguised form a still further prediction, namely, that Basilius will fulfill the prophecy through actions taken in order to escape its fulfillment.

In this respect startlingly similar to *Oedipus Rex*, in both *Arcadia*s a main character fulfills a prophecy concerning his own future by seeking to escape it. Like Oedipus, Basilius equivocates with the prophecy, a fact his counselor Philanax points out when he tries to dissuade Basilius from leaving his throne and fleeing into the forest. Again like Oedipus, by this very act Basilius shows that he both does and does not give the prophecy credence. He exhibits sufficient belief in its inevitability to take drastic measures to escape it. But putting the point just this way discloses the other side of his equivocation: by attempting to avoid the predicted occurrences, Basilius betrays the fact that he does not believe in their inevitability. One might say that, given Basilius's general weakness of mind, this equivocation merely symptomizes an irrational confusion. But if Basilius's attempt to escape his doom is irrational, the fact that this attempt triggers the main plots of both *Arcadia*s demonstrates that it is a pregnant and significant irrationality. For what Basilius flees is not just the specific events that the oracle prophesies; what he flees is the apparent incomprehensibility of the prophecy itself. He seeks to escape a situation where differentially opposed situations both turn out to be true. How is it possible to be both dead and alive? How can a love be both natural and unnatural? How can he commit adultery with his own wife?

In the new *Arcadia* the reader first hears of the oracular prediction that drove Basilius from his throne when Kalander explains the king's actions to Musidorus early in Book 1:

> Now then, our Basilius (being so publicly happy as to be a prince, and so happy in that happiness as to be beloved prince, and so in his private blessed as to have so excellent a wife, and so over-excellent children) hath of late taken a course which yet makes him more spoken of than all these blessings; for having made a journey to Delphos and safely returned, within short space he brake up his court and retired himself, his wife, and children into a certain forest hereby which he calleth his desert, wherein, besides a house appointed for stables and lodgings for certain persons of mean calling who do all household services, he hath builded two fine lodges. (p. 17)

Basilius leaves the government of Arcadia to his trusted counselor Philanax, who gives Basilius essentially the same advice Sidney has him give in the old *Arcadia*. He exhorts Basilius to depend on his own virtue rather than soothsayers to determine his future. Furthermore, he discloses one of the essential marks of oracular prediction that the main plot of the new *Arcadia* will illustrate: "these kind of soothsayers—since they have left us in ourselves sufficient guides —[are] nothing but fancy, wherein there must either be vanity or infallibleness, and so, either not to be respected, or not to be prevented" (p. 21). As I have already suggested, Basilius's attempt to thwart the predictions demonstrates that he adheres to both of Philanax's alternatives. In believing that he can escape them, he treats the predictions as "not to be respected," while this belief shows him sufficiently convinced of their inevitability as to want to escape them.

Philanax points out that in the very act of trying to avoid catastrophe Basilius may well incur it: "Why should you deprive your self of government for fear of losing your government, like one that should kill himself for fear of death?" Then Philanax predicts that in depriving his daughters of suitors Basilius may bring about the very "unnaturalness" the oracle predicts if he allows them suitors:

> Once, certain it is: the god which is god of nature doth never teach unnaturalness. And even the same mind hold I touching your banishing them from company, lest I know not what strange loves should follow. . . . Now to fall to a sudden straitening them, what can it do but argue suspicion, a thing no more unpleasant than unsure for the preserving of virtue? Leave women's minds, the most untamed that way of any. See whether any cage can please a bird, or whether a dog grow not fiercer with tying? What doth jealousy but stir up the mind to think what it is from which they are restrained? For they are treasures, or things of great delight, which men use to hide for the aptness they have to catch men's fancies; and the thoughts once awaked to that, harder sure it is to keep those thoughts from accomplishment than it had been before to have kept the mind (which being the chief part, by this means is defiled) from thinking. (pp. 21–22)

It turns out that the constraints Basilius imposes on his daughters —made all the more irksome in the new *Arcadia* after the heroism demonstrated during their imprisonment—trigger both daughters' willingness to elope with their lovers.

Sidney does not tell either the reader or Philanax the content of the oracle until the end of Book 2, at which point events have so come about that Basilius believes the predictions already fulfilled in an unexpectedly harmless manner. These predictions are now revealed to have been the following:

> Thy elder care shall from thy careful face
> By princely mean be stol'n and yet not lost;
> Thy younger shall with nature's bliss embrace
> An uncouth love, which nature hateth most.
> Both they themselves unto such two shall wed,
> Who at thy bier, as at a bar, shall plead
> Why thee (a living man) they had made dead.
> In thy own seat a foreign state shall sit.
> And ere that all these blows thy head do hit,
> Thou with thy wife adult'ry shall commit.
>
> (pp. 295–96)

In comparing this prophecy with Philanax's advice, the reader notices that both contain similar paradoxes, and Basilius finds himself trapped within them. If he heeds the Delphic oracle and tries to escape it, he will, Philanax predicts, fulfill it anyway. But if he ignores the oracle, as Philanax counsels, he can presumably expect the predictions to come true also. At its profoundest level the threat of the oracle lies in its insistence not only that contradictory events will happen (which is bad enough) but that they *can* happen, that there is a dialectical logic that makes them possible. Like Musidorus, Pyrocles, and many characters of the subplots, Basilius flees the dialectical logic that pursues him as a consequence of his inability to assimilate and synthesize the various competing differentials that govern the text of his own future. It is therefore wholly appropriate that the origin of the Arcadian plot, the inaugurating event from which everything else flows and which dictates its overall structure, should be the delivery to the King of Arcadia of a text which affirms the coexistence of differentially opposed events. The prediction thus stands literally as the "fore-conceit" of the whole work, the basic ground-plan governing the essential events of the main plot. As such, it maintains an equivocal existence: it is a text that both summarizes the plot (synecdoche) and exists within that plot as a part of it (metonymy).

Dwelling outside the fictive text it controls, the prediction functions as the author's own fore-conceit. Dwelling, on the other hand, within the fictive world of the text, it governs it specifically as a prediction issuing from a supernatural agency. Sidney argued in *A Defence of Poetry* "the skill of the artificer standeth in that *idea* or fore-conceit of the work, and not in the work itself. And that the poet has that *idea* is manifest, by delivering them forth in such excellency as he had imagined them."[11] In generating the main plot of the fictive Arcadian world, while standing outside this fictive world and summarily recording Sidney's own fore-conceit of the work, the oracular prediction presents the reader with a perspectival paradox in which the freedom of Basilius's choices and the determinism of the oracular predictions dialectically interact. Because Basilius's attempts to escape the oracle's predictions only lead to their fulfillment, both dimensions of the oracular text fuse uncannily together. Sidney's fore-conceit exerts formal control over his fictive world by entering that world and inaugurating actions—Basilius's freely willed rejection of this predictive summary of his own biography—that obey this formal control by seeking to escape it.

As both a metonymical part of the plot it generates and a synecdochal text summarizing this plot, the oracular text presents interpretive problems on two different levels: that of the characters in the fiction, and that of the reader's engagement with Sidney's text. Both are challenged to interpret a text that asserts the mutual implication between mutually exclusive opposites. And both are invited to discover the dialectical rules that "disambiguate" the text. The events themselves of the main plot—completed only in the old *Arcadia*—disambiguate the oracle in a limited fashion, by making explicit the causal links binding together mutually exclusive texts and motivations. But though the oracle predicts these events, the events do not explain the oracle. The dialectical logic implicit in the predictions demands not merely fulfillment but interpretation and understanding. The main plot focuses, at this level, on Basilius's failure as an interpreter of texts. It is therefore quite appropriate that Sidney should include in both old and new *Arcadia*s an episode wherein Basilius erroneously believes that the oracular prediction has in fact already been fulfilled. His error is one of interpretation because he does not understand the rules governing his actions and those of the characters about him.

This episode is preceded by the peasants' revolt against Basilius and Pyrocles' heroic actions in putting it down. During this episode Pyrocles, still disguised as Zelmane, manages to preserve Pamela and Philoclea from the wrath of the rebels and afterward sits in Basilius's throne in order to placate the rebels with a cunningly contrived oration. All of these events Basilius, to his delight and relief, interprets as fulfilling the oracular prediction:

> Basilius returned into the Lodge, thus by himself construing the oracle: that, in that he said his elder care should by princely mean be stolen away from him and yet not lost, it was now performed, since Zelmane had as it were robbed from him the care of his first-begotten child—yet was it not lost, since in his heart the ground of it remained; that his younger should with nature's bliss embrace the love of Zelmane because he had so commanded her for his sake to do—yet should it be with as much hate of nature, for being so hateful an opposite to the jealousy he thought her mother had of him; the sitting in his seat he deemed by her already performed; but that which most comforted him was his interpretation of the adultery, which he thought he should commit with Zelmane, whom afterwards he should have to his wife. The point of his daughters' marriage, because it threatened his death withal, he determined to prevent with keeping them, while he lived, unmarried. (pp. 296–97)

The reference to Philoclea is to Basilius's suborning his younger daughter earlier to bear his messages of love to Pyrocles.

The significance of this passage lies in the ironic interplay between Basilius's conviction that he now commands his own destiny because he has interpreted the oracle correctly and the reader's awareness of important facts that Basilius remains ignorant of, namely, the presence of the two princes on the scene and their wooing his daughters. Sidney's care to relocate the text of the oracle from the beginning of the old *Arcadia* to this episode at the end of Book 2 in the new *Arcadia* reinforces this ironic interplay. Coming at the beginning of the old *Arcadia*, it casts its influence forward over the main plot, silently awaiting fulfillment and elucidation at the end. However, by withholding the oracle until the point in Book 2 of the new *Arcadia* where Basilius gives it an erroneous interpretation, Sidney focuses the reader's attention on the specific problem of interpretation itself. The oracle is partially fulfilled and therefore all the more mysterious. Ignorant of the future events that will elucidate the oracle, the reader must admit at least the plausibility of Basilius's interpretation. But this admission is necessarily tempered by the reader's possessing crucial information that Basilius does not, namely, that his daughters are already about to fulfill the clauses concerned with wooing. How much credibility, then, can the reader allow Basilius's interpretation? The point is that the reader cannot be sure. And at the center of this uncertainty lies the realization that interpretation may be at once plausible and wrong. This bare insight by itself is not remarkable. But coupled with the information the reader has already gathered from the first two books of the new *Arcadia*—which includes all the episodes and character analyses I have discussed in Part One and so far in Part Two—this insight presents problems that become the more dense the more they are examined.

The center of the new *Arcadia*'s concern is the interpretation of texts themselves: whether this interpretation be the reader's recuperating the differentially structured style of the new *Arcadia*, the work's paradoxical plot, or its juxtaposition of different generic materials, values, and rules. If the ultimate goal of the work is a final text in which are reconciled the central oppositions that constitute it —epic heroism/pastoral eroticism, freedom/determinism, concupiscible/irascible, and most profoundly, mutual exclusion/mutual implication—then the radical obstacle to this reconciliation lies in the blindness of all concerned, readers and characters alike, to the dialectical rules that make such a reconciliation possible and intelligible. In this respect, then, the reader undergoes an interpretive agon in reading the new *Arcadia* which replicates a similar agon undergone by the host of characters, major and minor, in the fictive Arcadian world itself.

A third and final reference is made to the oracle near the end of the Book 3 fragment in the new *Arcadia*. Not only does this reference, occurring within what is apparently Sidney's very latest writing, reiterate his plan to conclude the new *Arcadia* with some form of the ending of the old, but it reinforces my insistence on the oracle's central function in generating and structuring the main plot. After Queen Helen of Corinth removes Amphialus's wounded body from Cecropia's castle, Anaxius and his brothers remain to carry on resistance to Basilius's siege. Anaxius falls in love with Pamela and proposes marriage by a messenger to her father. Basilius turns once again to the oracle at Delphos for guidance. He sends Philanax, who has consistently doubted the significance of oracular predictions, to consult the oracle:

> . . . the spirit that possessed the prophesying woman with a sacred fury attended not his demand, but, as if it would argue him of incredulity, told him not in dark, wonted speeches, but plainly to be understood, what he came for, and that he should return to Basilius and will him to deny his daughters to Anaxius and his brothers, for that they were reserved for such as were better beloved of the gods; that he should not doubt, for they should return unto him safely and speedily; and that he should keep on his solitary course till both Philanax and Basilius fully agreed in the understanding of the former prophecy; withal, commanding Philanax from thence forward to give tribute, but not oblation, to human wisdom. (p. 457)

Given all we know already about the original prophecy, the following comments are suggested by this passage. First, the "former prophecy" is clearly the text of the first prediction given in both *Arcadia*s. Second, by instructing Basilius to continue his "solitary course," the oracle in effect asks Basilius to continue his attempted frustration of this prediction by remaining in the forest. Third, the marriage of his daughters to Musidorus and Pyrocles, obliquely referred to here, will (as we discover in the old *Arcadia* ending) result from nothing else than Basilius's sustained attempt to escape the oracle. We must conclude, in short, that the oracle instructs Basilius to continue attempts to frustrate the original prediction in order that it be fulfilled.

It should by now be apparent that Sidney has wittily engaged one of his own main characters—Basilius—in a form of perverse and unwitting complicity in writing the *Arcadia*. The oracular prediction as both (authorial) fore-conceit and (fictional) generator of plot balances uncannily on the borderline that divides the literary work into fictive action made by an author and an action done by fictive agents.[12] We ordinarily assume the logical incommensurability between the two worlds inhabited by the author and his characters, an incommensurability that is not violated by, but in fact makes possible, trompe l'oeil fictions in which both seem to cross this line (as in Part 2 of Don Quixote, where the fictive world contains Part 1 of the novel and someone who has read it, whom Don Quixote meets and with whom he discusses it[13]). In both old and new *Arcadias* the case is complicated by the fact that the authorial fore-conceit is not only replicated within the fiction as an oracular prediction, but the main plot of the fiction comes into existence through Basilius's freely willed rejection of his prediction. It would seem, however, that Sidney has discovered an economical device for rendering mutually supportive these elements in his plot that one might presume to be irreconcilable. Sidney's problem was in a sense every author's problem: how to construct a plot in which characters obey his fore-conceit, but do so in actions that are freely chosen and motivated. Sidney solves this problem by inserting the fore-conceit of his plot into the plot, patently converted into an oracular prediction. The fore-conceit thus "predicts" in the domains of both authorial control and fictive plot— does each only by doing both—and in this fashion Sidney manages to reconcile freedom and constraint in both dimensions. Basilius fulfills the oracular prediction (i.e., Sidney's fore-conceit) through actions intended to escape and thwart it, and it is clear to reader and characters alike by the end (in the conclusion of the old *Arcadia*) that these actions have been at once totally free and totally determined.

It should also be apparent by now that within my own interpretive perspective on the new *Arcadia* the question of oracles per se, their believability or nonsensicality, is not what Sidney is getting at. Whatever Sidney's personal opinion of oracles as "dreams which the [pagan] poets indeed superstitiously observed,"[14] the presence of the oracle in the work is not intended to trigger in the reader a consideration of whether or not it is possible to predict future events. Rather, the oracle is primarily a device that motivates and regulates the main plot of the new *Arcadia* (as it does that of the old *Arcadia*).

And its "message" to the reader dovetails with the complex message of the whole: namely, the problem of understanding any kind of text, oracular or otherwise, when this text renders human actions in differential form. Existing equivocally both within the work's fictive world and outside of it as the keystone of the author's own ground-plan, the oracle "predicts" nothing else than what Sidney himself "predicts," that is, what Sidney predicts and predicates of life in general: that the structure of human character and the actions this structure generates obey the dialectical rules governing the texts of human lives structured differentially.

Section 3

The recomposition of the old *Arcadia* as the 1593 composite text

This section and the next take up the question of what kind of work the new *Arcadia* is. This problem has been much worked over in the critical and scholarly literature on the work, and for good reason. Not only does it display a bewildering mixture of genres, most particularly of epic and pastoral, but it raises also the different but related question of why Sidney chose to recompose the relatively simple pastoral comedy of the old *Arcadia* as a mixed-genre production in the new *Arcadia*.

I have already indicated that the mixed generic structure of the new *Arcadia* bears a radical import for the meaning of the whole work. The main additions to the old *Arcadia* in the new lie in two major areas: the retrospective narratives about Musidorus's and Pyrocles' adventures in the eastern Mediterranean prior to their arrival in Arcadia; and the whole of Book 3, concerning Amphialus and the imprisonment of the two heroines and Pyrocles in Cecropia's castle. In contrast with the pastoral material that wholly makes up the plot of the old *Arcadia*—also present in the new—these two massive additions represent an extended composite portrayal of the two heroes' epic undertakings. The first recounts their various enterprises during the period that precedes the beginning of the main plot, and the second their equally heroic ventures while under the yoke of erotic passion.

The significance of this generic expansion depends on understanding what exactly Sidney did when he followed up the old *Arcadia* by composing the new but keeping most of the old as its central core. Because the conflict between the values of epic heroism and pastoral eroticism is highlighted in the new *Arcadia*, the juxtaposition of different generic forms and their system of value judgments becomes thematically significant in the new *Arcadia*. The new *Arcadia* represents neither a revision nor a displacement of the old *Arcadia*, but rather Sidney's disclosing thematic and characterological potentials latent in the earlier work, foregrounded and made problematic by being embedded in a greatly expanded context. The fact that, despite all these changes and additions, Sidney did not significantly alter the original fore-conceit of the old *Arcadia*—the oracular prediction—indicates that the conclusion of the old *Arcadia* was to be retained along with the rest of the main plot.[15]

Such a work, though imperfect, is what we find in the 1593 composite *Arcadia* brought out by Sidney's sister: the incomplete torso of the 1590 new *Arcadia*, which breaks off in mid-sentence somewhere near the end (presumably) of Book 3; followed by Books 3–5 for the most part as they occur in the earlier work. Does the 1593 composite *Arcadia* represent in the main Sidney's plan in revising the old *Arcadia* as the new? This question breaks down into two separate questions: the first bibliographical and the second interpretive. The bibliographical question concerns the final form Sidney planned for the new *Arcadia*, while the interpretive question deals with whatever intelligible meaning this final form conveys. And since in this final form the mixture of genres is made thematically significant, the meaning of the bibliographical evidence must be read in the context of this significance. In turn, the plausibility of this significance depends on a plausible interpretation of the bibliographical evidence itself, and for that reason this section takes up the first question: what did Sidney intend to be the final form of the new *Arcadia*?

In this connection I shall argue the following points: Sidney from first to last during the composition of the new *Arcadia* planned to end

the work with the central events of old *Arcadia* Books 3–5.[16] Whatever changes he might have intended in the details of the latter, there
are sufficient indications in the new *Arcadia* fragment of 1590 that
the general outline of the old *Arcadia* conclusion was to be retained:
Basilius's supposed death at the hands of Gynecia; the guilt of Musidorus and Pyrocles in seizing opportunities for elopement and love
making, respectively; the trial of the two princes by Euarchus, who is
ignorant of their identity; their condemnation, the timely reawakening of Basilius, and the general reconciliation. Consequently, I shall
argue further that the 1593 composite text joining the 1590 fragment
of the new *Arcadia* to Books 3–5 of the old represents not only the
closest thing we have to Sidney's original plan in revising the old *Arcadia* but also a reasonable approximation of this plan. In summary,
then, my argument in the remainder of Part Two seeks to account
for the mixed generic nature of the new *Arcadia* by integrating this
dimension of the work with those I have already discussed. In this
respect, the juxtaposition of epic and pastoral and comic-erotic texts
in the new *Arcadia* replicates on the global level of the whole work
the differentials developed on the local level of individual passages
discussed in Part One.

Jean Robertson in her edition of *The Countess of Pembroke's Arcadia
(The Old Arcadia)* surveys all the material both printed and in manuscript connected with both *Arcadia*s. What follows here is a summary
of her conclusion regarding the composition of both works, with
addition of Skretkowicz's views given in the footnotes.

The old *Arcadia* was begun at Wilton, the country home of Sidney's
sister the Countess of Pembroke, some time after 1577, probably
between March and August, 1580 (pp. xv–xvi). The first version
was finished in the spring of 1581 and revisions were begun during 1581–82 (p. xvii). Robertson adopts William Ringler's division
of the extant old *Arcadia* manuscripts into five groups representing
five distinguishable stages of revision of the work, the fifth of which
exhibits material that also finds its way into the new *Arcadia* fragment of 1590 (pp. lii–lvi).[17] Some time between 1581–82 and 1584
(p. lvii), Sidney commenced the composition of the new *Arcadia*.[18]
After Sidney's death in 1586 his close friend Fulke Greville, assisted
possibly among others by John Florio, brought out an edition of the

new *Arcadia* fragment in 1590, which breaks off at mid-sentence in Book 3. Greville in a letter to Sir Francis Walsingham, Sidney's father-in-law, in November, 1586, says that the printer Ponsonbie approached him with the information that another printer was going to print "Sir philip sydneys old arcadia." [19] Ponsonbie asked Greville if this projected printing was being done with "yor honors consent or any other of his frends." Greville says that he told Ponsonbie that he knew nothing of this matter and writes Walsingham to tell him of another work:

> Sir I am lothe to reneu his memori vnto you, but yeat in this I might presume, for I haue sent my lady yor daughter [Sidney's widow] at her request, a correction of that old one don 4 or 5 years since which he left in trust with me wherof ther is no more copies, & fitter to be printed then that first which is so common, notwithstanding euen that to be amended by a direction sett doun vndre his own hand how & why, so as in many respects espetially ye care of printing it is to be done with more deliberation. . . . (Ringler, p. 530)

Greville's publication in 1590 of the "correction" of the old *Arcadia* included chapter divisions that Sidney had not made in the manuscript in Greville's possession, as well as eclogues "chosen and disposed as the overseer thought best." [20]

Sidney's sister, the Countess of Pembroke, aided by several editors, in turn brought out in 1593 the text of 1590 plus Books 3–5 of the old *Arcadia*. A number of changes were made in 1590 as well as in the last books of the old *Arcadia* in order to bring both texts into some conformity with each other. These include name changes—Cleophila of the old *Arcadia* becomes Zelmane, while Basilius is promoted from duke to king—but the most important changes involve the insertion into the old *Arcadia* text of two extended passages not present in the original manuscripts of that work. The first substitutes a new and extended ending for Book 3, where Pyrocles clandestinely enters Philoclea's bedroom, while the second inserts a long passage regarding the troubles and travels of Euarchus before he arrives in Arcadia. These two passages, Robertson speculates, were included in the "direction" Greville speaks of in his letter to Walsingham (p. lx), for they seem to be authorial. Because these passages are important later on in my discussion of Sidney's recomposition of the *Arcadia*, I shall not discuss them here, except to point out that they appear to confirm (contra Robertson's conclusion) Sidney's intention to complete the new *Arcadia* with the old *Arcadia*'s ending (see Appendix).

The composite *Arcadia* of 1593, while being the edition known to readers generally from that time down to Bertram Dobell's recovery of two manuscripts of the old *Arcadia* in 1907 and 1909,[21] has never seemed satisfactory to anyone, including its own editors. Hugh Sanford's preface to the 1593 edition says as much:

> The disfigured face, gentle reader, wherewith this work not long since appeared to the common view, moved that noble lady, to whose honour consecrated, to whose protection it was committed, to take in hand the wiping away those spots wherewith the beauties thereof were unworthily blemished. But, as often in repairing a ruinous house, the mending of some old part occasioneth the making of some new; so here her honourable labour begun in correcting the faults, ended in supplying the defects; by the view of what was ill done guided to the consideration of what was not done. Which part with what advice entered into, with what success it hath been passed through, most by her doing, all by her directing, if they may be entreated not to define, which are unfurnished of means to discern, the text (it is hoped) will favourably censure. But this they shall, for their better satisfaction, understand, that though they find not here what might be expected, they may find nevertheless as much as was intended, the conclusion, not the perfection of *Arcadia*; and that no further than the author's own writings, or known determinations, could direct. Whereof who sees not the reason, must consider there may be reason which he sees not. Albeit I dare affirm he either sees, or from wiser judgements than his own may hear, that Sir Philip Sidney's writings can no more be perfected without Sir Philip Sidney than Apelles' pictures without Apelles. . . . Whom albeit it do not exactly and every lineament represent; yet considering the father's untimely death prevented the timely birth of the child, it may happily seem a thank-worthy labour, that the defects being so few, so small, and in no prin-

cipal part, yet the greatest unlikeness is rather in defect than in deformity. (Robertson, pp. xlix–l)

Sanford here throws down a challenge to the editors of the 1590 edition and initiates a battle that has perhaps yet to be won by either side. John Florio, who may have been part of Greville's editorial team, replied to Sanford's preface by calling attention to its unsatisfactoriness in his dedicatory preface to volume two of his Montaigne translation (1603), addressed to the Countess of Rutland, Sidney's daughter, and Penelope Rich:

> I know, nor this, nor any I have seen, or can conceive, in this or other language, can in aught be compared to that perfect-unperfect *Arcadia*, which all our world yet weepes with you, that your all praise-exceeding father (his praise-succeeding Countesse) your worthy friend (friend worthiest Lady) lived not to mend or end-it: since this end wee see of it, though at first above all, now is not answerable to the precedents: and though it were much easier to mend out of an originall and well corrected copie, than to make-up so much out of a most corrupt, yet see we more marring that was well, then mending what was amisse.[22]

The fact that in the 1593 edition the spliced-on conclusion of the old *Arcadia* "is not answerable to the precedents" has been universally acknowledged from Florio's time down to our own. What exactly Florio meant by this phrase, however, is perhaps not as obvious as some have taken it to be. For the most part, Sidney scholars and critics since then, insofar as they align themselves with Florio's adverse opinion, take him to mean that the two parts are ill matched by reason of their divergent tones and concerns.[23] That another interpretation is possible of Florio's word "answerable" is indicated by Sir William Alexander's addition in the 1613 reprinting of the 1593 version of a transitional passage linking the unfinished Book 3 of 1590 with the beginning of the old *Arcadia* Book 3 as given in 1593. Alexander is aware, as he says, that "what conclusion it should have had, or how far the work have been extended (had it had his last hand thereunto) was only known to his own spirit, where only those admirable images were (and nowhere else) to be cast" (Robertson, p. 448).

Nevertheless, his addition of a transitional passage was intended to compensate for the following:

> Here we are likewise utterly deprived of the relation how this combat [between Pyrocles and Anaxius] ended, and how the ladies by discovery of the approaching forces were delivered and restored to Basilius; how Dorus returned to his old master Dametas. All which unfortunate maim we must be content to suffer with the rest. (Ibid.)

Alexander's insertion is stuff poor enough.[24] But it should be noted here that Florio's charge (presuming Alexander knew of it) that the conclusion was "not answerable to the precedents" would have meant to Alexander not that there was an irreconcilable discrepancy between the two parts taken as distinct narratives, but more narrowly that there existed no bridge between them composed by Sidney himself.[25] Alexander's difficulties in composing such a bridge were real enough, but they derive rather from his ineptitude than from any inherent irreconcilability between the two segments.

However Sidney intended to bridge the gap between the new *Arcadia* material of Book 3 and Book 3 of the old *Arcadia*, passages already present in the 1590 edition indicate beyond any reasonable doubt that such a conjunction was in his mind throughout his composing the new *Arcadia*. The first is, of course, the original prediction of the oracle, which is repeated with some additions and changes in the new *Arcadia*. As in the old *Arcadia*, the prediction sets in motion and governs the actions of the main plot in the new *Arcadia*. Confirming this central indication of Sidney's plan is the passage describing Gynecia's nightmare taken over from the old *Arcadia*, but with a significant addition. In the old *Arcadia* (Robertson, p. 117) Gynecia dreams she sees Pyrocles-Cleophila at the top of a hill, and when she arrives there, "she found nothing but a dead body which seeming at the first with a strange smell so to infect her as she was ready to die likewise, within a while the dead body (she thought) took her in his arms and said: 'Gynecia, here is thy only rest.'" This passage is repeated in the new *Arcadia* in most of its details. But one significant detail is altered: "she found nothing but a dead body—like unto her husband" (p. 277), a detail which Sidney apparently added to bring this foreshadowing dream into stricter alignment with the oracle, and consequently with the ending he envisioned for the new *Arcadia* itself.

In addition, there are two references in the new *Arcadia* Book 3 to Gynecia's and Basilius's infatuation with Zelmane-Pyrocles, which mainly serve to keep before the reader's mind this central element of the main plot, and which also imply Sidney's sustained intention to return to that plot after the conclusion of the imprisonment episode. The first is the following:

> Basilius himself came forth, and brought forth the fair Gynecia with him—who was gone into the camp under colour of visiting her husband and hearing of her daughters, but indeed, Zelmane was the saint to which her pilgrimage was intended, cursing, envying, blessing, and in her heart kissing the walls which imprisoned her. (p. 399)

In the second passage Sidney says that it was primarily fear for Zelmane's life that caused Basilius to give up the siege:

> He [Basilius] would have proceeded on, when Gynecia came running in, amazed for her daughter Pamela—but mad for Zelmane; and falling at Basilius' feet besought him to make no delay, using such gestures of compassion, instead of stopped words, that Basilius (otherwise enough tender-minded) easily granted to raise the siege which he saw dangerous to his daughters—but indeed, more careful for Zelmane, by whose besieged person the poor old man was straitly besieged. (p. 418)

All of these passages appear well into the body of Sidney's recomposed *Arcadia*, all indicate the consistency with which Sidney held to his fore-conceit, and all point unequivocally toward the conclusion found in the last three books of the old *Arcadia*.

If one wants to argue from decorum alone, it would appear that the violation of decorum occurs rather between the erotic comedy of the old *Arcadia* Books 1 to 3 and the two concluding books of the same work. If these last two books exhibit a transformation of pastoral erotic comedy into tragicomedy, then—assuming the new *Arcadia*'s commitment to mixed genres throughout—these latter two books fit much better the new *Arcadia* than the old. And if one must speculate, it is more plausible that as Sidney proceeded in composing the old *Arcadia*, it became increasingly clear to him that, by the time he arrived at Book 4, he had a significantly different work on his hands. It is not unreasonable to take old *Arcadia* Books 4 and 5 as in reality preparation for the writing of the new *Arcadia*, something which Sidney nevertheless did not undertake until after a certain period of tinkering with the old, as the manuscripts investigated by Sidney's Oxford Press editors illustrate.

The extensive revisions registered in the successive old *Arcadia* manuscripts do not necessarily lead to the conclusion that Sidney tried but failed to revise his earlier work to his own satisfaction, and only then proceeded to drop it in favor of the new *Arcadia*. On the contrary, such revisions suggest exactly the opposite hypothesis: that the new *Arcadia* grew out of Sidney's sustained preoccupation with the old, registered in his retaining so much of it in the first two books of the new *Arcadia*. The assumption of Sidney's Oxford editors (Ringler, Robertson, Skretkowicz) is that this latter revision yielded in the new *Arcadia* a work wholly different from the old *Arcadia* (which it admittedly is generically), and by the same token severed the new *Arcadia* from the old *Arcadia* in all other respects as well. Sidney's careful amalgamation of new *Arcadia* narratives with the old *Arcadia* main plot and the retention of the Delphic oracle as the work's "fore-conceit" indicates that this is not the case. The new *Arcadia* represents not a repudiation of old *Arcadia*, but rather an expansion of the framework of the old *Arcadia* main plot to contain the vast and varied subordinate narratives that constitute the new *Arcadia* materials.[26]

This in turn suggests that there is no "*New Arcadia*" as distinct from the "*Old Arcadia*," as the usual designations in the *Arcadia* literature have it. I have consequently refused to incorporate "old" and "new" as adjectival indicators of sharp distinction into my rendering of these titles in my analysis. The new *Arcadia* is only the old *Arcadia* expanded, with the plot framework of the earlier work remaining in place from first to last. All of this is implied in my contention that the 1593 version gives the basic form of what Sidney was planning, even if that particular version is significantly faulty in its arrangement of the eclogues and dubious in its editorial intervention in textual details.[27]

From the perspective of my argument in this study, the closest approximation to a perfect version of the new *Arcadia* would combine (1) the 1590 new *Arcadia* in Skretkowicz's edition, (2) the text of the old *Arcadia* in Robertson's edition for Books 3–5, plus (3) insertions of material regarding Pyrocles-Philoclea and Euarchus's journey to Arcadia given by Robertson in her apparatus (pp. 236–37, 355–57).

I critique elsewhere (see the Appendix) Robertson's reading of the textual evidence, as well as Skretkowicz's apparent agreement with her in his edition of the new *Arcadia*. Her finding it "inconceivable" that the 1593 composite *Arcadia* should reflect Sidney's final intentions is finally not a matter of such evidence but of interpretation, more specifically, interpretation of Sidney's deliberate violations of generic decorum. When Sidney combined old *Arcadia* passages with new material in the new *Arcadia* Books 1 and 2, he fused the heroic and the pastoral-erotic in ways that no less violated decorum than did his sister in splicing the old *Arcadia* ending onto the 1590 fragment. Such transgressions are consistent from the beginning of the new *Arcadia*, and I have shown in this section that they were to continue to the end. So far the bibliographical evidence will take us. What it will not tell us is why Sidney chose to do this, and this, the second central question which Part Two must answer, is taken up in the final two sections of this book.

Section 4

The reconciliation of epic heroism and pastoral love

The interplay of generic ingredients in the new *Arcadia* makes the following point: the values, motivations, and actions of the heroic life embodied in the epic romance both exclude and consequently imply the values, motivations, and actions of the erotic life embodied in the pastoral genre.[28] The deeds and sufferings of the two princes show that their attempts to define themselves according to the text of epic romance necessarily entails rejecting the text of the erotic pastoral. But this rejection also implies mutual implication, and rejection of love in the name of heroism dialectically implies enslavement to love and abandonment of heroism.

Sidney's juxtaposition in the new *Arcadia* of epic and pastoral genres mediates and replicates the two heroes' struggle to achieve textual wholeness, which has one major obstacle to overcome: the rules that determine textual intelligibility are divisive rather than unitive. The well-formed text (and self) excludes all terms that oppose those central ones constituting that text. Some of the portraits examined in Part One indicate that a character who does not harmonize the (potentially) competing parts of his or her identity will have to confront a perpetual agon, a continual self-division. Obedience to the rule of noncontradiction—the founding condition of an intelligible and well-formed text of the self—may compel the self to confront those elements intrinsic to it which it has had to reject as the price of its well-formedness. Governing this return of the repressed are the rules of dialectic that explain how such exclusions unwittingly imply what they exclude. These rules (which I have listed at the end of Part One, particularly rules E and F) are various consequences of the central rule, by which mutual exclusion both excludes and implies mutual implication.

Sidney introduces the problem of generic purity and its violation in Musidorus's debates with Pyrocles about the relative worth of heroic and erotic pursuits. In arguing that it is impossible for human males simultaneously to embrace both, Musidorus transforms the boundary lines drawn by the theoretical purism of Renaissance genre theory into the lines that demarcate the conflict he and Pyrocles suffer between their previous lives of heroic endeavor and their present enslavement to love in Arcadia. At the beginning of their heroic adventures Pyrocles and Musidorus are shown making a conscious choice to imitate (with an important difference) classical models of heroism:

> they determined in unknown order to see more of the world, and to employ those gifts esteemed rare in them to the good of mankind; and therefore would themselves (understanding that the King Euarchus was passed all the cumber of his wars) go privately to seek

exercises of their virtue, thinking it not so worthy to be brought to heroical effects by fortune or necessity (like Ulysses and Aeneas) as by one's own choice, and working. (p. 179)

And it is against such models of heroical effort that Musidorus measures Pyrocles' falling away into the role of lover in the debates examined above in section one. The arguments against mixed genres in Italian Renaissance literary criticism often assumed that genre divisions reflect divisions in the domains of nature and society, and this assumption allowed Sidney to map his two heroes' divided identities onto the generic anomalies posed by a mixed genre fiction. The problems of generic purity and its transgression become thus the vehicle through which Sidney allows Musidorus and Pyrocles to textualize their struggle to unite the opposing imperatives of heroism and eros.

Rosalie Colie sums up Renaissance genre theory as at once a classification of literary "kinds" and a map of the areas of human existence as the Renaissance sorted them out, when she speaks of "the *social* force and function of the kinds, as abbreviations for a 'set' on the world, as definitions of manageable boundaries, some large, some small, in which material can be treated and understood."[29] Bernard Weinberg's survey of Italian Renaissance literary criticism discloses many justifications of generic purity on the basis of "natural" divisions between different kinds of human experience. For instance, Weinberg paraphrases a commentary on Horace's *Ars poetica* by Giovanni Britannico da Brescia (1518) as holding that "the universal principle of appropriateness is merely a transposition into literary terms of the notion that things of the same kind are assorted by nature and such things as would not be put together by nature must not be combined by art."[30] Weinberg also cites Tasso on the indecorum of mixing high and low actions and characters (2:1077) in *Delle differenze poetiche* of 1587, a sentiment echoed in the 1590 *Apologia* of Giason Denores: "for a mixed form would either have to have two actions, in which case it would sin against unity, or it would have to combine opposite things in one action, in which case it would sin against nature" (2:675).

The appeal to the norm of nature curiously brings into the same camp those critics who find the 1593 composite *Arcadia* indecorous, and Musidorus himself, who finds Pyrocles' erotically induced androgyny unnatural. Both arguments assume that nature and (therefore) literary genres must render the different "kinds" of human experience mutually exclusive. That Sidney did not view either case this way is demonstrated on the one hand by the vicissitudes suffered by his two heroes, and on the other in his recomposing the new *Arcadia* as an overtly mixed-genre production. Colie speculates that Scaliger was Sidney's source for his statement on mixed genres in the *Defence* and goes on to say:

> Without losing sight of the specific requirements for generic division, Scaliger at the same time defends the propositions that everything utterable has its genre, and that a complex, large, inclusive utterance may require mixture of the kinds. That is, I think Scaliger recognizes the principle of invariancy, which assures a given genre its subject and style, and in some cases shape also, as well as the inclusiveness dictated by belief in the *paideia*; within his genre-system, he allows for counter-genericism too.[31]

Whether or not Sidney took this hint from Scaliger, it seems to me clear that Sidney assumes the "principle" of "invariancy" in order to play off against it his conviction that "a complex, large, inclusive utterance may require mixture of the kinds." In a sense, then, the new *Arcadia* is at once an attack on Renaissance notions of generic decorum and a revision of Renaissance notions of human identity that this decorum institutionalizes. Decorous order in both cases means a nondialectical exclusion of disruptive opposites, a hierarchical sundering of "above" and "below," of flesh and spirit, of action and passion, of moral good and evil. But the texts of this decorous order are all nondialectical texts, which achieve (false) security from disruption by their matching countertexts through obeying the imperatives of a differential discursive structure regulated by noncontradiction.

The material in Books 1 and 2 of the new *Arcadia* taken over from the corresponding books of the old *Arcadia* is generally changed only in being no longer placed in the mouth of an omniscient narrator, but instead distributed to various characters within the fiction itself. This dispersion of viewpoint in the new *Arcadia* is matched by a dispersal of the narrated events in the temporal dimension of chronology. Whereas the old *Arcadia* presents us with a more or less continuous parallel between narrative order and the order of events themselves, in the new *Arcadia* narration runs backward and forward across this order. The latter opens with the shipwreck of the two princes off the coast of Laconia and proceeds to their initial adventures in Arcadia and falling in love. Book 2 then is partly devoted to recounting events preceding the shipwreck in retrospective narratives put variously in the mouths of Musidorus, Pyrocles, and Pamela. Book 3, on the other hand, once again matches the sequences of narration and chronology. In addition to this dislocation of narrative sequence, we have also another essential change in the new *Arcadia*: the oracular prediction is not told the reader until the end of Book 2, whereas in the old *Arcadia* the oracle is one of the first pieces of information relayed by the omniscient narrator. In general, then, several major events and sequences of events are narrated before their causal antecedents are disclosed.

A significant result of this dispersion is that the two princes conform their narrations to the conventions of the romance epic, and it is specifically as "epic romance" tales of themselves that they recount their adventures to their inamorata. By locating their epic recitals within the perspectives and voices of a shepherd and a bisexual "amazon" who dwell in a pastoral love comedy, Sidney suggests that both discourses define each other by a dialectical doubleness of mutual exclusion and mutual implication.

More broadly, by relinquishing a privileged narrative voice, Sidney implements a discovery he appears to have made while composing the last two books of the old *Arcadia*. This discovery is registered in Philanax's vengefully biased account of the two princes' motives in coming to Arcadia and wooing the two princesses. This account affirms a central fact of the new *Arcadia*: that characters' actions are wholly a function of the discourses in which they are textualized. In the old *Arcadia* the reader possesses a privileged viewpoint from which he can recognize the discrepancies between his own knowledge of the princes' actions and the large degree to which these actions will bear Philanax's biased interpretation. In the new *Arcadia*, however, this juxtaposition is no longer between the actual events themselves and a specific text that gives their meaning, but rather between two different texts.[32]

This juxtaposition is most fully worked out in the tale Musidorus, disguised as the shepherd Dorus, tells Pamela of his adventures.[33] Sidney gives us a complex nest of tales, one inside of another. The outermost tale is Musidorus's account to Pyrocles of how he narrates his own adventures to Pamela in the third person, bringing their conclusion down to the present where the prince Musidorus disguised as a shepherd attempts to woo the haughty Pamela. By leading his tale up to the actual point of his telling it to her, he discloses that the teller of the tale and its subject are in fact the same person.

Musidorus must convey to Pamela the information that he is not the shepherd Dorus but rather Musidorus prince of Thessaly in such a way as not to betray himself to the ever-watchful eyes of Dametas, Mopsa, and Miso. His method is first to convey the message that he has a message to convey. He does this by inviting Pamela to perceive the disproportion between the Petrarchan text he addresses to Mopsa and the blindingly obvious facts of Mopsa's own unprepossessing person. This disproportion is intended to inform Pamela that neither text nor lover are as they appear. In the old *Arcadia*, where the omniscient narrator is able to give us Pamela's own hidden reactions to this preposterous wooing, Sidney makes overt what we might call the hermeneutic principle that Musidorus relies on:

> But the more she marked the expressing of Dorus's affection towards Mopsa, the more she thought she found such phrases applied to Mopsa as must needs argue either great ignorance or a second meaning in Dorus; and so to this scanning of him was she now content to fall, whom before she was resolved to banish from her thoughts. (Robertson, p. 99)

In the new *Arcadia*, however, which limits the perspective on this whole episode to what Musidorus himself can observe and infer, this information is omitted. Musidorus is left to wonder aloud to Pyrocles whether she has decoded his elaborately encoded message or not. This situation allows Sidney to postpone disclosure of Pamela's real thoughts to a point late in Musidorus's narrative of his own epic tale, when in a poignant moment Pamela suddenly realizes who the teller is, and Musidorus in turn understands that she has achieved this recognition.

For my present purposes, the most important point about the Mopsa episode is that it exhibits a ludicrous contrast between two different, indeed opposed, textualizations of Mopsa's attractions. Early in the new *Arcadia* Kalander describes Mopsa for Musidorus in a comic poem written about her by "a pleasant fellow of my acquaintance" setting forth "her praises in verse" (p. 18). This poem parodies the Petrarchan blazon of the beloved's physical features, in the manner we are familiar with in Donne's Elegy 2, "The Anagram." It consists of praise generated by all the wrong things. She is, it would seem,

Like great god Saturn, fair, and like fair Venus, chaste;
As smooth as Pan; as Juno, mild; like goddess Iris, fast;
With Cupid she foresees, and goes god Vulcan's pace,
And for a taste of all these gifts, she steals god Momus' grace;
Her forehead, jacinth-like; her cheeks of opal hue;
Her twinkling eyes, bedecked with pearl; her lips as sapphire, blue;
Her hair like crapal stone; her mouth, O, heavenly wide;
Her skin like burnished gold; her hands like silver ore untried.

                                                    (p. 18; ll. 21–28)

As the lovers and Titania demonstrate in *A Midsummer Night's Dream*, anyone becomes beautiful and lovable if one happens to see her as such, and can invent a text that objectifies and substantiates this vision. The reader may or may not be expected to remember this poem when he encounters Musidorus's song to Mopsa later on in Book 2:

        Since so mine eyes are subject to your sight,
        That in your sight they fixed have my brain;
        Since so my heart is filled with that light,
        That only light doth all my life maintain;

        Since in sweet you all goods so richly reign,
        That where you are no wished good can want;

149

Since so your living image lives in me,
That in myself your self true love doth plant;
  How can you him unworthy then decree,
  In whose chief part your worths implanted be?

(pp. 129–30)

Even more perhaps than Musidorus's eclogues concluding the various books or acts in the old *Arcadia* does this piquant situation reveal Musidorus's total immersion in the text of the erotic pastoral: his enacting the role of a shepherd singing polished verse to a rustic lass. Amorous song is followed by amorous speech:

"The song being ended, which I had often broken off in the middest with grievous sighs which overtook every verse I sang, I let fall my harp from me, and casting my eye sometime upon Mopsa, but settling my sight principally upon Pamela, 'And is it the only fortune, most beautiful Mopsa,' said I, 'of wretched Dorus, that fortune must be the measure of his mind? Am I only he that, because I am in misery, more misery must be laid upon me? Must that which should be cause of compassion become an argument of cruelty against me? Alas, excellent Mopsa, consider that a virtuous prince requires the life of his meanest subject, and the heavenly sun disdains not to give light to the smallest worm. O Mopsa, Mopsa! If my heart could be as manifest to you as it is uncomfortable to me, I doubt not the height of my thoughts should well countervail the lowness of my quality. Who hath not heard of the greatness of your estate? Who seeth not that your estate is much excelled with that sweet uniting of all beauties which remaineth and dwelleth with you? Who knows not that all these are but ornaments of that divine spark within you which, being descended from heaven, could not elsewhere pick out so sweet a mansion? But if you will know what is the band that ought to knit all these excellencies together, it is a kind of mercifulness to such a one as is in his soul devoted to those perfections." (p. 130)

The reader and—as Musidorus hopes—Pamela both perceive in this speech a delightful intertextuality, wherein mingle praise, the lover's discomfort, and covert protestations of his own princely identity.

Having repeated to Pyrocles this text in which he loads onto Mopsa a heavy layer of irony, Musidorus as it were retextualizes Mopsa once again, but this time for Pyrocles' ears only:

> "Mopsa (who already had had a certain smackering towards me) stood all this while with her hand sometimes before her face, but most commonly with a certain special grace of her own, wagging her lips and grinning, instead of smiling. But all the words I could get of her was (wrying her waist, and thrusting out her chin), 'In faith, you jest with me! you are a merry man indeed!'" (p. 131)

Juxtaposed here are text and countertext—a second discourse composed of these terms differentially excluded by the first. Musidorus's strategy is essentially that employed by Andromana in seducing her husband, the King of Iberia, to enmity against his son Plangus: both utter a text that is intended to elicit in the receiver its own countertext. Just as Andromana's praise dialectically generates condemnation in the king, Musidorus's complimenting Mopsa is intended to evoke in Pamela the consciousness of all those terms of dispraise excluded by the first text, and therefore implied by them. Musidorus's speech marks a sundering not between text and reality so much as between two texts: between the speech itself and all the other texts —typified by the poem Kalander recites earlier—in which Pamela would reasonably expect Mopsa to be textualized. Musidorus's irony operates like irony in general: by exploiting the dialectical generation of mutual implication out of mutual exclusion, the text of praise generates a countertext of dispraise.[34]

Having cut loose from Mopsa his text of praise by the ingenious method of first attaching it to her, Musidorus invites Pamela to see it floating free and to wonder to whom it might appropriately be applied. Because he has deprived himself of a narrator able to give an immediate account of Pamela's reactions to this bizarre episode, Sidney can now portray her own comments delivered in a deliciously straight manner: "'I will not deny,' answered the gracious Pamela, 'but that the love you bear to Mopsa hath brought you to the consideration of her virtues, and the consideration may have made you the more virtuous, and so the more worthy'" (p. 132). The hypothetical note sounded by "may" here, and her recognition that it must be love indeed that can find such beauties in so unlikely an object, is the only hint we are given of what Pamela may really be thinking. She otherwise delivers herself of a lengthy exhortation to Musidorus that if he indeed loves Mopsa, he must confirm it with honorable intentions. Musidorus cannily seizes on the question of his worthiness, to tell a story of a prince who found it necessary to take on the disguise of mean estate in order to woo the woman he loves.

From here follows the beginning of Musidorus's tale of himself and Sidney's introduction of the first subplots. The story concerns the two princes Musidorus and Pyrocles, who having been raised according to the conventions of the "education of princes" embodied in the text of Xenophon's *Cyropaedia*, find themselves next fallen into the Heliodoran world of *An Aethiopian History*, wherein they enact various feats of salvific Herculean heroism. It is in this tale, joined later by the tale that Pyrocles tells Philoclea, that Sidney manages to import into the new *Arcadia* a radically essential ingredient lacking in the old *Arcadia*: the two heroes' narration of epic romance juxtaposed against their present immersion in pastoral erotic comedy.

Before taking up the significance of this central point for Sidney's latter work, however, I must unpack the complex nest of texts that constitutes Musidorus's epic story, and the significance of this multi-leveled textualization for the new *Arcadia*. In his story Musidorus's purpose is essentially the same as Astrophil's in sonnet 45: to communicate the fact of divided identity, and to invite pity and consequently love: "I am not I, pity the tale of me." We can see in *Astrophil and Stella*, in fact, a full-dress rehearsal for the textual complexities of this episode in the new *Arcadia*, and examining some of these complexities in the earlier sonnet sequence will throw into relief Sidney's purposes in the later work. In both cases we have a lover telling a tale to his beloved, where the tale is both an account of his love and an instrument for wooing.[35] The sonnets are intended to win Stella's love, but they do so by telling the story of how "Astrophil" strives to win the love of "Stella." Astrophil attempts to win Stella's love by giving her sonnets that recount his various emotions, thoughts, and actions during the process of his wooing. In other words, the relation between the sonnet texts as instruments-of-love and the same texts as story-of-love keep receding as *mise en abîme* in a hall of mirrors. The narrative constantly pursues the wooing—the "actual" situation in which Astrophil addresses the sonnets to Stella —in that whatever the sonnets tell has already been enacted in the past, while the writing of the sonnets takes place in the present. We are not allowed to forget, however, that the only account we have of this "present" is within the sonnets themselves, which makes the poems curiously self-reflexive and circular. The tale they tell is the tale they enact: the writer-as-lover himself consistently textualizes himself as the lover-as-writer. There is no wooing situation outside of the poems themselves, and consequently the deictic, referential dimension of these poems, like that in Musidorus's tale, has a peculiar doubleness. On the one hand, they gesture toward a transtextual, "real-life" situation, and in this respect the distance between poem-as-story and poem-as-instrument-of-wooing is sharply maintained. On the other hand, this deixis is circumscribed within the poetic texts themselves, since they recount their own presentation or recital to Stella. And from this perspective the poem-as-story and the poem-as-instrument-of-wooing maintain a fluid state of oscillating separation and fusion.

The teller of the tale cannot be divorced from the discourse in which he textualizes himself. Musidorus like Astrophil locates himself within one text in order to deliver himself of another text, and the reader is required to make distinctions among various texts nesting one inside another. Such nesting is registered in a continual oscillation between first-person and third-person viewpoints. All of this can be diagramed as a series of embedments:

[Narrator (third person) [Musidorus telling Pyrocles (first person) [Musidorus telling Pamela (first person) [The story of Musidorus's adventures (third person)]]]].

In this recursive sequence Musidorus takes on three different roles. He tells Pyrocles in his "own person" the story he told Pamela while disguised as the shepherd Dorus. Within that tale Musidorus is portrayed putatively in his "own person" once again. I put "own person" in quotation marks, however, to highlight the problem of Musidorus's identity in relation to these various roles. Is it in fact accurate to say that the Musidorus who recounts this episode to Pamela is identical with the subject of Dorus's tale? The answer to this question can be only a rather vertiginous yes-and-no. The Musidorus of whom Dorus speaks to Pamela is still the hero of epic romance, a character heroically dedicated to overcoming Heliodoran disasters in a world of high adventure. The gap between these two identities corresponds exactly to the gap between the values, motivations, and actions of epic romance on the one hand and those of pastoral erotic comedy on the other. For the Musidorus who tells this tale has doffed the role of the Musidorus who enacts it and taken on the love-dominated role of the shepherd Dorus. The identity he thus presents to Pyrocles is redolent of the same self-awareness that bedevils Pyrocles himself: the consciousness of both heroes that they are now very different persons than they were.

The embedment of texts—graphed above—diagrams the division of identities Musidorus has undergone and still suffers from. The total narrative situation here, with stories nesting inside stories, adds up to a complex textualization of the act of narration—of textualization—itself, and therefore of the complex, divided identity of the story teller also. Musidorus is one text (the text of enamored shepherd) reciting another text (the text of the romantic epic). The notion, in other words, that Musidorus is really the same Musidorus hiding behind the disguise of Dorus is called into question and invalidated because his love for Pamela has transformed him into a living denizen of a pastoral love comedy.[36]

Ultimately, as Musidorus brings his tale down to the present moment, we witness through Pamela's eyes the paradox of two moral identities superimposed on the same person. Musidorus's tale of himself and his act of telling it become indistinguishable when Pamela recognizes that the latest act of the tale of the heroic prince is his telling it to her in the role of enamored shepherd. This doubling of identities is ironically announced through Musidorus's original purpose in telling his story to Pamela: to disclose in the person standing now before her the subject of his story. It is a story about causes and origins: it answers the question Who am I and how did I get here? Its purpose is to unmask the teller himself, who attempts to step outside the frame of his story and show himself for who he "really is"—

Musidorus, prince of Thessaly. But in the end that teller is not present either, but only another text, the text of the erotic shepherd, a role which he has been compelled to take on by the force of his love. The story he has told is, in fact, a story of alienation from self, of a fissure thrust through the integrity of his previous identity. As Pyrocles tells Philoclea, equivocating on Musidorus's fate after the shipwreck that brought both of them to Arcadia, "I may truly say he is lost, since he is no more his own" (p. 276). Consequently, the means that Musidorus uses to confirm his princely identity to Pamela—the story of his falling in love and abandonment of the heroic life—confirms just the opposite: that his "disguise" as Dorus signals a real identity. And if this is the case, then the gulf between romance epic and pastoral love comedy, and between the divided selves that Musidorus hopes in this fashion to reunite, remains unclosed.

By taking on the role of an enamored shepherd in a pastoral love comedy, Musidorus can now tell the story of Musidorus the hero of an epic romance. It is as if he could tell the tale of himself only when he was no longer enacting it, which in turn suggests that the partial and incomplete values and motivations of epic romance can be envisioned only within the perspective of the genre that stands differentially paired against it. We have here, then, a narrative situation curiously like that in *The Faerie Queene*, where the shepherd poet of *The Shepheardes Calender* is presented in the prologue of Spenser's epic as its narrator.

Pyrocles' new identity as the amazon Zelmane likewise raises problems of textualization, this time of a rather piquant sort: by pronouns of what gender is he to be called? This problem is not faced by the characters who credit Pyrocles' disguise, such as Basilius and, for a while, Philoclea. It is a problem rather for the narrator, either when he speaks of Pyrocles in his own voice or refers to Pyrocles in a narrative text that renders the perspective of those who know of the disguise or have pierced it, such as Musidorus or Gynecia. Sidney consciously confronted the pronoun gender problem when he transferred the initial description of the disguised Pyrocles from the old to the new *Arcadia*. The two passages are for the most part identical, but one significant change occurs in this passage: "Upon her body she ware a doublet of sky-colour satin covered with plates of gold, and as it were, nailed with precious stones, that in it she might seem armed" (p. 68). This passage from the new *Arcadia* revises the following in the old *Arcadia*: "Upon his body he ware a kind of doublet of sky-colour satin, so plated over with plates of massy gold that he seemed armed in it" (Robertson, p. 26). Furthermore, both descriptions from this point on continue to use feminine and masculine pronouns, respectively.

In deciding to use the feminine forms in the later work, Sidney gives us a choice consistent with deemphasis on the omniscient narrator. In the old *Arcadia* the chatty narrator says:

> . . . thus did Pyrocles become Cleophila [Pyrocles' adopted name in the old *Arcadia*]—which name for a time hereafter I will use, for I myself feel such compassion of his passion that I find even part of his fear lest his name should be uttered before fit time were for it; which you, fair ladies that vouchsafe to read this, I doubt not will account excusable. (Robertson, p. 27)

The narrator's text continues briefly after this to refer to Pyrocles-Cleophila as "he" and "him," changing to feminine forms from there on out. But the moment the disguised Pyrocles is introduced in the new *Arcadia*, feminine forms are the rule. In other words, Sidney had to choose between naming the disguised Pyrocles from the viewpoint of an omniscient narrator—which privileged position he overtly relinquishes—and naming him according to the viewpoint of those who see him only from the outside.

In addition, Sidney doubtlessly directs the feminine pronouns to apply accurately to Pyrocles, since he has now oscillated like Musidorus from his previous wholly masculine, epic identity to that of effeminate lover. There is thus a kind of double irony in this disguise, since it manifests rather than hides an inner reality, while it is Pyrocles' conviction that he is "really" a man disguising himself as woman. As he tells Musidorus during their debate: "Neither doubt you because I wear a woman's apparel I will be the more womannish [Feuillerat], since, I assure you, for all my apparel there is nothing I desire more than fully to prove my self a man in this enterprise" (p. 74). The spelling "womannish," which depends on the traditional false etymology for "woman" as "woe-man," possibly derives from the old *Arcadia* foul papers that Greville had from Sidney himself, and from which the 1590 fragment was set (Skretkowicz, p. lxvi).[37] If this is so, it only emphasizes Pyrocles' conviction that however much he may be "transformed in show, but more transformed in mind" (p. 69), he still retains his essential masculine identity.

Nor is this conviction without substantial foundation. The problem that arises is how and where to draw the boundary lines between three distinct perspectives that yield three different versions of this disguise: the perspective of those who, ignorant of the disguise itself, see Pyrocles only as a woman; that of Pyrocles, for whom the disguise is sharply separated from his real, masculine identity; and that sponsored by the dialectical structure of the male-female relation, and the epic-pastoral relation cognate with it, which the composite, mixed structure of the new *Arcadia* imposes on Pyrocles. The anomaly which the narrator notes overtly in the old *Arcadia*, and which is displaced onto the reader in the new *Arcadia*, can be summed up in the simple question of just which gender form of third-person personal pronouns is appropriate to Pyrocles? Either masculine or feminine form seems at once appropriate and inappropriate. In the third perspective, within which Pyrocles is a kind of hermaphroditic oxymoron created dialectically by his univocal commitment to his masculine, heroic role, the problem of pronoun gender becomes particularly difficult for both narrator and reader. But no matter where we insert the probe of our discussion into this business of a man disguised as a woman, who is really a kind of male-female who wants others to take him as a woman while believing himself to be wholly masculine, we encounter a sense of anomaly. Pyrocles' situation simultaneously asserts and effaces the sexual difference, a paradox that the text can register only by always being incorrect no matter which pronoun gender it employs. The problem of differentiality—the condition of discursive meaning itself—is thus raised at all levels: Pyrocles' textualization of himself, others' textualization of him, the narrators' textualization of these first two. We can see then that this "glitch" in the text itself, a point where in one's traversal of it one always hits a snag, where one must replace the "she" with a "he" which must then be replaced with a "she," raises in yet another way the basic dialectical crisis that the text enacts continuously: the dynamic process in which a statement entails its opposite, effacing the differential gaps that make meaning possible in order to establish meaning, while (at the same time) affirming these gaps as the necessary condition of their own transgression.[38]

The history of Musidorus and Pyrocles from their births up to the very moment when Pamela and Philoclea bid them tell it is initiated by an oracular prediction. Musidorus is the son of Dorilaus, prince of Thessaly, and the sister of King Euarchus of Macedon. Dorilaus having been killed in repelling the invasion of the King of Phrygia, both cousins are brought up by Euarchus according to the dictates of the Xenophonic text of the "education of princes."

> . . . for almost before they could perfectly speak they began to receive conceits not unworthy of the best speakers; excellent devices being used to make even their sports profitable, images of battles and fortifications being then delivered to their memory, which, after, their stronger judgments might dispense; the delight of tales being converted to the knowledge of all the stories of worthy princes, both to move them to do nobly, and teach them how to do nobly, the beauty of virtue still being set before their eyes, and that taught them with far more diligent care than grammatical rules; their bodies exercised in all abilities both of doing and suffering, and their minds acquainted by degrees with dangers; and in sum, all bent to the making up of princely minds. . . . (pp. 163–64)

This text, imitated from Xenophon's *Cyropaedia*, is of course Musidorus's own account of his education and Pyrocles'. Since the two princes progress from childhood to manhood through a series of stages demarcated according to different source texts, the Arcadian narrative in which their careers are recounted merely replicates the texts of these careers as they enact them.[39] Further, the history of Musidorus and Pyrocles becomes a series of deferrals of rejected texts. For example, the Heliodoran heroic romance, the text that grows out of and supplants the Xenophonic text of their education, is only the deferral of the Sannazaran pastoral text that it excludes and that ultimately comes to displace it. Textual wholeness, if not deferred indefinitely for Sidney as for Jacques Derrida, must yet attend the global unfolding of the differentials that constitute the total, complete texts of the two princes' lives.[40] And since differentiality includes mutual implication as well as mutual exclusion, the lives of Musidorus and Pyrocles can achieve moral integrity only dialectically, through a progress that defers and, in deferring, covertly moves toward this integrity. And this deferral is registered in the new *Arcadia* as a series of displacements: from Xenophonic text to Heliodoran text to Sannazaran text. The first is displaced in a fashion intended to remind the knowledgeable reader of the opening of the *Athiopian History*, so that the text of the princes' heroic life commences similarly with a shipwreck (pp. 165ff.). The Heliodoran text will end the same way, marking the boundary across which Musidorus and Pyrocles move into the text of the erotic pastoral at the very beginning of the new *Arcadia*: another shipwreck.[41]

Marking both princes in their peregrinations through the Middle East is their immunity to the complex dialectics enslaving the many persons whom they save or fight. As several critics have pointed out, the human evil and disorder the two princes encounter in their Heliodoran adventures break down into two significant categories: public disorders of ruling and private disruptions due to erotic passion.[42] Often, as in the cases of Erona and Andromana, the two types are joined and interrelated. The point, however, is that the immunity the two princes enjoy during this period is in reality only the deferral of their own involvement in broils of a similar sort to come later. With the return of the repressed, and their immersion in the text of erotic pastoral, they find themselves increasingly involved in the political disruptions in and around Arcadia: Pyrocles' leadership of the Laconian rebels, where we first meet him; his deflection of the rebellion that closes Book 2; the involvement of both princes in the Cecropia-Amphialus episode that dominates Book 3; and finally their own direct violation of family and state institutions when—following the old *Arcadia*—Musidorus elopes with Pamela, the heir to Basilius's throne, and Pyrocles seduces (or almost seduces) Philoclea.

Sidney constructed the fictive world of the new *Arcadia* as a synthesis of distinct times, places, and cultures within the Mediterranean basin, each represented by and in its own representative text and genre. Thus for instance, the world of the two princes' travels narrated in Book 2 is the late Hellenic but still pre-Roman world of the eastern Mediterranean and Asia Minor found in the *Histories* of Polybius.[43] It is noteworthy that Polybius is one of the main ancient sources of information about the actual Arcadia in Greece. Superimposed not inconsistently on this world defined in military and dynastic terms is the romance world of Heliodorus. The two princes during this time move easily from one to the other, as shipwrecks and misadventures thrust them successively into one political imbroglio after another. The Arcadian world of the main plot, that which is taken over generally intact from the old *Arcadia*, remains a mixture of Roman comedy intrigue and erotic pastoral derived as much from Renaissance pastiche of classical and medieval sources as from these sources themselves. The heroic episodes that take place within this world, climaxing with the siege of Cecropia's castle and the extended episode of Amphialus, derive from chivalric romance of the Arthurian and Charlemagne varieties.[44]

The sustained and systematic intertextuality Sidney imposed on the generically purer old *Arcadia* tells us that for him there is no Arcadian world divorced from the diverse texts out of which it is constituted. It is literally a utopia, a "nowhere" at a textual site where converge texts torn out of the coordinates that divide various cultures and the texts that constitute them, and united in a single intertextuality. Where else may knights from medieval chivalric romance encounter shipwrecks from Heliodorus and scheming princes from Polybius, not to mention a Plautine senex and Theocritean shepherds? As Harry Berger, Jr., has persuasively argued regarding *The Faerie Queene*,[45] the new *Arcadia* is a discursive archeology, the result of layering texts derived from over a thousand years of human history in the Mediterranean basin, the boundaries between which the two princes successively cross as their own identities—the textualizations of their human selves—shift from one to another. Though it is perhaps not wholly inappropriate to argue that in Pyrocles and Musidorus ontogeny replicates phylogeny, like Joyce's cosmic hero in *Finnegans Wake*, Sidney's heroes—and indeed all his characters—exhibit a substantial identity that continually threatens to dissolve back into the cultural texts that constitute them.

For these reasons it is inappropriate to demand a clear generic identification for the new *Arcadia*, and to find it in various Renaissance theories of genres, as do Myrick, Davis, and others. Within the perspective of my own argument, the genre(s) of the new *Arcadia* are not a matter of structure only but of function as well. The category of genre illuminates not simply the materials out of which it is made but also the significance of these materials whereby they become vehicles of meaning in their own right.

We must conclude that the indecorum some critics discover in the new *Arcadia*, and particularly that which arises from the imperfectly joined segments in the composite 1593 *Arcadia*, is planned by Sidney. It was indeed as a critique of pure generic distinctions which cannot accommodate the dialectics of human moral identity that Sidney re-composed the old *Arcadia* as the new. By exploiting the established identification of specific generic conventions with equally specified categories of human behavior, Sidney was enabled to create a multi-faceted fiction in which fuse the world of human ethical choice and action, the rhetorical and generic resources through which men tex-tualize this world, and the purely verbal world of his own Arcadian fiction.[46]

Section 5

The conclusion of the *Arcadia*

The new *Arcadia* fragment breaks off during the fight between Pyro-cles and Anaxius. We can see that up to this point heroism and eros have oscillated in Pyrocles and Musidorus without resulting in any sort of reconciliation or harmony. In Book 3, as in the rescue of the princesses from wild animals in Book 1 and from rebels in Book 2, Pyrocles and Musidorus continue to maintain the separation between love and war, although for them heroism has always been the ally of love and not its enemy. The dialectical transgression of the dif-ferential gap separating love and war has, on the other hand, been played out by Amphialus. For him throughout, his passion for Philo-clea has been a flame consuming the various objects of his friendship and affection, and in Book 3 the love/war differential generates a continual onslaught on Philoclea grounded in his love for her.

And Musidorus and Pyrocles are not to remain immune to the

malign potentiality of this differential. In the broader perspective of the epic/pastoral dialectic which the new *Arcadia* proposes to abrogate, such an abrogation is apparently not possible until the two princes themselves come to suffer the fate of Amphialus, at least to the extent of allowing their erotic passions so to master their heroic identities that both corrupt rather than aid each other. Within this broad synoptic perspective, another demarcation of the new *Arcadia*'s narrative land-mass becomes visible. I am referring to the parallels between Amphialus's kidnapping of both daughters in the new *Arcadia* Book 3, and similar actions by the two heroes in that later work's projected ending. All three characters are driven by their erotic passions to acts of public disruption. For when Pyrocles and Musidorus in that latter episode plan to kidnap the princesses, they repeat Amphialus's essential actions and bring down on themselves the wrath of justice. And the fact that Pyrocles and Musidorus fight to free their respective beloveds from Amphialus, only to repeat his actions in the following episode, is another vector pointing to Sidney's intention in the new *Arcadia*. Up to the point where Amphialus is incapacitated and the two princesses freed, the princes have continued to enact their epic roles of salvific heroism, which have been uneasily superimposed periodically in disguised form on their other disguises as shepherd and amazon, respectively. In the old *Arcadia* ending, then, Euarchus as bringer of justice and punisher of crime plays Pyrocles and Musidorus to the princes' Amphialus. More broadly, in attempting to exhaust the central dialectical possibilities that the epic/pastoral and war/love differentials evoke, Sidney sees that it is not enough to exhibit the two princes merely leaving the heroic life for that of passion, or oscillating between the two. It is also necessary to preface and prepare for the final reconciliation of both genres and their respective values by first enacting and purging still another possibility: the mutual corruption of each value by the other. Eventually Musidorus and Pyrocles must unite eros and heroic endeavor in a way that realizes the final displacement deferred from the moment of their births: that by which the education of princes must imply education in love as well.

It is dialectically appropriate that Euarchus, under whose benign wisdom they grew up and were educated, should come to confront and judge this ultimate stage of this education, and find in the shepherd and the transvestite a moment of recognition that he cannot accommodate or accept. The judgments Euarchus passes on his son and nephew are and can only be those which Musidorus and Pyrocles would previously have passed on themselves. Euarchus, whose education of the young princes has written that seminal text of their lives which by dialectical revolution lowering has led them to become the opposite of themselves, must confront his nephew and son not only with a condemnation of them but also an implicit adverse judgment of himself.

The value of old *Arcadia* Books 3–5 in interpreting the conclusion Sidney planned for the new *Arcadia* must necessarily be limited. That he rethought some of the earlier work in relation to its new uses is demonstrated by the two extended passages present in Books 3 and 5, respectively, of the composite *Arcadia* of 1593 but absent from the old: a new ending of Book 3 (the scene between Pyrocles and Philoclea; Robertson, pp. 236–37), and a large insert detailing the travels of Euarchus before coming to *Arcadia* (ibid., pp. 355–57). The only thread leading us through this labyrinth remains the revised oracle given at the end of Book 2 of the new *Arcadia*, reinforced by the various indications in the later work that this oracle provides the scenario for its conclusion. My argument regarding this conclusion therefore must be limited to what can reasonably be inferred from the revised oracle. In addition, certain points can be made about sections of the old *Arcadia* ending which are consistent with what I have said about the new *Arcadia*, and though their form in the earlier work might well not have been what Sidney finally intended, this earlier form is not inconsistent with the later work. In this perspective I shall suggest that one reason for writing the new *Arcadia* was specifically to provide a way of leading into the old *Arcadia* ending, which as I have already argued can more readily be seen rather as inconsistent with the early books of the old *Arcadia* than with those of the new.[47]

In this connection, then, I shall discuss three episodes: (1) Philanax's speeches during his prosecution of Gynecia and the two princes, which illustrate how the same set of circumstances and actions may plausibly be given different and incompatible meanings; (2) Euarchus's condemnation of his son and nephew, which turns out to be the final twist of the dialectical logic the new *Arcadia* has abundantly illustrated throughout; (3) finally, the two princes revealed as malefactors in a good cause, at once violators of Arcadian law and the saviors of the two princesses from their unjust bondage. In the context of one another, the actions of Pyrocles, Musidorus, Euarchus, and Philanax all become ethically ambiguous because derived from a nondialectical reading of the texts of human action and motivation. The comedy of Basilius's belated resurrection will then manifest itself as Sidney's final wry comment on what the narrator at the end of the old *Arcadia* calls the "uncertain[ty]" of "mortal judgements" (Robertson, p. 416).

What exactly the old *Arcadia* ending would have looked like had Sidney recomposed it is something we shall never know. The evidence suggests that little would have been changed, although much might have been added: this at any rate was the author's general practice in recomposing old *Arcadia* Books 1 and 2 as the corresponding books of the new *Arcadia*. Since the revised oracle retains most of the details of the first version while adding others, Sidney was not free to change very much in the sequence of events in old *Arcadia* Books 3–5, where they exhibit a high level of careful coordination and mutual dependence.[48] It is thus impossible to detach the intrigue comedy of old *Arcadia* Book 3 from the final work—as those offended by its lack of decorum vis-à-vis the bleakness of new *Arcadia* Book 3 would like to do—because this comedy sets up and accounts so very precisely for all the actions that lead to the trial episode. Sidney's plan to keep the discovery, indictment, trial, and condemnation of the princes and Gynecia pretty much as in the first version is further indicated by two apparently authorial revisionary passages that appear for the first time in the 1593 composite *Arcadia*, which respectively concern Euarchus's journey to Arcadia, and the two princes' attempted liaisons with Basilius's daughters (see Appendix).[49]

What follows then is a discussion of certain central episodes in the old *Arcadia* ending in order to show the appropriateness of their having been kept by Sidney, presuming that this was his plan. Far from there being a sharp discrepancy between the new *Arcadia* fragment and the old *Arcadia* ending, there are several significant patterns that might well have been carried over from the later work to the ending of the earlier. And I take this to suggest that it was specifically the ending of the earlier work that set in motion Sidney's creation of the later as a context in which the thematic implications of the earlier work would be more completely fulfilled. These central episodes include Philanax's prosecution speech, the ironies attending Euarchus's judgment and condemnation of his own son and nephew, and the significance of the fact that Pyrocles and Musidorus are in fact pardoned by Basilius of real crimes. My point in each case will be quite simply that each continues and completes a central concern that I have already examined in this part of my study and in Part One.

Philanax begins his prosecution of Pyrocles by saying that the crimes he has confessed are so heinous that the auditors "will rather imagine you hear some tragedy invented of the extremity of wickedness than a just recital of wickedness indeed committed" (Robertson, p. 386). And it is indeed as a tragedy of conspiracy and bloodshed of the Senecan variety that Philanax proceeds to textualize the information about their arrival and life in Arcadia provided him by the two princes. Philanax's is a conspiratorial view which assumes that none of the events in the denoument of the intrigue plots could have occurred without human will and intention. This central presupposition undergirding Philanax's argument is ironically highlighted by his willingness to entertain, though but for a moment, the possibility that "in these foretold things fortune might be a great actor perchance to an evil end, yet to a less evil end all these entangled devices were intended" (p. 389). It is unclear whether Philanax is thinking of the oracle, the seriousness of which he had originally denied. It is certain that nowhere else in his speech does Philanax refer to this oracle, doubtless because he now as then refuses to take such things seriously.

Philanax's way of textualizing these events is typical of all conspiracy-mongers: it takes the form of the negative question, "How else could such things have happened?"

Had she [Gynecia], who showed her thoughts were so overruled with some strange desire as, in despite of God, nature, and womanhood, to execute that in deeds which in words we cannot hear

165

without trembling? Had she, I say, no practice to lead her unto
it? Or had she a practice without conspiracy? Or could she conspire without somebody to conspire with? And if one were, who
so likely as this, to whom she communicated, I am sure, her mind;
the world thinks, her body? (pp. 388–89)

The entailments of this argument unfold to Philanax's vision as un-
challengeable. What is so seductive (and ironic) about such reason-
ing, in context of the congeries of erotic intrigue, mistaken identity,
and simple inadvertence that brought about this state of affairs, is
that it makes at least as much sense as the facts themselves. Philanax
presents his audience with a well-formed text in which words and
statements each univocally and analytically imply the next. Philanax,
in other words, exhibits in the trial the same blindness to the dialectical interaction between human persons and fate that he had refused
to accept in rejecting Basilius's belief in the oracle at the beginning
of the plot. Sidney allows Philanax to become himself one of the instruments of the oracular prediction, a not surprising irony when we
consider how Basilius's attempts to thwart the oracular prediction
have fulfilled them.

Philanax continues to construct his interpretation, and as he does
so the reader can only acquiesce in his contention that the evidence
can bear the interpretation he gives it:

But let Gynecia's action die with herself. What can all the earth
answer for his [Pyrocles'] coming hither? Why alone, if he be a
prince? How so richly jewelled, if he be not a prince? Why then a
woman, if now a man? Why now Timopyrus, if then Cleophila
[Zelmane in the new *Arcadia*]? Was all this play for nothing? Or
if it had an end, what end but the end of my dear master? Shall
we doubt so many secret conferences with Gynecia, such feigned
favour to the over-soon beguiled Basilius, a cave made a lodging, and the same lodging made a temple of his religion, lastly
such changes and traverses as a quiet poet could scarce fill a poem
withal, were directed to any less scope than to this monstrous mur-
der? O Snaky ambition which can wind thyself in so many figures
to slide thither thou desirest to come! (Robertson, p. 389)

Philanax's version of Pyrocles' actions assumes that they are motivated by political ambition. In this he appropriates events that origi-
nate in the text of erotic pastoral and reinterprets them in a text that
corresponds to several the reader and the two princes have encountered during the latter's Heliodoran wanderings. That is, Pyrocles
and Musidorus are accused of acting in Arcadia in the manner of
the kings of Phrygia and Pontus, Andromana, Antiphilus, and the
bastard son of the King of Paphlagonia: their actions are powered
by a mixture of political ambition and ethical unscrupulousness.
That the reader knows this is not the case only serves to highlight
the realization of how vulnerable are actions and motivations of
one genre (erotic pastoral) to retextualization in another—political
tragedy. Furthermore, it is not simply a question of appearance versus
reality. We likewise perceive that Philanax does not merely misinter-
pret actions that are "really" guiltless in themselves. Rather, Pyrocles
and Musidorus have in fact committed crimes against Arcadia, and
their condemnation will exhibit a certain justice. But in accordance
with the new *Arcadia*'s larger concern with evolving a textual wholeness of human life dialectically out of fragmented and competing
texts, the textual slide that has already carried the two princes from
Xenophonic *paideia* through Heliodoran epic adventure to Sannazaran erotic pastoral is now about to deposit them in another generic
world, that of tragedy.

Consequently, however factually wrong Philanax may be in his
accusations, he is structurally right: he follows a recognizable decorum in textualizing the actions of the princes as intrigues leading to
tragic death and usurpation. After Philanax has finished his opening
indictment, Pyrocles speaks in his own defense. This is followed by
the two letters written by Philoclea and Pamela to Philanax urging
him to relent in his prosecution. Philanax suppresses them (p. 398),
delivers an answer to Pyrocles' speech, and is followed in turn by
Musidorus's defense. This sequence concludes with Euarchus's final
statement and his condemnation of the two princes. In this sequence
it becomes essentially the word of one side against that of the other.
Nor is this an inappropriate climax for the new *Arcadia*, considering
its dominant concern with the mixing and juxtaposition of different
texts.

Pyrocles' defense rests on the facts of the pastoral comedy already known to the reader in the first two books. The weightier material of Musidorus's speech, however, brings both princes' actions into a more ambiguous light than any participants in the trial can be aware of. Philanax accuses Musidorus of conspiring with Pyrocles to remove the heir of Arcadia's throne in order to coerce Arcadia's obeisance once Basilius is dead (p. 399). This charge is consistent with Philanax's conviction that political ambition lies behind all of these events. What is interesting here is not merely that he is wrong, which of course he is, but that in an odd way he is right.

Musidorus raises for the reader the question of how to interpret his and Pyrocles' attempted abduction of the two princesses, by focusing unwittingly on the parallels between this abduction and the actions of Cecropia and Amphialus in new *Arcadia* Book 3. He begins by calling attention to the services both he and Pyrocles have rendered the royal family in saving the princesses from wild animals and from the revolt of the peasants:

> Either think them now dead, or remember they live by us. And yet full often this telltale [Philanax] can acknowledge the loss they should have by their taking away, while maliciously he overpasseth who were their preservers. Neither let this be spoken of me as if I meant to balance this evil with that good, for I must confess that saving of such creatures was rewarded in the act itself, but only to manifest the partial jangling of this vile pickthank. But if we be traitors, where was your fidelity, O only tongue-valiant gentleman, when not only the young princesses but the duke himself was defended from the uttermost peril, partly by me, but principally by this excellent young man's both wisdom and valor? (p. 401) [50]

Musidorus climaxes his account of their services to Basilius and his family by saying: "But you will say I persuaded her to fly away. Certainly I will for no death deny it, knowing to what honour I should bring her from the thraldom, by such fellows' counsel as you, she was kept in" (p. 402). Here the pattern of parallels that Sidney apparently intended to establish in recomposing the old *Arcadia* comes into high relief. We remember that Musidorus and Pyrocles were com-

pelled to take on their disguises specifically because Basilius had in-
sisted on keeping his daughters sequestered from suitors. It was then
the "thraldom" imposed by Basilius himself—contested by Philanax
originally—that set the stage for all the succeeding events. Musidorus
and Pyrocles end up playing the roles of both rescuer and abductor.
In eloping with the two princesses and rescuing them from the imprisonment imposed by their father, Pyrocles and Musidorus attempt
to reenact the rescue of their loved ones from Cecropia's castle. By
the same token, they are being accused by Philanax of acting like
Cecropia in abducting them. Actions textualizable under the sign of
love are available to being textualized under the sign of political ambition. According to the dialectical rules for reading itself that the new
Arcadia has consistently elicited from the reader, these opposing texts
import the following: both readings of these actions are appropriate,
because it was impossible for the princes to elope with the princesses
in the name of love without at the same time committing a political offense. In other words, these opposing texts not only exclude
each other, they also imply each other.[51] Therefore, it should come
as no surprise that Musidorus and Pyrocles should enact the roles
simultaneously of Cecropia, Amphialus, and of saviors in their attempted abduction/rescue of the princesses. Pyrocles and Musidorus
are thus both abductors *and* saviors, both guilty *and* innocent, which
means that both they and Philanax are correct in their arguments.
And the problem is that there is no one present at the trial, including
(crucially) Euarchus, capable of constructing a dialectical metatext
in which the above points become sayable and intelligible.[52]

Euarchus's summing up and judgment (pp. 406ff.) conforms in its
inclusions and exclusions precisely to Philanax's own interpretation
of the matter:

> But now let us see how these young men (truly for their persons
> worthy of pity, if they had rightly pitied themselves) do go about
> to mitigate the vehemency of their errors. Some of their excuses
> are common to both, some peculiar only to him that was the shep-
> herd; both remember the force of love, and as it were the mending
> up of the matter by their marriage. If that unbridled desire which is
> entitled love might purge such a sickness as this, surely we should

have many loving excuses of hateful mischiefs. Nay rather, no mis-
chief should be committed that should not be veiled under the
name of love. For as well he that steals might allege the love of
money, he that murders the love of revenge, he that rebels the love
of greatness, as the adulterer the love of a woman; since they do
in all speech affirm they love that which an ill-governed passion
maketh them to follow. But love may have no such privilege. That
sweet and heavenly uniting of the minds, which properly is called
love, hath no other knot but virtue; and therefore if it be a right
love, it can never slide into any action that is not virtuous. (pp.
406–407)

It is in the closing sentence of this passage that we perceive how
much the strength of Euarchus's virtues—so carefully laid out for
the reader in previous passages—becomes the limitation as well of
his vision. Of course we cannot reasonably expect him to guess that
the prisoners before him are his son and nephew, since he thinks
them dead. And for their own part, the two princes have decided to
maintain their disguises to "cover the shame of their royal parentage"
(p. 385) if they should be executed:

> Wherein the chief man they considered was Euarchus, whom the
> strange and secret working of justice had brought to be the judge
> over them—in such a shadow or rather pit of darkness the wormish
> mankind lives that neither they know how to foresee nor what to
> fear, and are but like tennis balls tossed by the racket of the higher
> powers. (pp. 385–86)

But even when Euarchus discovers whom he has condemned, after
the timely arrival of the shepherd whose place Musidorus had originally taken, he remains consistent in his judgment:

> If rightly I have judged, then rightly have I judged mine own chil-
> dren, unless the name of a child should have force to change the
> never-changing justice. No, no, Pyrocles and Musidorus, I prefer
> you much before my life, but I prefer justice as far before you.
> While you did like yourselves, my body should willingly have been
> your shield; but I cannot keep you from the effects of your own

doing. Nay, I cannot in this case acknowledge you for mine; for never had I shepherd to my nephew, nor never had woman to my son. Your vices have degraded you from being princes, and have disannulled your birthright. Therefore, if there be anything left in you of princely virtue, show it in constant suffering that your unprincely dealing hath purchased unto you. (pp. 411–12)

By this point in the action Sidney has carefully poised the reader in a dilemma of judgment that allows apparently no escape. We cannot disagree with Euarchus's condemnation at the trial, since it is based on actions that both princes have admitted. On the other hand, we are aware in ways that Euarchus is not of the greater complexity of forces that have joined to create this situation. Unlike Euarchus, Sidney has required us to see, both in the main plot and in the numerous subplots, the labyrinthine paths that the texts in which men and women constitute themselves and one another may take. If in fact "never-changing justice" is really Euarchus's concern—that is, a judgment that takes account of and is wholly adequate to the dialectical rules that Sidney has shown governing the text of the Arcadian world—then it is precisely this kind of justice that he does not, and cannot, mete out. Guiltily, they have offended against Basilius, but what they have abrogated was Basilius's own unjust sequestering of his daughters. But the matter, in the context of the whole *Arcadia*, does not rest there. It rather lies in the reader's understanding of the complex dialectic governing the princes' careers from their birth down to this present moment, wherein he and she have been allowed to witness the dialectical interface between the rules that govern their successive textualizations and the freedom with which they chose, at each step of the way, to embark on behavior that is noble rather than ignoble, motivated by love and generosity rather than hatred, meanness, or ambition.

Euarchus can no more perceive the mixed nature of the princes' guilt than he can recognize in them kin to himself once he discovers who they are. When he says "I cannot in this case acknowledge you for mine; for never had I shepherd to my nephew, nor never had woman to my son," he exhibits in addition his incapacity to understand the dialectics of heroism and eros. In castigating them for no

171

longer acting "like themselves," he raises once again the vexed question of Musidorus's and Pyrocles' true identities. And if Euarchus has educated his son and nephew in the heroic ideals of Xenophonic *paideia,* then he must bear some of the responsibility for their transformation. For the consequence of their acting "like" themselves has been nothing other than their vulnerability to erotic passion and to the identities/disguises which Euarchus finds so alien to their true selves—and to himself.[53]

When Basilius awakens, as William A. Ringler has correctly pointed out, the charge of regicide has been obviated. But that Euarchus's condemnation of the princes for abduction remains unmitigated, as Ringler also contends, is not it seems to me the case:[54]

> At length, remembering the oracle, which now indeed was accomplished (not as before he had imagined), considering all had fallen out by the highest providence, and withal weighing in all these matters his own fault had been the greatest, the first thing he [Basilius] did was with all honourable pomp to send for Gynecia. (Robertson, p. 416)

It is important to understand just what is being said in the light of my whole discussion of the main plot. Basilius recognizes that the mischances which led to his supposed death, as well as the planned abduction of the two princesses, were such that "his own fault had been the greatest." When Basilius understands that the oracle has been fulfilled, he recognizes also his own complicity in bringing this fulfillment about. In this regard, he must also be understood to recognize that what Musidorus and Pyrocles are condemned for was nevertheless the result of his own faulty actions. We must conclude that Euarchus's judgment is appropriately abrogated, since the condition of prior justice violated by the princes was itself chimerical—something which of course Euarchus could not have been expected to know.

We are left, finally, with the blithe comedy with which Sidney has contrived to end this enormously complex exploration of human texts and their dynamic movement toward either fragmentation or harmony. The awakening of Basilius is doubtless a violation of tone, as many critics have noted, a violation particularly baffling if we consider how far Sidney went in the new *Arcadia* to deepen the dark complexity of this work in comparison with the old *Arcadia*. Is it feasible or appropriate that the dialectics of the main plot, otherwise so dense in their development of the textual interplay that constitutes human psychological and moral identity, should be resolvable by a palpable stage trick, a bare-faced deus ex machina? What are we to make of this ending, which seems to transform the complexity of human relations, and particularly the free will/determinism dialectic that regulates the whole main plot, into a mere facade, an appearance with no substance behind it?

To answer this question we come back to what it was specifically about the oracle Basilius seemed most to fear: not merely the events which it predicted, but the uncanny paradoxes that characterize these events. Basilius fled the darkness and obscurity of the oracular text itself, the violation of well-formed textuality in paradoxes that predicted events normally excluded by the rule of noncontradiction. In fleeing the oracle, Basilius runs to embrace it, not only in his love for the hermaphroditic Pyrocles—himself a matrix of textual anomalies —but as regards the total main plot in which he enmeshes everyone around him. What the oracle can now be seen from hindsight to have predicted was no dire event, but the appearance of dire events behind which masked no such thing. Though Basilius's daughter was to be stolen, yet she would not be lost; the younger was to embrace an unnatural love that would yet be attended by "Nature's bliss"; Basilius would be dead and yet alive; and the only adultery he would commit is with his wife. We may even go so far as to say that had Basilius committed himself totally to belief in the oracle he would have had nothing to fear, since the oracle insists that, despite its paradoxical statements, there is ultimately nothing fearsome in what it predicts.

Basilius cannot grasp the text of the oracle because he is unable to understand a text which makes its own dialectical structure explicit, in which mutual exclusion both excludes and implies mutual implication. What Basilius does not originally understand is what the reader learns all along in reading the new *Arcadia*: the dialectical rules that govern the differential structuring of human verbal discourse. We can see then that rhetorical figuration at the microcosmic level of the work finally coalesces with the macrocosmic dimension of the work's main plot: like the reader, Basilius finally learns to read the new *Arcadia*, the history of his own life, or a part of it.

One can perhaps best understand the decorum of the conclusion —its appropriateness in relation to all that has gone before—by seeing it as an example of new comedy reconciliation, such as Northrop Frye describes in his classic essay on the subject.[55] The final marriage between young hero and heroine and the reconciliation all round that yields replacement of an old order of paternal repression by a new order of social harmony and freedom is ultimately a kind of dialectical function of the obstacles to this replacement which the new order must overcome. In this respect we can achieve renewed understanding of the enormous breadth of Sidney's vision, in which he reconciles the new comedy intrigues and characters of Roman comedy with the utopian thrust of both pastoral and epic romance. It is perfectly true, as Frye says (p. 79), that "the opponent is usually the father (senex)." But Stanley Cavell has more recently called attention to ways in which the new comedy plot dovetails with elements from the traditional romance in a fashion easily recognizable in the *Arcadia*. On the one hand, he points out that "the classical obligations of the father in romance are to provide his daughter's education and to protect her virginity. These obligations clearly go together: say they add up to suiting her for marriage. Prospero describes or enacts his faithfulness to these obligations toward Miranda with didactic explicitness."[56]

On the other hand, Cavell also points out that

comic resolutions depend upon an acquisition in time of self-knowledge; say this is a matter of learning who you are. In classical romance this may be accomplished by learning the true story of your birth, where you come from, learning the identity of your parents. In comedies of remarriage [and this applies also to marriage per se in the *Arcadia*] it requires learning, or accepting, your sexual identity, the acknowledgement of desire. Both forms of discovery are in service of the authorization or authentication of what is called marriage. (pp. 589–90)

Regarding the father figure in romance, which corresponds to the senex in new comedy, this "acknowledgement of desire" means that "acceptance by the father of the daughter's sexuality, which means of her separation from him, her human equality with him, is part of the happiness of these women, of their high capacities for intelligence, wit, and freedom" (ibid.).

The new *Arcadia* shows that the father's desire to protect his daughter's virginity in preparing for her marriage may yield to the desire to keep her from marriage in order to protect her virginity. Philanax clearly foreshadows the new comedy plot to ensue when he warns Basilius in the beginning of the dialectics that generate desire out of its suppression and prepare daughters' revolt from their father's tyranny. Basilius's removal of his daughters from courtship and marriage generates the kind of dialectical return of the repressed that Philanax predicts, and that sets in motion the intrigues of the new comedy. The new comedy plot of the old *Arcadia*, which concludes with Basilius's final relinquishing his daughters to their betrothed lovers, circumscribes and gives birth to an elaborate interplay of heroic and pastoral in the new *Arcadia* that builds specifically on the clash of indecorum implicit therein. This clash also creates a new decorum, constructed out of Sidney's grasp of the vast range of possible human actions implicit in new comedy, heroic romance, and erotic pastoral that could never be contained within any one of these forms. The dialectics that bring about the birth of a new order of marriage and freedom out of reactions to the rigidities of the old order governed by the father figure become, in Sidney's vision, paradigmatic of the central problem of human living in general: the integration of action and contemplation, of heroic endeavor and erotic fulfillment, of eros and civilization. And in obedience to this vision Sidney was compelled to exploit and remake several traditional genres in which these elements of human existence were historically textualized in isolation from one another.

As long as this isolation subsists, as long as human beings refuse the dialectics that govern their textualization of their moral identity and insist on building this identity out of partial, incomplete acceptance of some and rejection of other elements all implicit in this identity, just so long must the entanglements of the Arcadian plots remain unresolved. But once recognized and accommodated, the dialectics of human textualization at that moment cease and disappear as if they had never been. In a comment that applies exemplarily to the conclusion of the new *Arcadia*, Northrop Frye says:

> In a typically festive conclusion all previous conflicts are forgiven and forgotten. In ordinary life this phrase is seldom a moral reality, because it is usually a contradiction: to forgive an offense implies that the offense was real; to forget it implies that something in it was not, and forgetting is not a voluntary act as forgiveness is. To forget implies a break in the continuity of memory, a kind of amnesia in which the previous action is put out of our reach. Normally, we can forget in this way only when we wake up from a dream, when we pass from one world into another, and we often have to think of the main action of a comedy as "the mistakes of a night," as taking place in a dream or nightmare world that the final scene suddenly removes us from and thereby makes illusory.[57]

When Basilius awakens from his sleep—a sleep induced by a potion which was mistaken for an aphrodisiac by his wife—we are presented with just such a festive achievement of a new world as Frye describes. The sexual comedy, or nightmare, that Basilius's rejection of sexuality has engendered is not so much resolved as dissolved. The reawakening of Basilius not only to life but to his own folly is like a Chinese rope puzzle: a mass of impenetrable tangles, save for the single strand which when pulled dissolves the tangle instantly into clearness and simplicity. In the conclusion of the new *Arcadia* we recognize nothing that the oracle has not already predicted—and the nothing that the oracle has predicted. For what the oracle predicted was in fact much ado about nothing.

Behind the appearance of tragedy—the texts of Philanax and Euarchus—and in his fears of Basilius also, and in her self-recriminations of Gynecia too, there is nothing at all. Beyond the expectation of tragedy all things are brought clear and serene again: and that too was what the oracle predicted. The simplicity with which the knot of near tragedy dissolves in joy and reunion of loved ones is Sidney's vision of a paradisal state wherein the dialectical tensions constituting human identity are finally relieved and brought to placid calm.

Appendix

The editors of the *Arcadia* material for the Oxford University Press, William A. Ringler, Jr., Jean Robertson, and Victor Skretkowicz, are agreed that Sidney did not intend to conclude the new *Arcadia* with the old *Arcadia* ending. Ringler, in his edition of Sidney's poems, consistently treats the 1593 version as rendering the complete narrative thread of the new *Arcadia* from beginning to end and refers to the new *Arcadia* oracle as indicating a conclusion with a trial scene (pp. 378–79). Nevertheless, Ringler still argues that "we should read the *New Arcadia* in a text based only upon the narrative part of 90 corrected by Cm [the Cambridge MS], the *Old Arcadia* in a text based upon St [St. Johns College, Cambridge, MS] and corrected by the other manuscripts." (His argument that the new *Arcadia* oracle is sufficiently different from the old *Arcadia* version I have responded to in an earlier note to Part Two.)

Victor Skretkowicz, in his recent edition of the new *Arcadia*, is surprisingly elliptical on an issue of such importance to his text. Skretkowicz says, "The addition to A [old *Arcadia* foul papers] of the bulky manuscript of [new *Arcadia*] Book III left the remaining section in need of radical revision in plot, character, and style. To fulfill the predictions of the oracles within this new framework would necessitate a serious reconsideration of the romantic plot. . . . For [revising] the prose, he [Sidney] could return to the old Books III–V, or could invent a new ending. He did neither" (p. lxxiv). He also says (p. lxxv) that "the change in method at this point [completion of new *Arcadia* Book 2], from adaptation of old material to fresh composition, corresponds to the enormous gap in thematic unity between the rest of Book III and this appendix" (i.e., OA ending in 1593). Also relevant is Skretkowicz's statement on p. lxxviii: "It had been a work in progress, reaching one plateau in the *Old Arcadia* and another in the *New Arcadia*. The unfinished remains of the foul copy are preserved in the appendix to 93. Above all, their incomplete nature indicates how great was the chasm between the level actually achieved and Sidney's ultimate goal." Skretkowicz does not specify why the romantic plot would need "reconsideration" after the composition of new *Arcadia* Book 3, but his reference to "the enormous gap in thematic unity" between new *Arcadia* and old *Arcadia* ending suggests that he accepts Jean Robertson's more developed position on that matter. The same interpretation could be drawn from his discovering the "great . . . chasm" between Sidney's goal and its actual achievement, putatively reflected in the old *Arcadia* ending of the 1593 version.[1]

Jean Robertson's argument in her edition of the old *Arcadia* is founded on her notion of artistic and aesthetic decorum. Her argument in general is that the old *Arcadia* conclusion, in continuing the comedy of the first two books, is tonally inconsistent with the traumatic events of the new *Arcadia* Book 3:

> It is inconceivable that after the sufferings of the princesses in the "captivity episode" Sidney would have attempted to return to the *Old Arcadia* story without very considerable changes. As Florio remarked of the 93 composite version, "this end we see of it, though at first above all, now is not answerable to the precedents." (p. lx)

Regarding Basilius's second consultation with Delphi, she says:

> Sidney inserted a second oracle near the end of the unfinished Book III of the *New Arcadia*, in which Basilius is told that his daughters will shortly be released from captivity, and he is to "keep on his solitary course, till both Philanax and Basilius fully agreed in the understanding of the former prophecy." . . . But I do not think we should deduce from this that Sidney intended to conclude his story with the *Old Arcadia* ending as it stood. (ibid., footnote)

It is difficult to understand what Sidney's plan could have been, if it was other than "to conclude his story with the *Old Arcadia* ending as it stood." The "very considerable changes" Robertson envisions in the earlier passage would, presumably, have had to conform to the indications I have already cited, however much else was changed. The oracle and Gynecia's dream specifically refer to Basilius's death, as well as to the wooing of Basilius's two daughters by the two princes, Basilius's adultery with his wife, and Euarchus's judgment passed while sitting on Basilius's throne. In short, taking all these allusions together, we can reasonably conclude that the events of old *Arcadia* Books 3–5 form a unit that begins in farce, proceeds through near tragedy, and concludes with reconciliation.

Robertson nevertheless refuses to see the implications of the bibliographical evidence at hand straight on in her analysis of the two extensive inserts into the old *Arcadia* ending which are not present in any of the old *Arcadia* manuscripts, but which do appear in the 1593 version. These two passages include a new ending for Book 3, where Pyrocles is shown quite definitely not consummating his love for Philoclea; and a lengthy account of Euarchus's travels before arriving at Arcadia in time to be sought out to judge the trials of the two princes and Gynecia. Robertson believes (I think rightly) that these passages are authorial and represent reliable indications of the kinds of changes Sidney might have intended in the old *Arcadia* ending when he attached it to the new *Arcadia* (p. lx).

Furthermore, her summaries of these passages are correct: The passage concerning Euarchus shows him believing the princes dead from Plangus's report that they had died in a shipwreck, and ignorant as well of events in new *Arcadia* Book 3. The new ending of the old *Arcadia* Book 3 has Pyrocles only fall asleep on Philoclea's bed, an action far short of any further sexual involvement (as in the old *Arcadia*). What should be noted about all of the above changes is that collectively they only confirm Sidney's continued intention to conclude the new *Arcadia* with the judgment scenes of the old *Arcadia*, an intention worked out sufficiently before Sidney left off composition as to require a carefully revised ending for old *Arcadia* Book 3. And yet, out of all this Robertson can only conclude that the old *Arcadia* ending was not intended to conclude the new *Arcadia*. One reason for this deduction is Euarchus's ignorance of the new set of events in new *Arcadia* Book 3:

> This suggests that the revised account of the journey in 93 was written after the *New Arcadia* Book II was completed, but before the *New Arcadia* Book III had been composed. (p. lxi)

> Thus the major changes in Books III–V of the *Old Arcadia* as printed in 93 are interrelated, and were probably either made or their nature indicated by Sidney himself. They were probably intended, not for the *Old Arcadia*, but for the *New Arcadia* as it stood before the new Book III was written. (p. lxii)

Robertson's argument goes this way: Sidney's intention to complete the recomposed *Arcadia* with the old *Arcadia* ending lasted up to the completion of Book 2 of the later work. At that point he presumably altered totally his purpose, composed Book 3—or changed his course while composing it—and this accounts for Euarchus's ignorance of events in new *Arcadia* Book 3 in the extended passage concerning him inserted into the 1593 Book 5.

To these contentions several points can be adduced in response. First, the fact that Euarchus has not yet learned that Plangus's report of Musidorus's and Pyrocles' deaths is false proves nothing. In fact, Euarchus's continued belief that his son and nephew are dead is consistent with Sidney's having this report circulated generally through the eastern Mediterranean and Asia Minor during the time taken up by new *Arcadia* Books 1–3. Furthermore, Euarchus's ignorance is indispensable to what Sidney was in fact planning for the ending, namely, the whole trial business wherein Euarchus unwittingly condemns both princes to death on the general presumption that they could not possibly be before him, having been already killed.

Second, if Robertson wants to base her argument against the old *Arcadia* ending on what is essentially her own sense of what is proper and improper, probable and improbable, then her argument is susceptible to judgment on the same basis. By her own admission, Sidney intended to keep the main plot of the *Arcadia* down at least to the point where he finished writing Book 2 of the new *Arcadia*. She could hardly argue otherwise, given Sidney's great care to mingle material from the first work in carefully rewritten form with material indigenous to the second. But for us to accept her contention, we must also accept at least the probability of the following scenario: Sidney abides by his original plan, which commits him to intricate ligatures between old and new material, through the writing of the first two books of the new *Arcadia*, and he does not see that there is an indecorum in joining these materials until he finishes Book 2. Despite this perception, he inserts into new *Arcadia* Book 3 two references to Gynecia's and Basilius's infatuation with Zelmane, and a reaffirmation of the original oracular prediction. It is only near or at the point where Book 3 breaks off that Sidney decided to act on his sense of this indecorum—presumably gnawing at his artistic conscience throughout the composition of this book—and leave the work unfinished. Does it seem probable that a plan as carefully carried out as the revisions, additions, rearrangements of material mediating between the two *Arcadia*s indicate, should yet assume an ending that Sidney began to see as nonviable only after he had already written between one-third and one-half of the whole? Ultimately, it is a question of the critic's notion of what is probable and decorous versus Sidney's own notion, since in view of the evidence against Robertson's contention (as well as those of Ringler and Skretkowicz) it is only her sense of violated decorum that causes her to discount this evidence. And once one puts the question on these grounds, the scholar must perforce give way.

Notes

Notes to the Introduction

1 Studies of the *Arcadia* that interpret it mainly according to what it shares with its context include much of the monograph-length work done on it. Works that particularly emphasize context include: Kenneth Myrick, *Sir Philip Sidney as a Literary Craftsman* (Lincoln: University of Nebraska Press, 1965; orig. pub. 1935); Forrest G. Robinson, *The Shape of Things Known: Sidney's "Apology" in Its Philosophical Tradition* (Cambridge: Harvard University Press, 1972); Richard C. McCoy, *Sir Philip Sidney: Rebellion in Arcadia* (New Brunswick: Rutgers University Press, 1979); M. S. Goldman, *Sir Philip Sidney and the Arcadia* (Urbana: University of Illinois Press, 1934); A. C. Hamilton, *Sir Philip Sidney: A Study of his Life and Works* (Cambridge: Cambridge University Press, 1977); Dorothy Connell, *Sir Philip Sidney: The Maker's Mind* (Oxford: Oxford University Press, 1977); Walter R. Davis, "A Map of Arcadia: Sidney's Romance in its Tradition," in *Sidney's Arcadia* (New Haven: Yale University Press, 1965); Jon S. Lawry, *Sidney's Two "Arcadias": Pattern and Proceeding* (Ithaca, N.Y.: Cornell University Press, 1972); Andrew D. Weiner, *Sir Philip Sidney and the Poetics of Protestantism: A Study of Contexts* (Minneapolis: University of Minnesota Press, 1978); Mark Rose, *Heroic Love: Studies in Sidney and Spenser* (Cambridge: Harvard University Press, 1968).

2 Cited by E. M. W. Tillyard, *The English Epic and Its Background* (New York: Oxford University Press, 1954), p. 299.

3 *The Common Reader* (2d ser.) (New York: Harcourt, Brace, 1948), pp. 42, 45.

4 Tillyard, *The English Epic*, p. 300; R. W. Zandvoort, *Sidney's Arcadia: A Comparison between the Two Versions* (Amsterdam: N. V. Swets & Zeitlinger, 1929), p. 177; Myrick, *Sir Sidney as a Literary Craftsman*, pp. 178–79.

5 Richard A. Lanham, "The Old Arcadia," in *Sidney's Arcadia* (New Haven: Yale University Press, 1965), pp. 317 and passim.

6 Cited by Hoyt H. Hudson in his edition of John Hoskins's *Directions for Speech and Style* (Princeton: Princeton University Press, 1935), p. xxii; emphasis in the original.

7 Ibid.

8 J. E. Spingarn, ed., *Critical Essays of the Seventeenth Century*, 3 vols. (Bloomington: Indiana University Press, 1957), 1:187.

9 *The Poems of Richard Lovelace*, ed. C. H. Wilkinson (Oxford: Clarendon Press, 1930), p. 68.

10 Quoted in Lanham, "The Old Arcadia," p. 183.

11 Sir Philip Sidney, *The Countess of Pembroke's Arcadia (The Old Arcadia)*, ed. Jean Robertson (Oxford: Clarendon Press, 1973), p. xvi.

12 Sir Philip Sidney, *The Countess of Pembroke's Arcadia (The New Arcadia)*, ed. Victor Skretkowicz (Oxford: Clarendon Press, 1987).

13 Modern editions include Albert Feuillerat, ed., *The Prose Works of Sir Philip Sidney*; 4 vols. (Cambridge: University Press, 1965; orig. pub. 1912), vols. 1 and 2; and Sir Philip Sidney, *The Countess of Pembroke's Arcadia*, ed. Maurice Evans (Harmondsworth: Penguin Books, 1977).

14 Scholars who adhere to one or both of these opinions include the following: Elizabeth Dipple, "The Captivity Episode and the *New Arcadia*," *Journal of English and Germanic Philology* 70 (1971): 418–31; Joan Rees, "Fulke Greville, and the Revisions of *Arcadia*," *Review of English Studies* 17 (1966): 54–57; Nancy R. Lindheim, "Vision, Revision, and the 1593 Text of the *Arcadia*," *ELR: English Literary Renaissance* 2 (1972): 136–47; A. C. Hamilton, *Sir Philip Sidney*, p. 158; Richard Lanham, "The Old Arcadia," pp. 400–401; Jean Robertson in her introduction to *The Countess of Pembroke's Arcadia*, pp. lx–lxii.

15 Sir Philip Sidney, *A Defence of Poetry*, in Katherine Duncan-Jones and Jan Van Dorsten, eds., *Miscellaneous Prose of Sir Philip Sidney* (Oxford: Clarendon Press, 1973), p. 79: ". . . for any understanding knoweth the skill of each artificer standeth in that *idea* or fore-conceit of the work, and not in the work itself. And that the poet hath that *idea* is manifest, by delivering them forth in such excellency as he hath imagined them."

16 Dorothy Connell in *The Maker's Mind*, p. 140, also notes the decisive importance of Sidney's retaining the oracular predictions in the new *Arcadia* and concludes that "in effect, Sidney has committed himself to the task of

forcing the action back into its old path." Also agreeing with the minority opinion that the composite 1593 version of the *Arcadia* represents at least in general Sidney's final intention is Myrick, *Sir Philip Sidney as a Literary Craftsman*, p. 161; Peter Lindenbaum, "Sidney's *Arcadia*: The Endings of the Three Versions," *Huntingdon Library Quarterly* 34 (1971): 205–18; and Thelma N. Greenfield, *The Eye of Judgment: Reading the "New Arcadia"* (Lewisburg, Pa.: Bucknell University Press, 1982), p. 118. William A. Ringler, Jr., ed., *The Poems of Sir Philip Sidney* (Oxford: Clarendon Press, 1962), argues (pp. 372, 378, 383) that the version of the oracle that appears in the new *Arcadia* is significantly different from that in the old. Ringler's argument is taken up in Part Two, section three. Although he does not discuss the troublesome conjunction of old and new *Arcadia*s in the composite version of 1593, R. W. Zandvoort avers that "the original draft stands to the revision as a first sketch to a finished composition," *Sidney's Arcadia*, p. 102. Though it is generally now agreed that the old *Arcadia* was a completed work, and Robertson's study of the manuscripts confirms a period of tinkering with this version before Sidney began the new *Arcadia*, Zandvoort has his hand on part of the truth, at least to the rather high degree to which Sidney retained the plot of the old *Arcadia* as the circumscribing main plot of the new.

17 The problem of the genre of the new *Arcadia* (as well as that of the old) has long been a topic for discussion. It has also been a question muddied by the different perspectives from which the matter of genre has been raised. One may begin with Renaissance literary theory, particularly Italian, and note Sidney's divergence from or compliance with a more or less rigidly segregated table of generic types. Or one may be concerned with the relevance of the genres included in the work to its meaning. Once again, the problem of indebtedness and influence to specific works in different genres may be the starting point. Or, finally, it is possible to take up two or even three of these approaches in tandem. Without specifying at the moment the different approaches taken by specific scholars, I will only note the various generic labels that have been affixed to the new *Arcadia*. Myrick, *Sir Philip Sidney as a Literary Craftsman*, p. 114, suggests that Sidney "may still have thought of the *Arcadia* as a more modest sort of heroic poem, differing from the epic in certain obvious ways, but resembling it in structure and in fundamental purpose." The central problem, as Margaret E. Dana has noted, "Heroic and Pastoral: Sidney's *Arcadia* as Masquerade," *Comparative Literature* 25 (1973): 308, is that "Sidney has juxtaposed the most prestigious of all literary genres of the Renaissance —the heroic poem—with the humblest—pastoral." Victor Skretkowicz,

"Sidney and Amyot: Heliodorus in the Structure and Ethos of the *New Arcadia*," *Review of English Studies* 27 (1976): 173, argues that "under the influence of Heliodorus, Sidney completely abandoned the classical five-act dramatic structure of the *Old Arcadia* in favour of the Heliodorian heroic," an opinion held likewise by S. L. Wolff, *The Greek Romances in Elizabethan Prose Fiction* (New York: Columbia University Press, 1912), p. 328. One can see so far that two more related ways of asking the genre question are available: one that queries the theoretical separation between epic or heroic poetry and pastoral in Renaissance literary theory, and one that distinguishes between the classical epic and the romance as variously practiced by late Hellenistic, medieval, and Renaissance writers. On this latter question, Goldman, *Sir Philip Sidney and the Arcadia*, p. 158, declares simply that the new *Arcadia* is "an heroic romance." Similarly, Lawry, *Sidney's Two "Arcadias,"* pp. 14–15, sees both versions as heroic poems. Most convincing on this line of argument is Alan D. Isler, "Heroic Poetry and Sidney's Two *Arcadias*," *PMLA* 83 (1968): 368–79, who says that neither Renaissance theory nor Sidney saw a distinction between the heroic subject matter indigenous to both epic and romance, an opinion that nevertheless must be balanced off by Bernard Weinberg's extensive account of the sixteenth-century quarrel in Italy between adherents of Ariosto and Tasso, respectively, in which the differences between classical epic and Ariostan romance were much at issue: *A History of Literary Criticism in the Italian Renaissance*, 2 vols. (Chicago: University of Chicago Press, 1961), 2: 954–1073. The issue is of course further complicated by Sidney's clear debts to Sannazaro's *Arcadia* and Montemayer's *Diana*, the originators of that hybrid genre, the pastoral romance. Thus Hamilton, *Sir Philip Sidney*, in agreeing with Lawry that old and new *Arcadias* are both heroic poems (p. 125), further argues that the new *Arcadia* combines the pastoral romance of Montemayor with the heroic romance of Heliodorus. On the other hand, in the best summary of the sources, Walter Davis, "A Map of Arcadia," p. 5, overtly separates the work from the classical epic tradition and calls it a pastoral romance. Also excellent in analyzing Sidney's debts is Arthur F. Kinney, *Humanist Poetics: Thought, Rhetoric, and Fiction in Sixteenth-Century England* (Amherst: University of Massachusetts Press, 1986), pp. 245ff. Finally, consistent with his mainly ironic view of the rhetoric in both works, Richard A. Lanham, "The Old Arcadia," p. 398, calls the new *Arcadia* a "comic epic."

18 A. C. Hamilton, "Sidney's *Arcadia* as Prose Fiction: Its Relation to Its Sources," *ELR: English Literary Renaissance* 2 (1972): 30. Hamilton bases his general approach on Lanham's comment in "The Old Arcadia" that

"in studying the *Old Arcadia*, genres rather than particular works and source areas are most important."

19 As Kenneth Myrick argues (*Sir Philip Sidney as a Literary Craftsman*, p. 173), when he sees Minturno as Sidney's guide and justification.

20 Rosalie L. Colie, *The Resources of Kind: Genre-Theory in the Renaissance*, ed. Barbara K. Lewalski (Berkeley: University of California Press, 1973), pp. 86, 115.

21 Stephen J. Greenblatt, "Sidney's *Arcadia* and the Mixed Mode," *Studies in Philology* 70 (1973): 274. Greenblatt's later work, *Renaissance Self-Fashioning: From More to Shakespeare* (Chicago: University of Chicago Press, 1980), deals at length with the understanding and exploitation of role playing in the Renaissance. Self-fashioning, as Greenblatt develops the concept, intersects with my own argument that human reality both real and imitated is constituted from the linguistic codes made available by culture itself. In the case of the *Arcadia*—which Greenblatt does not discuss—I argue the central importance of rhetorical figuration as a resource for constituting the self, a focus which diverges from Greenblatt's own concern with self-fashioning in an agonistic context defined by social and political codes of stratification and conflict.

22 See Hiram Haydn's extensive discussion of these issues in his chapter "The Courtly Tradition of Love and Honor," in *The Counter-Renaissance* (New York: Grove Press, 1960), pp. 555–618.

23 Edgar Wind, *Pagan Mysteries in the Renaissance* (New York: W. W. Norton, 1968), "Virtue Reconciled with Pleasure," pp. 81–96.

24 Arthur K. Amos, Jr., *Time, Space, and Value: The Narrative Structure of the "New Arcadia"* (Lewisburg, Pa.: Bucknell University Press, 1977), p. 188.

25 In a statement that to some extent prefigures my discussion of the two heroes in Part Two, Elizabeth Dipple, "Harmony and Pastoral in the *Old Arcadia*," *ELH: English Literary History* 35 (1968): 318, says that "they are, in short, heroes of an absolutely literary nature, answering the highest demands of the epic romances, the sonnet sequences, and Florentine neo-platonic dialogues."

26 Wolff, *The Greek Romances in Elizabethan Prose Fiction*, p. 358. Cf. George Philip Krapp, *The Rise of English Literary Prose* (New York: Oxford University Press, 1915), p. 374.

27 Ian Watt, "Elizabethan Light Reading," in *The Age of Shakespeare*, ed. Boris Ford (Harmondsworth: Penguin Books, 1955), p. 123.

28 George Puttenham, *The Arte of English Poesie*, ed. Gladys Doidge Willcock and Alice Walker (Cambridge: Cambridge University Press, 1936), p. 142.

29 Ibid., pp. 142–43.

30 See Seymour Chatman, *Story and Discourse: Narrative Structure in Fiction and Film* (Ithaca, N.Y.: Cornell University Press, 1978), where Chatman develops the Russian formalist distinction between the structures of a story's plot and those of the verbal medium in which these structures are encoded.

31 Sidney, *The Countess of Pembroke's Arcadia*, ed. Robertson, p. 29.

32 Nancy Lindheim, *The Structures of Sidney's "Arcadia"* (Toronto: University of Toronto Press, 1982), argues positions on these three topics that are generally incompatible with my own. Regarding antithetical figuration and the conflict between the demands of active heroism and contemplative eros, Lindheim sees Sidney calling for the disappearance of opposites in the name of perfection: "Perfection resolves—no, dissolves—all contraries, superseding elements originally worked out as some sort of antithesis. Sidney insists on the conflict before he makes it disappear" (p. 167). And although like myself she grants the decisive significance of the old *Arcadia* oracle as it reappears substantially the same in the new *Arcadia*, she believes it necessary for the reader to pick and choose among the incidents of old *Arcadia* Books 3–5, to find those which are tonally compatible with the deepened significance of the new *Arcadia* torso. I argue extensively against this position in Part Two. Finally, she says that "since one can see so many patterns operating simultaneously, and even particular incidents contributing to several different schemes, it is illusory to seek the single structural principle that governs the *Arcadia*" (p. 153). From my own perspective, the essential difference between my own dialectical schema—on the basis of which I believe it possible to elicit "a single principle that governs the *Arcadia*"—and Lindheim's nondialectical interpretation of the antithetical structures of the *Arcadia*, comes down to the following: Lindheim's position on the nature of logical antitheses and the global structures of the *Arcadia* itself involves only two possible options: simple oppositions and multiple structures, or simple fusion and mere repetitions of the same structure. And opposition for her equals the logical relation of mutual exclusion. As my extensive argument in Part One indicates, I believe that Sidney is working within a much more refined and discriminating logical schema, in which opposites are related as both mutually exclusive and mutually implicative, and consequently the alternative to antithesis is not at all its disappearance. Further, the dialectical schema I employ is capable of generating a broad variety of specific dialectical structures, a variety yet subsumable within the same schema. It is on the basis of this essential disagreement that Lindheim and I reach such consistently different conclusions regard-

ing aspects of the *Arcadia* on which we ask, for the most part, the same questions.

Notes to Part One

1 Bacon's objections to Ciceronian style assumed several paradigms, including the traditional distinction between high, middle, and low styles. In arguing for the value of the low style, Bacon criticized the figures characteristic of the high style and found the figures of perspicuity and concision of the former style much more to his liking; Rosamond Tuve, *Elizabethan and Metaphysical Imagery: Renaissance Poetic and Twentieth-Century Critics* (Chicago: University of Chicago Press, 1947), p. 232n. From the viewpoint of Bacon and other anti-Ciceronians in Sidney's own time, the notion of "normal" style was superimposed on the stylistic characteristics of the *genus humile*, from which the figures of the high style could only appear to be deviations.

2 Abraham Fraunce, *The Arcadian Rhetorike*, ed. Ethel Seaton (Oxford: Basil Blackwell, 1950), p. 26.

3 George Puttenham, *The Arte of English Poesie*, ed. Gladys Doidge Willcock and Alice Walker (Cambridge: Cambridge University Press, 1936), p. 137.

4 Quintilian, *The Institutio Oratoria*, trans. H. E. Butler, 4 vols. (Cambridge: Harvard University Press, 1921), 3:353–55.

5 For a more extensive, theoretical discussion of historicism's practice of paraphrasing a literary work by discovering another literal, nonliterary work into which to translate it, see my article "The Authentic Discourse of the Renaissance," *Diacritics* 10, no. 1 (1980): 77–87.

6 See P. Albert Duhamel, "Sidney's *Arcadia* and Elizabethan Rhetoric," *Studies in Philology* 45 (1948): 134–50. Both Perry Miller in *The New England Mind: The Seventeenth Century* (Boston: Beacon Press, 1961), chap. 7, "The Uses of Reason," pp. 181ff.; and Walter Ong in *Ramus, Method, and the Decay of Dialogue* (Cambridge: Harvard University Press, 1958), passim, treat extensively Ramus's method of writing and reading based on discovering the genus-species structure underlying the unfolding of the argument. In contemporary terms, there would be for Ramus no distinction between surface and deep structures, since a correct argument would display overtly the logical ligatures binding together the succession of propositions. But in a way that distantly (and simplistically) foreshadows Sidney's stylistic practice in the *Arcadia*, Ramus calls attention to the ways in which reading entails the recuperation not merely of the meaning of an argument but the metatextual rules that govern and structure it.

I might point out also in parenthesis that Ramism gives us today a curious prefiguration of modern structuralism, to the degree at any rate that both feature such recuperations as a preface to the discovery of meaning.

7 Citations of the new *Arcadia* are from Sir Philip Sidney, *The Countess of Pembroke's Arcadia (The New Arcadia)*, ed. Victor Skretkowicz (Oxford: Clarendon Press, 1987). Skretkowicz has modernized both spelling and punctuation, and I have occasion to cite Albert Feuillerat, ed., *The Prose Works of Sir Philip Sidney*, 4 vols. (Cambridge: Cambridge University Press, 1912), vol. 1, which reproduces the spelling and punctuation of the original. Citations from the old *Arcadia* are from Sir Philip Sidney, *The Countess of Pembroke's Arcadia (The Old Arcadia)*, ed. Jean Robertson (Oxford: Clarendon Press, 1973).

8 The shipwreck description has drawn a number of comments and is perhaps the single most cited passage in the *Arcadia*. See John F. Danby, *Poets on Fortune's Hill* (London: Faber and Faber, 1952), p. 49. Brother Simon Scribner, in his useful study *Figures of Word-Repetition in the First Book of Sir Philip Sidney's "Arcadia"* (Washington: Catholic University of America Press, 1948), p. 64, notes the function of sequence in communicating the division of the ship's parts; he says that "the implication is one of complete ruin, and the implication is powerfully reinforced by the use of the figure. The thought is not complete until the third member is reached." Kenneth Myrick, *Sir Philip Sidney as a Literary Craftsman* (Lincoln: University of Nebraska Press, 1965), pp. 186–87, is likewise conscious of the ways in which the sequence of the passage presents us with a kind of "phenomenology" (my word) of the reader's perception of the scene. Finally, Forrest G. Robinson, *The Shape of Things Known: Sidney's "Apology" in Its Philosophical Tradition* (Cambridge: Harvard University Press, 1972), pp. 147–48, attempts to derive from this passage support for his belief that Sidney in the *Arcadia* features structural relations that are predominantly spatial rather than verbal. Although Robinson's very useful argument generally parallels my approach in emphasizing that Sidney dealt with highly articulated structures of information that were intended to be reconstructed in the reader's mind with equal articulation, I decisively diverge from him when he says, summarizing his main argument: "In effect then, Sidney is only secondarily interested in the strictly verbal side of poetry and places the burden of emphasis on the simultaneously concrete and abstract pictures that those words produce in the reader's mind" (pp. 103–104). I should note, further, that the priority and dominance of verbally articulated relationships over spatially arranged structures is implicitly witnessed in Robinson's discussion of

the shipwreck passage, when he says: "each modification renders the scene more disastrously heavy with human implication and thus narrows and clarifies our moral focus. At the same time, of course, the series of modifications, like the paradoxes and antitheses, is a verbal reminder that we are in the presence of a very discriminating narrator." Though she shares Robinson's belief in the dominance of the visual in the new *Arcadia*, Thelma Greenfield has noted the forms of stylistic precision that are the subject of Part One; Thelma N. Greenfield, *The Eye of Judgment: Reading the "New Arcadia"* (Lewisburg, Pa.: Bucknell University Press, 1982), pp. 96–99.

9 The arrangement of Kalander's garden corresponds to late sixteenth-century fashions. Cf. Bruce R. Smith, "Landscape with Figures: The Three Realms of Queen Elizabeth's Country-house Revels," *Renaissance Drama*, 8 n.s. (1977): 57–115. The segmentation and consequent potentiality for confusion among different areas of a total garden is envisioned by Sir Henry Wotton in *The Elements of Architecture* (1624): "I have seene a *Garden* (for the maner perchance incomparable) into which the first Accesse was a high walke like a *Tarrace*, from whence might bee taken a generall view of the whole *Plott* below; but rather in a delightfull confusion, then with any plaine distinction of the pieces" (Smith, "Landscape with Figures," p. 65). Sidney may, in fact, have been describing Penshurst.

10 Another way of analyzing this passage is to note that "veins" involves a *catachresis*, the metaphorical transfer of a term from a literal to a metaphorical meaning that nevertheless becomes literal in its own right. Like "leg" which names the vertical support of a table, "veins" is a standard term for the visible lines in marble. Nevertheless both "leg" and "veins" in such usage are metaphorical. Sidney in effect unmetaphors the word "vein" when he calls attention to the actual figure represented in the marble, while also remetaphoring the term in citing the viewer's inability to distinguish physiological and marmoreal veins. Both speaker and reader are thus caught in an oscillation between the literal and metaphorical meanings of the term, where the metaphorical meaning is also literal. Sidney's use of "veins" in this sense predates the earliest *OED* entry of 1663.

11 A theoretical explanation of "countertext" that relates the concept to the structuralist model operative in my analysis of the new *Arcadia* appears in Michael McCanles, "The Dialectical Structure of Discourse," *Poetics Today* 3, no. 4 (1982; published 1984): 21–37.

12 The "reader" functions in this book as an idealized model of text reception characterized by knowledge of (1) the rules that make a given text read-

able, and (2) knowledge of the second-order rules necessary to discover
the first rules. In this respect the notion of "reader response" I assume
here is not indebted to that formulated by Hans Robert Jauss, *Toward an
Aesthetic of Reception*, trans. Timothy Bahti, introduction by Paul de Man
(Minneapolis: University of Minnesota Press, 1982); and Wolfgang Iser,
The Act of Reading: A Theory of Aesthetic Response (Baltimore: The Johns
Hopkins University Press, 1978), which features sociological determiners
of reading practices. The "reader" I discuss here derives rather from that
described by Jonathan Culler in *Structuralist Poetics: Structuralism, Lin-
guistics, and the Study of Literature* (Ithaca, N.Y.: Cornell University Press,
1975), pp. 113ff. and passim, which projects readership as a function
of knowing the various grammars—linguistic, rhetorical, generic—that
allow one to understand a specific kind of verbal text.

13 Ernest Hemingway, *The Sun Also Rises* (New York: Charles Scribner's
Sons, 1926), pp. 216–17.

14 On the question of Sidney's indebtedness to Theophrastus, see John Buxton, "Sidney and Theophrastus," *English Literary Renaissance* 2 (1972):
79–82. John Hoskins, *Directions for Speech and Style*, ed. Hoyt H. Hudson
(Princeton: Princeton University Press, 1935), p. 41, said that Sidney was
indebted to Theophrastus's character sketches. While there were several
continental editions of Theophrastus available to Sidney, Robinson points
out (*The Shape of Things Known*, p. 207) that the first English edition,
Joseph Hall's *Characters of Vertues and Vices*, was not published until 1608,
some twenty-four years after the probable date of composition of the new
Arcadia. Buxton argues nevertheless that Sidney might well have known
editions that were limited to the first twenty-three Theophrastan characters (p. 79). Questions of debt, however, are irrelevant, since neither
Theophrastus nor the English character books modeled on Theophrastus
published after Sidney's death exhibit the complex rhetorical figuration
and logical dialectics typical of Sidney's character sketches.

15 Aristotle, *Nichomachean Ethics*, II.6, 1106b, in *The Basic Works of Aris-
totle*, ed. Richard McKeon (New York: Random House, 1941), p. 958. On
Sidney's large debt to both the *Politics* and *Ethics* of Aristotle, see Arthur F.
Kinney, *Humanist Poetics: Thought, Rhetoric, and Fiction in Sixteenth-Century
England* (Amherst: University of Massachusetts Press, 1986), pp. 263ff.
In general, conceptions of the ethical structures informing the *Arcadia*
tend to the dichotomous and moralistic in one direction, and the aware-
ness of ambiguity and indeterminacy in the other. Adherents to the first
include Walter R. Davis, "A Map of Arcadia: Sidney's Romance in Its
Tradition," in *Sidney's Arcadia* (New Haven: Yale University Press, 1965);

Jon S. Lawry, *Sidney's Two "Arcadias": Pattern and Proceeding* (Ithaca, N.Y.: Cornell University Press, 1972); and Andrew D. Weiner, *Sir Philip Sidney and the Poetics of Protestantism: A Study of Contexts* (Minneapolis: University of Minnesota Press, 1978). These studies view the *Arcadia* from the perspective of generally Christian-platonic traditions and contexts, and conclude that it is primarily a fictional handbook directed against the vices of private passion and political irresponsibility. Adherents to the second perspective include Nancy Lindheim, "Sidney's *Arcadia*, Book II: Retrospective Narrative," *Studies in Philology* 64 (1967): 159–86; Elizabeth Dipple, " 'Unjust Justice' in the Old Arcadia," *Studies in English Literature* 10 (1970): 83–101; Dorothy Connell, *Sir Philip Sidney: The Maker's Mind* (Oxford: Oxford University Press, 1977); Arthur K. Amos, *Time, Space, and Value: The Narrative Structure of the New Arcadia* (Lewisburg, Pa.: Bucknell University Press, 1977); and Greenfield, *The Eye of Judgment*, p. 57.

16 Sister Miriam Joseph, *Rhetoric in Shakespeare's Time* (New York: Harcourt, Brace, and World, 1962), p. 324. For antithetical figuration see also Richard A. Lanham, *A Handlist of Rhetorical Terms: A Guide for Students of English Literature* (Berkeley: University of California Press, 1969), pp. 12 and passim. Lindheim, *The Structures of Sidney's "Arcadia"* (Toronto: University of Toronto Press, 1982), pp. 35ff., discusses only the figures *antimetabole* and *correctio,* which name inversions of previously stated ideas, as expressions of Sidney's interest in antithetical relationships. She is not concerned with the wider variety of antithetical figures present in the Arcadian styles, since within her reductionist argument antithetical rhetorical figures are used by Sidney only "to establish and then overturn distinctions" (p. 35).

17 I am indebted to A. J. Greimas, *Sémantique structurale: Recherche de méthode* (Paris: Librairie Larrouse, 1966), for a theoretical examination of the ways in which extended texts are governed by the differentially paired semantic markers of key terms in the text, and of practical applications to specific texts. See also the same author's *Maupassant: La Sémiotique du texte: Exercices pratiques* (Paris: Éditions du Seuil, 1976).

18 It is generally agreed that a main purpose of the Book 2 narratives is to illustrate a variety of ethical complexities that parallel in different degrees the moral conundrums in the main plot. Amos, *Time, Space, and Value,* says that "the difficulties with the either/or categories arise partly from the ethical complexity built up through the temporal emphasis of Book II. As the causal chains became more and more intertwined, the princes' choices became more and more ambiguous" (p. 138). Walter R. Davis,

"Thematic Unity in the *New Arcadia*," *Studies in Philology* 57 (1960): 123–43, argues that these episodes collectively teach the princes the liaison between private passions and public disorder. Combining both viewpoints is Nancy Lindheim, "Sidney's *Arcadia*, Book II: Retrospective Narrative," who finds the narratives offering "morally perplexed examples of 'right' actions done for wrong reasons, and conversely, 'wrong' actions done for right reasons. The basic morality of the *Arcadia* resides in these episodes —values and beliefs are always being challenged by other seeming goods and outside forces, and must be held actively if they are to be held at all" (p. 85).

19 Cf. Seneca, *De clementia, Moral Essays*, trans. John W. Basore, 3 vols. (London: Heinemann, 1928), 1:395–97.

20 René Girard, *Deceit, Desire, and the Novel*, trans. Yvonne Freccero (Baltimore: The Johns Hopkins Press, 1965), pp. 10–14.

21 For an analysis of a treatment of love as power similar to Sidney's, see Michael McCanles, "Love and Power in the Poetry of Sir Thomas Wyatt," *Modern Language Quarterly* 29 (1968): 145–60.

22 Skretkowicz registers a similar recognition by isolating the following phrases as direct quotations of Andromana's speech embedded in Pamela's narrative: ("Such a kingly entertainment! such a kingly magnificence! such a kingly heart for enterprises!"). I have chosen to follow Feuillerat here, since Pamela's narrative text is shot through with reproductions of Andromana's text as free indirect discourse and it is therefore inappropriate to isolate—as Skretkowicz's punctuation does—these particular phrases as if they were the only citations of Andromana's text occurring here.

23 E. M. W. Tillyard, *The English Epic and Its Background* (New York: Oxford University Press, 1954), p. 319, finds Amphialus "a truly tragic character," as does A. C. Hamilton, *Sir Philip Sidney* (Cambridge: Cambridge University Press, 1977), p. 139, who observes that "even his virtues seem to undo him." See also Greenfield, *The Eye of Judgment*, p. 41. A more common view, consistent with attempts to impose a simplistic, dichotomous ethic on the *Arcadia*, is Davis's, in "Thematic Unity in the *New Arcadia*," p. 142, who sees in Amphialus a classic exemplar of passion's conquest of reason, a view echoed and developed by Lawry, *Sidney's Two "Arcadias."*

24 *Sic* Feuillerat, vol. 1, p. 366, spelling modernized. Skretkowicz inserts a comma between "pretty" and "intricate," but there is no reason to doubt the 1590 reading. The *OED* indicates 1565 as the earliest use of "pretty" as an intensifying adverb.

25 The old *Arcadia* ending in the 1593 version concludes with a reference to future events and includes among these "stories of . . . Helen and Amphialus" (Robertson, p. 417). This inclusion is absent from the original old *Arcadia* conclusion and suggests that the 1593 editors may have had among the instructions received from Fulke Greville some indication that Sidney envisioned Amphialus as saveable. Robertson (p. lx) believes that Sidney's sister received from Greville the "direction" he had inherited from Sidney for further development of the new *Arcadia* revision, as well as the manuscript copy of the work itself. It is difficult to understand why the 1593 editors should have inserted this reference without Sidney's own indication, given the apparent mortality of Amphialus's wounds as described in the text.

26 Erona's obsessive love of the worthless Antiphilus creates a plot context in which similar double binds thrive. Antiphilus is captured by Tiridates, who seeks Erona's love and who threatens to kill Antiphilus unless she yields to him. The dialectics of the situation are almost predictable: "she [was] drawn to two contraries by one cause (for the love of him commanded her to yield to no other; the love of him commanded her to preserve his life), which knot might well be cut, but untied it could not be; . . ." (p. 207).

27 (New Haven: Yale University Press, 1965), p. 343.

28 Richard A. Lanham, *Style: An Anti-Textbook* (New Haven: Yale University Press, 1974), and idem, *The Motives of Eloquence: Literary Rhetoric in the Renaissance* (New Haven: Yale University Press, 1976).

29 Pierre Guiraud, "Immanence and Transitivity of Stylistic Criteria," in *Literary Style: A Symposium*, ed. Seymour Chatman (London: Oxford University Press, 1971), pp. 18–19.

30 Roland Barthes, "Style and its Image," in *Literary Style*, ed. Chatman, p. 4.

31 In this connection see John M. Ellis's extensive critique of the deviationist approach in *The Theory of Literary Criticism: A Logical Analysis* (Berkeley: University of California Press, 1974), pp. 165ff.; Stanley E. Fish, "How Ordinary Is Ordinary Language," *New Literary History* 5 (1973): 41–54; and Tzvetan Todorov, "The Place of Style in the Structure of the Text," in *Literary Style*, ed. Chatman, pp. 29–44.

32 Nils Erik Enkvist, "On the Place of Style in Some Linguistic Theories," in *Literary Style*, ed. Chatman, p. 54. Umberto Eco makes an interesting defense of rhetorical figures as deviations from the viewpoint of information theory in *La struttura assente: Introduzione alla ricerca semiologica* (Milan: Bompiani, 1968), p. 86. Eco argues that only the nonredundant, i.e., the relatively unexpected, segment of a message carries information,

and consequently rhetorical figures carry information only to the degree that they cannot be predicted by the reader on the basis of normally expected usage. Eco's argument in general derives from the formalist notion of "automization" versus "deautomization" (p. 79); also John Burbank and Peter Steiner, eds., *The Word and Verbal Art: Selected Essays by Jan Mukařovský* (New Haven: Yale University Press, 1977), pp. 68–69, where the aesthetic use of any element means deautomization, i.e., violation of normal pattern.

33 See Gérard Genette's essays "L'envers des Signes" and "Figures" in *Figures* (Paris: Éditions du Seuil, 1966), pp. 185–221, for a critique of figuration as deviation and an argument for figuration as a secondary system of structures built on, i.e., deriving from, "normal" speech patterns. Jacques Derrida, "White Mythology: Metaphor in the Text of Philosophy," *New Literary History* 6 (1974): 5–74, examines the assumption of a "proper" and "natural" language lying behind metaphor, into which metaphor must be translated. Derrida's remarks critique the assumptions lying behind a deviationist theory of style, as does Paul De Man's main argument in *Allegories of Reading: Figural Language in Rousseau, Nietzsche, Rilke, and Proust* (New Haven: Yale University Press, 1979). De Man says: "All rhetorical structures . . . are based on substitutive reversals, and it seems unlikely that one more reversal over and above the ones that have already taken place would suffice to restore things to their proper order. One more 'turn' or trope added to a series of earlier reversals will not stop the turn towards error" (p. 113). One of these assumptions is that there exists a normative, nonfigured use of verbal language, which is the "proper" verbal medium in which the meanings of rhetorical figures are to be articulated and recovered. Such language use is in fact a sociological phenomenon, determined by the social and political forces that establish the "official," i.e., dominant texts and codes of a society. See Michael McCanles, "Criticism is the (Dis)closure of Meaning," *What Is Criticism?* ed. Paul Hernadi (Bloomington: Indiana University Press, 1981), pp. 268–79, for an analysis of "literal" meaning as determined by a given culture's notion of a dominant language of the "natural."

34 M. A. K. Halliday, "Linguistic Function and Literary Style: An Inquiry into the Language of William Golding's *The Inheritors*," in *Literary Style*, ed. Chatman, p. 339. See also Todorov, "The Place of Style," in ibid., p. 36.

35 Rosemond Tuve, *Elizabethan and Metaphysical Imagery: Renaissance Poetic and Twentieth-Century Critics* (Chicago: University of Chicago Press, 1947), p. 110.

36 Puttenham, *The Arte of English Poesie*, p. 159. Neil Rudenstine's comment on this passage in *Sidney's Poetic Development* (Cambridge: Harvard University Press, 1967), pp. 56–57, sees it in effect naming a conception of style as derivation.

37 Halliday, "Linguistic Function and Literary Style," in *Literary Style*, ed. Chatman, p. 359.

38 From Estienne's *Paradoxes, ce sont propos contre le commun opinion: debatus, en forme de declamations fore[n]ses* (Paris, 1553); quoted in Warner G. Rice, "The Paradossi of Ortensio Lando," *University of Michigan Publications in Language and Literature*, vol. 8 (Ann Arbor: University of Michigan Press, 1932), p. 67; my translation.

39 A. E. Malloch, "The Techniques and Function of the Renaissance Paradox," *Studies in Philology* 53 (1956): 191–203.

40 Rosalie L. Colie, *Paradoxia Epidemica: The Renaissance Tradition of Paradox* (Princeton: Princeton University Press, 1966), p. 7.

41 John E. Hollingsworth, *Antithesis in the Attic Orators from Antiphon to Isaeus* (Menasha, Wis.: George Banta, 1915).

42 John Lyly, *Euphues: The Anatomy of Wit, Euphues and His England*, ed. Morris William Croll and Harry Clemons (New York: Russell and Russell, 1964; orig. pub. 1916), p. 25.

43 Ibid., p. xxvi.

44 George Williamson, *The Senecan Amble: A Study in Prose Form from Bacon to Collier* (Chicago: University of Chicago Press, 1966), p. 88.

45 Hoskins, *Directions for Speech and Style*, ed. Hudson, p. 36.

46 Jonathan Culler, "Paradox and the Language of Morals in La Rochefoucauld," *Modern Language Review* 68 (1973): 28.

47 For a full development of the argument outlined here, see Michael McCanles, "The Dialectical Structure of Discourse," *Poetics Today* 3, no. 4 (1982; published 1984): 21–37.

48 Translated by Paul Shorey, in *The Collected Dialogues of Plato*, ed. Edith Hamilton and Huntingdon Cairns (New York: Pantheon Books, 1961), p. 638.

49 *Literary Criticism: Plato to Dryden*, ed. Allan H. Gilbert (Detroit: Wayne State University Press, 1962), p. 71.

50 Ibid., p. 361.

51 Baxter Hathaway, *Marvels and Commonplaces: Renaissance Literary Criticism* (New York: Random House, 1968), pp. 47–48.

52 On the fusion of description and mimesis, see Gérard Genette, "Boundaries of Narrative," *New Literary History* 8 (1976): 1–13.

53 Some discussions of free indirect discourse include the seminal work of

Mikhail Bakhtin, *Problems of Dostoefsky's Poetics,* trans. R. W. Rotsel (Ann Arbor, Mich.: Ardis, 1973); Seymour Chatman, "The Structure of Narrative Transmission," in *Style and Structure in Literature: Essays in the New Stylistics,* ed. Roger Fowler (Ithaca, N.Y.: Cornell University Press, 1975); Brian McHale, "Free Indirect Discourse: A Survey of Recent Accounts," *PTL: A Journal for Descriptive Poetics and Theory of Literature* 3 (1978): 249–87; and two articles by Paul Hernadi: "Verbal Worlds Between Action and Vision: A Theory of Poetic Discourse," *College English* 33 (1971): 18–31, and "Dual Perspective: Free Indirect Discourse and Related Techniques," *Comparative Literature* 24 (1972): 32–43. For another treatment of free indirect discourse in a Renaissance text, cf. Michael McCanles, *The Discourse of "Il Principe,"* Series Humana Civilitas No. 8, The Center for Medieval and Renaissance Studies, UCLA (Malibu, Calif.: Undena Publications, 1983).

54 In his seminal essay "The Function of Language in Psychoanalysis," the modern structuralist psychologist Jacques Lacan gives us a post-Freudian version of Sidney's perspective on the textualization of the self. Lacan notes that for Freud "the dream has the structure of a sentence." For this reason Lacan is led to conceive of dreams and of the discourse in which the dreamer recounts his dreams as governed by the available forms of rhetorical figuration: "The important part begins with the translation of the text [by the analyst], the important part which Freud tells us is given in the [verbal] elaboration of the dream—in other words, in its rhetoric. Ellipsis and pleonasm, hyperbaton or syllepsis, regression, repetition, apposition—these are the syntactical displacements; metaphor, catachresis, autonomasis, allegory, metonymy, and synecdoche—these are the semantic condensations in which Freud teaches us to read the intentions —ostentatious or demonstrative, dissimulating or persuasive, retaliatory or seductive—out of which the subject modulates his oneiric discourse"; in *The Language of the Self* by Anthony Wilden (New York: Delta Books, 1975), pp. 30, 31.

55 Nancy S. Struever, *The Language of History in the Renaissance: Rhetorical and Historical Consciousness in Florentine Humanism* (Princeton: Princeton University Press, 1970), p. 125.

Notes to Part Two

1 Renato Poggioli, *The Oaten Flute: Essays on Pastoral Poetry and the Pastoral Ideal* (Cambridge: Harvard University Press, 1975), p. 253: "The two most important divisions of the pastoral are the pastoral of innocence and the

pastoral of love. . . . Of these two, the pastoral of innocence claims a sort of primacy or priority, since bucolic love is but a quest for innocence in happiness itself." Poggioli says earlier (p. 42), "happiness means in pastoral terms always one and the same thing: the fulfillment of the passion of love, the consummation of man's erotic wishes, as much as unhappiness means exactly the opposite, the rejection or denial of his heart's desire." For extended application of Poggioli's categories to Sidney, see Myriam Yvonne Jehenson, *The Golden World of the Pastoral: A Comparative Study of Sidney's "New Arcadia" and d'Urfé's "L'Astrée"* (Ravenna: Longo Editore, n.d.).

2 The active/contemplative life differential was a major categorical division of human experience for Renaissance culture. And as one might expect of a differential funding such a wealth of complex texts, the differential subsumes relations of both mutual exclusion and mutual implication. Thus Mark Rose successively explores traditional lore that opposes heroism and eros in "Sidney's Womanish Man," *Review of English Studies* 15 (1964): 353–63; and that which sees eros as inspiring humankind's highest feats in *Heroic Love: Studies in Sidney and Spenser* (Cambridge: Harvard University Press, 1968), pp. 48–49. There were available mythic stories that confirmed both views, the most significant on the side of mutual exclusion being that of the distaff Hercules: spinning in woman's clothing having been enslaved to love of the nymph Omphale. The legendary choice Hercules makes of heroism over eros was reinterpreted by Dürer as the choice between virtue and pleasure; see Eugene M. Waith, *The Herculean Hero in Marlowe, Chapman, Shakespeare and Dryden* (New York: Columbia University Press, 1962), pp. 47–49 and passim; Edgar Wind, *Pagan Mysteries in the Renaissance*, rev. ed. (New York: W. W. Norton, 1968), "Virtue Reconciled with Pleasure," pp. 81–96. The difficulties in establishing a relation of mutual implication were seen to lie in the fact that the two modes of life were governed respectively by the two main affective powers of the soul, namely, the irascible and the concupiscible. Both Spenser and Tasso envisioned the problem in these terms, thus retextualizing Plato's own mythologizing of this formula in the *Phaedrus*. *The Faerie Queene* gives us excesses of the irascible in Pyrochles and of the concupiscible in Cymochles in Book II, as well as a reenactment of the distaff Hercules in Book V in the story of Artegall and Radigund; on the philosophical, ethical background of Spenser's Book II see Harry Berger, Jr., *The Allegorical Temper: Vision and Reality in Book II of Spenser's Faerie Queene* (New Haven: Yale University Press, 1957). Tasso's ex post facto allegorical reading of *Jerusalem Delivered* interprets Rinaldo as repre-

senting an excess of the irascible virtue, temporarily enslaved to the sensuous Armida, and finally tempered by reason figured in Godfrey; "The Allegory of the Poem," in Tasso, *Jerusalem Delivered*, trans. Edward Fairfax, ed. Henry Morley (London: George Routledge and Sons, 1890), pp. 436–43. In this connection see also Hiram Haydn, *The Counter-Renaissance* (New York: Grove Press, 1960), pp. 555ff. The reconciliation of Mars and Venus, represented in Renaissance painting, was already established as central in medieval courtly codes of love. As Rose says, *Heroic Love*, p. 49, "Musidorus' scorn for those 'gentle fooles' who speak of the 'gentle hart' constitutes a direct challenge to the literary and philosophical tradition reaching back to the troubadours. On the other side, Pyrocles' invocation of those 'notable men' who have considered love to be the 'highest power of the mind' is an appeal to the authority of the same tradition." The spiritualizing effects of love properly transmuted from the sexual to the contemplative were well known from Ficino's commentary on Plato's *Symposium* and the rhapsody it inspired in Bembo recorded at the end of Castiglione's *Courtier*. As we might expect, Shakespeare gives us both versions of the heroism/love differential in *Antony and Cleopatra*. D. M. Rosenberg, *Oaten Reeds and Trumpets: Pastoral and Epic in Virgil, Spenser, and Milton* (Lewisburg, Pa.: Bucknell University Press, 1981), produces evidence that suggests that the epic-pastoral opposition is partly based on the model of the Virgilian career, wherein the poet replicates the career of the hero, moving from pastoral contemplation to active heroism (pp. 53–54, 81–82, and passim). In this perspective the epic hero may enter briefly the pastoral "enclave," but such episodes either test his heroic mettle or provide visionary sustenance for his heroic quest. The case could be made that Sidney reverses this career pattern, launching his heroes first into heroic action and then later taking them into a pastoral setting. Thus Robert E. Stillman, *Sidney's Poetic Justice: "The Old Arcadia," Its Eclogues, and Renaissance Pastoral Traditions* (Lewisburg, Pa.: Bucknell University Press, 1986), pp. 127–28, notes that the eclogues in the old *Arcadia* illustrate "the ultimate impotence of courageous activity against the assaults of passion."

3 Louis Adrian Montrose, "Celebration and Insinuation: Sir Philip Sidney and the Motives of Elizabethan Courtship," *Renaissance Drama* 8 n.s. (1977): 3–35, argues that Sidney's masque *The Lady of May* (1578 or 1579) features the debate between action and contemplation: "Its debate structure is not a simple set of stated and related oppositions but a dialectical unfolding and revision of oppositions; its rhetorical intention is to move the audience from a situation of indecision between two antithetical ex-

tremes to a realignment that shows one term to incorporate, revise, and transcend the other" (p. 18). The facile ease of Musidorus's argument is prefigured by Sidney's assigning the debate on this subject to philosophers in *A Defence of Poesy*, whose sterile "wrangling" typically concerns such matters as "whether the contemplative or the active life do excell"; *Miscellaneous Prose of Sir Philip Sidney*, ed. Katherine Duncan-Jones and Jan Van Dorsten (Oxford: Clarendon Press, 1973), p. 93. Arthur F. Kinney, *Humanist Poetics: Thought, Rhetoric, and Fiction in Sixteenth-Century England* (Amherst: University of Massachusetts Press, 1986), pp. 231–32, places this theme in the context of humanist debate and ideology.

4 Musidorus does apparently know the story of Erona (which Philoclea tells Pyrocles). "Seeing the country of Lycia so much devoted to Cupid" (p. 205), Erona when she inherits the kingdom attempts to destroy all statues and pictures of the god of love. Her rejection of eros is suitably "punished" "when she was stricken with most obstinate love to a young man but of mean parentage in her father's court, named Antiphilus." Antiphilus of course does not reciprocate, and from this one-sided love develops one of the subplots of the new *Arcadia*, the only one in fact not resolved when Sidney left off writing.

5 Stillman, in *Sidney's Poetic Justice*, indicates that the eclogues function there to call into question the capacity of heroic virtues to deal with the passion of love. Stillman's analysis suggests that the additions of the retrospective narratives—present in ovo in the old *Arcadia* eclogues— were intended to develop the perspectives of the eclogues in the old *Arcadia* on the limitations and vulnerabilities of heroic endeavor. D. M. Rosenberg, *Oaten Reeds and Trumpets: Pastoral and Epic in Virgil, Spenser, and Milton* (Lewisburg, Pa.: Bucknell University Press, 1981), shows that the pastoral "enclave" in the epic, as he calls it, is primarily intended as a resting spot from heroic activity and as a visionary rendition of the perfect world toward which such activity labors. Rosenberg demonstrates that Virgil, Ariosto, Tasso, and Spenser all treat the pastoral retreat as a deviation from heroic activity. In contrast, Sidney in the new *Arcadia* makes the pastoral the domain where heroic virtues are not so much tested as they are in the epic, as critiqued and called into question. In this Sidney would be turning the priority of epic over pastoral on its head.

6 This paragraph is indebted to Roman Jakobson's reading of verbal discourse as a series of "metonymical displacements." See Roman Jakobson and Morris Halle, *Fundamentals of Language* (The Hague: Mouton, 1956), pp. 91ff. By metonymical displacement Jakobson means that the syntagmatic dimension of discourse is distinguishable from the paradigmatic

dimension in being composed of units which all relate to one another as parts of some projected totality. The paradigmatic dimension of discourse, which I have featured continually in my analysis of the differential sets implied by the passages and episodes already analyzed, is for Jakobson the realm of the metaphorical rather than metonymical and relates terms in the text to the class terms of larger extension. Consequently, reading any discourse requires a double recuperation: metaphorically, from individual terms to the larger class they fall under; and metonymically, from each successive unit (word or phrase) to the next, successively unfolding the totality of which all the units are a part. In the first instance the reader must recuperate the total paradigmatic set from which a given term or unit is selected, and in the second he must look toward the holistic set of which the discourse unfolds parts sequentially.

7 Critics who argue for the positive effects of the two heroes' sojourn in Arcadia include Elizabeth Dipple, "Metamorphoses in Sidney's *Arcadias*," *Philological Quarterly* 50 (1971): 47–62; Margaret E. Dana, "Heroic and Pastoral: Sidney's *Arcadia* as Masquerade," *Comparative Literature* 25 (1973): 308–320; and William Craft, "Remaking the Heroic Self in the *New Arcadia*," *Studies in English Literature: 1500–1900* 25 (1985): 45–67. More equivocal is Harold E. Toliver, *Pastoral Forms and Attitudes* (Berkeley: University of California Press, 1971), who argues that while Sidney presents an ultimately unbridgeable gulf between the heroic and the pastoral modes of living, nevertheless "the goal of their education is to discover a manner of engaging rusticity while remaining separate from it and essentially untransformed" (p. 57). Much less unequivocally critical of the heroes' pastoral adventure are Walter R. Davis, "A Map of Arcadia: Sidney's Romance in Its Tradition," in *Sidney's Arcadia* (New Haven: Yale University Press, 1965), and Andrew Weiner, *Sir Philip Sidney and the Poetics of Protestantism: A Study of Contexts* (Minneapolis: University of Minnesota Press, 1978), who agree in the kind of conclusion an essentially nondialectical frame of ethical reference would dictate: namely, that in falling in love Musidorus and Pyrocles abandon virtuous reason for sinful passion. In sympathy with these critics is David Kalstone, *Sidney's Poetry: Contexts and Interpretations* (Cambridge: Harvard University Press, 1965), p. 41–42.

8 Mark Rose, "Sidney's Womanish Man," p. 356, cites Barnaby Rich and Robert Burton for the belief that love turns a man effeminate.

9 On sources of androgyny in the new *Arcadia*, see Thelma N. Greenfield, *The Eye of Judgment: Reading the "New Arcadia"* (Lewisburg, Pa.: Bucknell University Press, 1982), pp. 60ff. Myron Turner, "The Heroic Ideal in

Sidney's Revised *Arcadia*," *Studies in English Literature* 10 (1970): 63–82, cites Pico della Mirandola on the derivation of Harmony from the union of Mars and Venus, and asserts that Sidney establishes "the necessity of a balance between the pride of the hero and the humility of the lover." Similarly, Elizabeth Dipple, "Metamorphoses in Sidney's *Arcadia*," p. 52, argues that the two heroes make a salutary discovery of an inner life when they enter Arcadia. Dorothy Connell, *Sir Philip Sidney: The Maker's Mind* (Oxford: Oxford University Press, 1977), finds the Arcadian experience a transition from well-knowing only to well-doing (p. 38). Finally, John F. Danby, *Poets on Fortune's Hill* (London: Faber and Faber, 1952), p. 56, says that "in Pyrocles [Sidney] would seem to be insisting that man is capable of a synthesis of qualities that includes the womanly yet avoids the hermaphroditic. The merely masculine prowess Musidorus argues for is a lesser thing than this: as Musidorus discovers when he in his turn submits to love in the person of Pamela—Basilius' elder daughter."

10 And those few who have noticed the importance of the predictions have not developed the point very far. The most significant statement on this matter remains S. L. Wolff's in *The Greek Romances in Elizabethan Prose Fiction* (New York: Columbia University Press, 1912), p. 321: "In fact, the fulfillment of the oracle is, as it were, a punishment inflicted upon Basilius for consulting an oracle at all. For the prediction is fulfilled by the very course that he takes to prevent its fulfillment. Had he remained at court, and allowed princely suitors access to his daughters, the one would not have needed to be 'by princely meane . . . stolne'; the other would not have embraced an apparently unnatural love, for Pyrocles would not have needed to disguise himself as a woman in order to court her [Philoclea]; and for the same reason there would have been no Zelmane for Basilius to fall in love with, and hence no rendezvous, no *quid-pro-quo*, no adultery, no potion, no apparent death of the King, and no trial of the princes at his bier." And, I might add, no *Arcadia*: Wolff inadvertently touches on the main point of my argument in this section, namely, that the oracular prediction is the fore-conceit of the Arcadian main plot, which comes about primarily through being resisted. Jean Robertson in the introduction to the Oxford edition of the old *Arcadia*, p. xxxiv, cites a remark by M. M. Lascelles to the effect that "the point of these stories [the main plot] seems to be that it is a man's efforts to avert his fate which fasten it upon him." Jon S. Lawry, Sidney's *Two "Arcadias": Pattern and Proceeding* (Ithaca, N.Y.: Cornell University Press, 1972), pp. 34, 35, notes that "all of [the prediction's] elements are golden and reasonable. They will reunite the king and queen, bring noble young princes and prin-

cesses together in marriage, and introduce the Macedonian monarch to Arcadia in a visit of alliance. It is only the 'fatal' attempt to bind or thwart the course of reason and governed nature that creates a painful deviant progress for those elements. . . . As human reason and divine providence together supply the foreconceit of the *Old Arcadia*, they also bring about the last golden laugh."

11 Duncan-Jones and Van Dorsten, eds., *Miscellaneous Prose*, p. 79.

12 Michael McCanles, "Mythos and Dianoia: A Dialectical Methodology of Literary Form," *Literary Monographs 4*, ed. Eric Rothstein (Madison: University of Wisconsin Press, 1971), pp. 4–5; and Michael McCanles, *Dialectical Criticism and Renaissance Literature* (Berkeley: University of California Press, 1975), pp. 216–27.

13 See in this connection Michael McCanles, "The Literal and the Metaphorical: Dialectic or Interchange," *PMLA* 91 (1976): 279–90.

14 *A Defence of Poetry*, in *Miscellaneous Prose*, p. 108. See in this connection, Kenneth Myrick, *Sir Philip Sidney as a Literary Craftsman* (Lincoln: University of Nebraska Press, 1965; orig. pub. 1935), p. 120; Marcus Goldman, "Sidney and Harington as Opponents of Superstition," *Journal of English and Germanic Philology* 54 (1955): 526–48; and Weiner, *The Poetics of Protestantism*, p. 56.

15 William A. Ringler, Jr., says (*The Poems of Sir Philip Sidney* [Oxford: Clarendon Press, 1962]) that the Delphic oracle revised for the new *Arcadia* indicates "a different denouement for the revised version of his story" (p. 372), i.e., different from that for the old *Arcadia*. In addition, he says that these changes "indicate that Pyrocles and Musidorus marry Philoclea and Pamela before their trial, and that the main point at issue in the trial is that they are accused of responsibility for the supposed death of Basilius rather than of violence toward the princesses" (p. 383). There is no basis for the first supposition regarding wedding's putatively preceding the trial. As for the second, one can only note that the main difference between old *Arcadia* and new *Arcadia* versions of the oracle is that the latter is more specific while including everything mentioned in the former. The added lines are the following:

> Both they themselves unto such two shall wed,
> Who at thy bier, as at a bar, shall plead
> Why thee (a living man) they had made dead.

This reference to a courtroom bar consisting of the bier on which Basilius's body lies is already present in the old *Arcadia* ("having only for their bar the table on which the duke's body lay," Robertson, p. 379), and this addition to the new *Arcadia* oracle merely foreshadows this text in the 1593 version. In addition, the elopement is just as surely predicted in the new *Arcadia* version as it is in the original version. In short, the two versions of the oracle predict the same conclusion, that given in old *Arcadia* Books 3–5.

16 The editor of recent Oxford edition of the new *Arcadia*, Victor Skret- kowicz, in an article, "Building Sidney's Reputation: Texts and Editors of the *Arcadia*," *Sir Philip Sidney: 1586 and the Creation of a Legend*, ed. Jan Van Dorsten, Dominic Baker-Smith, and Arthur F. Kinney (Leiden: E. J. Brill/Leiden University Press, 1986), pp. 111–24, says the following: "The manuscript that Greville received from Sidney . . . contained virtu- ally all of Sidney's work on the *Arcadia*. In composing the *'new' Arcadia*, Sidney reworked a complete copy of the *'old' Arcadia*, altering and add- ing words, phrases, and sentences, and writing in whole new passages of which the more lengthy were interleaved into that manuscript. Com- parison between the appendix to the *'new' Arcadia* [i.e., the old *Arcadia* ending grafted onto the new *Arcadia*] which was printed in [15]93 and the manuscripts of the *'old' Arcadia* reveals that excisions from the early form of the text correspond to materials adapted by the author either for the *'new' Arcadia* or elsewhere in the appendix itself. It therefore becomes clear that while writing the *'new' Arcadia* Sidney was using the same manuscript that was later to become printer's copy for the appendix in 93" (pp. 116–17). Later he says that "it is evident that Sidney himself was responsible for the alternation of the Third, Fourth, and Last Books of the *'old' Arcadia* during the process of revising and developing the nar- rative" (p. 121). These conclusions indicate that the latest editor of the *Arcadia* holds that Sidney clearly intended to conclude the *Arcadia* with the old *Arcadia* ending. However, Skretkowicz's statements here appear to conflict with those in his edition; see Appendix at the end of this book.

17 Ringler, *Poems of Sir Philip Sidney*, pp. 369ff.

18 Skretkowicz agrees with the substance of Robertson's arguments for this dating: "By 1584 those revisions which constitute the *New Arcadia* were substantially completed"; ". . . Sidney might have begun composition as early as 1582 and continued into 1584" (p. xlv). Skretkowicz disagrees with Ringler and Robertson on the extant manuscripts of the old *Arcadia* as representatives of Sidney's ongoing revisions climaxing with the com- position of the new *Arcadia*. He finds these to be copies of Sidney's own foul papers, rather than of scribal transcripts (pp. lxii and following).

19 Ringler, *Poems of Sir Philip Sidney*, p. 530.

20 Skretkowicz, p. lvii.

21 Ringler, *Poems of Sir Philip Sidney*, p. 364.

22 (London: Everyman's Library, n.d.), 2: 5.

23 Skretkowicz ("Building Sidney's Reputation") calls Florio's statement a "quibble" (p. 123) yet in the same article refuses to accept "literary unity in the 1593 text" (pp. 118–19).

24 Maurice Evans reprints Alexander's addition in his edition of the 1593 composite *Arcadia* (Harmondsworth: Penguin Books, 1977), pp. 595–625.

25 This narrower interpretation is supported by the editorial preface inserted before the old *Arcadia* Book 3 in the 1593 version: "How this combate ended, how the Ladies by the comming of the discovered forces were delivered, and restored to *Basilius*, and how *Dorus* againe returned to his old Master *Damaetas*, is altogether unknowne. What afterward chaunced, out of the Authors own writings and conceits hath bene supplied, as foloweth" (Feuillerat, 2: 218).

26 Ringler, for instance, speaks of "two different versions of the story" in the 1593 new *Arcadia* (*Poems of Sir Philip Sidney*, p. 379). But this is not accurate. What the 1593 version includes are two different stages of composition respectively for two halves of the same story.

27 The editors of the 1590 new *Arcadia* indicate their belief that the eclogues of the old *Arcadia* were intended by Sidney for the new as well. In the absence of clear authorial directions, the eclogues "have bene chosen and disposed as the over-seer thought best" (Feuillerat, 1: 4). As Ringler (*Poems of Sir Philip Sidney*, p. 372) indicates, the 1590 editors took over the eclogues from a late manuscript of the old *Arcadia*, and the editors of the 1593 version produced their own idiosyncratic arrangement (ibid., p. 378). The Cambridge MS of the new *Arcadia*, which derives either indirectly (ibid., p. 380) or directly (Skretkowicz, pp. lxv–lxviii) from Sidney's foul papers for recomposing the new *Arcadia*, contains no eclogues. Skretkowicz concludes: "But as the prose [in 1590] was stitched together and considerably altered by the editor, it must be regarded as the composition of that editor, with its genesis in A[5] but with no textual tradition behind it. The equally unauthorized version of the Eclogues in 93 has no claim to be further associated with the *New Arcadia*." (p. lxxx) Because of uncertainty as to the disposition Sidney intended for the eclogues in the new *Arcadia*, I have chosen to ignore these poems for the purposes of my analysis.

28 Joel B. Altman, *The Tudor Play of Mind: Rhetorical Inquiry and the Development of Elizabethan Drama* (Berkeley: University of California Press, 1978), pp. 8ff., envisions the *Arcadia* as a narrative extension of the

debate or dialogue form, the subject of which is precisely the active life of heroic endeavor versus retirement and the life of eros. Cf. also Humphrey Tonkin, *Spenser's Courteous Pastoral: Book Six of the "Faerie Queene"* (Oxford: Clarendon Press, 1972), pp. 18–20 and passim, which argues Spenser's similar attempt at reconciling the opposed agendas of chivalric romance and pastoral romance.

29 Rosalie L. Colie, *The Resources of Kind: Genre-Theory in the Renaissance*, ed. Barbara K. Lewalski (Berkeley: University of California Press, 1973), p. 115.

30 Bernard Weinberg, *A History of Literary Criticism in the Italian Renaissance*, 2 vols. (Chicago: University of Chicago Press, 1961), 1:93–94.

31 Colie, *Resources of Kind*, p. 28.

32 Davis ("A Map of Arcadia," pp. 164ff.) gives an extensive analysis of the differing versions of the princes' activities offered by Philanax, Pyrocles, and Musidorus, respectively.

33 Lawry (*Sidney's Two "Arcadias,"* pp. 201–202) foreshadows some of my argument here when he says that Musidorus's tale of himself "raises the question not only of the relationship of a fictive to an actual Cyrus, but also of the relationship of both to the 'essential' Musidorus. . . . The two lovers [Musidorus and Pamela] thus melt in and out of fiction and reality like Penelope and Odysseus at the close of the *Odyssey*. . . . As for [Musidorus], he acknowledges that he had once played 'well the part of a king in a tragedy at Athens.' He may now prove to have a prince's heart hid in a player's hide, even as, in repeating the role for Pamela, he had come almost to play himself while ostensibly playing a shepherd who was playing a prince."

34 Musidorus's poem is an example of the "paradoxical encomium," an ancient genre revived and much imitated in the Renaissance. See Henry Knight Miller, "The Paradoxical Encomium with Special Reference to Its Vogue in England, 1600–1800," *Modern Philology* 53 (1956): 145–78. As such, the poem would normally be discounted by the reader, since the paradoxical element in it invites recuperation as an example of what Wayne C. Booth called "stable irony," i.e., irony that allows praise to be read as dispraise; Wayne C. Booth, *A Rhetoric of Irony* (Chicago: University of Chicago Press, 1974), pp. 3ff. See also A. E. Malloch, "The Techniques and Function of the Renaissance Paradox," *Studies in Philology* 53 (1956): 191–203; Rosalie L. Colie, *Paradoxia Epidemica: The Renaissance Tradition of Paradox* (Princeton: Princeton University Press, 1966); and Walter Kaiser, *Praisers of Folly: Erasmus, Rabelais, Shakespeare* (Cambridge: Harvard University Press, 1963).

35 Richard A. Lanham, "Astrophil and Stella: Pure and Impure Persuasion," *ELR: English Literary Renaissance* 2 (1972): 100–15: "Great critics have disputed whether *Astrophil and Stella* tells a story, and if so what kind. This is a nonproblem. The work chronicles a series of attempts to persuade. This is a narrative of a sort, but of a peculiarly rhetorical sort" (p. 110). Stillman, *Sidney's Poetic Justice*, p. 191, links Musidorus's tale with this sonnet.

36 The complex message Sidney conveys through the princes' disguises is not exhausted either by saying, as does Margaret E. Dana, "Heroic and Pastoral: Sidney's *Arcadia* as Masquerade," that these disguises result from deliberate choice; or by Elizabeth Dipple's opposite contention in "Metamorphoses in Sidney's *Arcadia*" that the princes' disguises reflect real inner transformations. The fact of the matter seems to include both positions and then some. Clearly, a change of inner thought and emotions is undergone, and just as clearly the princes consciously take on their disguises. The important point, from the perspective of my argument, is that both inner changes and outward disguises (which ironically reflect these changes) are undergone unwillingly as something both princes are unprepared for, and are consequently vulnerable to. Total commitment to epic heroism is the dialectical cause of its opposite, pastoral eroticism. And this dialectic is registered in a division between inner (heroic) reality and outward (erotic) disguise, where the division itself with further scrutiny fades momentarily into a true harmony: what they show themselves to be, they really are. Because thrust unwillingly into love, the princes remain convinced that they are "merely disguised"; but because truly in love, they are not disguised at all. Ultimately, Sidney's purpose is to exhibit the princes' willing the necessary: consciously choosing the fusion of the heroic and the erotic, the initial refusal of which has thrust them into their present plight.

37 Skretkowicz modernizes this spelling, thereby eliding the double entendre implicit in the original.

38 Boris Uspensky, *A Poetics of Composition*, trans. Valentina Zavarin and Susan Wittig (Berkeley: University of California Press, 1973), pp. 18ff., distinguishes the various viewpoints registered by the different names that may be given the same character. For instance, formal names register the neutral perspective of an outsider, while nicknames register more intimacy. Regarding the pronouns assigned Pyrocles, it is difficult to tell how much of the ambiguities flowing from this assignment Sidney consciously controlled. There is, for instance, the apparently random oscillation back to male pronouns in new *Arcadia* Book 3, pp. 428, line 22

to p. 439, line 4, that interrupts the otherwise consistent use of female forms up to this point. We may arrive at the following, derived from a matrix of possible viewpoints registered by assigning these female forms: "she" and "her" registers two more or less incompatible viewpoints: (1) that taken by Pyrocles, Musidorus, Gynecia, and Philoclea, who are all cognizant of his biological maleness, as it were, and superimpose on this the consciousness of disguise; (2) that taken by the implied author himself, who assigns feminine forms to Pyrocles because the latter has, in some nonbiological sense, become truly effeminate. These viewpoints are incompatible because the first assumes that Pyrocles is "really" a male, while the second sees him as "female." I would suggest that Sidney counts on the reader's inability to assign either one of these viewpoints to the pronoun forms unequivocally to keep the reader aware of the larger issue of heroism versus eroticism.

39 Clearly, Euarchus, Musidorus, and Pyrocles have been reading *A Defence of Poetry*, where Sidney argues that "heroical" poetry, in which "as the image of each action stirreth and instructeth the mind, so the lofty image of such worthies most inflameth the mind with desire to be worthy, and informs with counsel how to be worthy"; *Miscellaneous Prose*, p. 98. In the perspective of my argument the plight of Musidorus and Pyrocles results ironically from their taking, as it were, Sidney's advice literally and conforming their lives to the conventions of various traditional genres, of which heroic poetry is one among several. A case can be made that the new *Arcadia*, composed presumably after the *Defence*, replicates the latter's argument for the moral effects on readers of reading heroic poetry, since Xenophon bestowed "a Cyrus upon the world" in order "to make many Cyruses"; ibid., p. 79. The new *Arcadia* thus would double the rhetorical effects of reading itself: not only providing the reader with images of heroic action to imitate, but imitating within itself the process of *mimesis*, whereby the two heroes become such because they have in turn imitated texts of classical and romance epics.

40 Jacques Derrida, *Speech and Phenomena, and Other Essays on Husserl's Theory of Signs*, trans. David B. Allison (Evanston, Ill.: Northwestern University Press, 1973), relates on the theoretical level the interplay between the differences that constitute meaning in a text, and the fact that the text in selecting some terms and rejecting others only defers the latter. Consequently *différence* is for him (as for Sidney) *différance* (deferral). See particularly the essay "Différance," pp. 129–60. Derrida's notion of textuality constituted from "difference deferred," like Jacques Lacan's textualization of Freud's repressed unconscious ("The Language of the Self")

both supply illuminating theoretical analogues to the global unfolding of Sidney's new *Arcadia*. For Lacan, the repressed equals the text of the Other, i.e., what I would call the countertext, which is made up of that text rejected by the conscious text of the Self. Mental health would correspond in Lacan's coordinates to Sidney's ideal textual wholeness, in which the diverse modes of human reality—a diversity articulated and confirmed by Renaissance theories of genre and style—are finally harmonized. For Sidney, Derrida, and Lacan alike—leaving aside the obvious differences—the fissures suffered by the human personality as the result of repressing parts of itself are distorted signs of health. And for all three the return of the repressed is both disruptive and potentially healing.

41 This point was noted by Nancy R. Lindheim, "Sidney's *Arcadia*, Book II: Retrospective Narrative," *Studies in Philology* 64 (1967): 167.

42 See Walter R. Davis, "Thematic Unity in the *New Arcadia*" *Studies in Philology* 57 (1960): 123–43; Arthur K. Amos, *Time, Space, and Value: The Narrative Structure of the New Arcadia* (Lewisburg, Pa.: Bucknell University Press, 1977), pp. 17–18.

43 In one of the major new passages found in the old *Arcadia* section of the 1593 composite (Book 5) that seem to be authorial, Sidney expands the account of Euarchus's travels preceding his coming to Arcadia. During part of this time he "was gone with some haste to visit that coast of his country that lay towards Italy: the occasion given by the Latins who, having already gotten into their hands, partly by conquest and partly by confederacy, the greatest part of Italy, and long gaped to devour Greece also (observing the present opportunity of Euarchus's absence and Basilius's solitariness), . . . were even ready to lay an unjust gripe upon it, which after they might beautify with the noble name of conquest" (Robertson, p. 355). Rome turned its attention toward Greece after Philip V of Macedon concluded a treaty in 215 B.C. with Hannibal, promising to aid Carthage against Rome in the second Punic War (*The Histories of Polybius*, trans. Evelyn S. Schuckburgh, 2 vols. [Bloomington: Indiana University Press, 1962], 1: 515). After Hannibal's defeat, Rome moved into Greece during the second century B.C. Although Sidney's account of the growing friction between Greece and Rome is of course wholly fictional, it is not inappropriate to point out that this particular passage would appear to localize the action of the new *Arcadia* some time during the last decade of the third and first decade of the second centuries B.C. On Sidney's treatment of the geography of the new *Arcadia*, see Peter Lindenbaum, "The Geography of Sidney's *Arcadia*," *Philological Quarterly* 63 (Fall 1984): 524–31.

44 Walter Davis's summary of sources in "A Map of Arcadia," pp. 46ff., is most useful. Major sources whether of specific incidents or of generic conventions include *Amadis of Gaul* and *Morte d'Arthur* among chivalric romances; Sannazaro's *Arcadia*, Montemayor's *Diana*, and Gil Polo's *Diana enamorada*, the sources of pastoral romance; and Heliodorus's *Aethiopian History* among late Hellenistic romances. Freda Townsend, "Sidney and Ariosto," *PMLA* 61 (1946): 97–108. The Roman comedy parallels are dealt with by Clark L. Chalifour, "Sir Philip Sidney's *Old Arcadia* as Terentian Comedy," *Studies in English Literature* 16 (1976): 51–63, and Robert W. Parker, "Terentian Structure and Sidney's Original *Arcadia*," *English Literary Renaissance* 2 (1972): 61–78.

45 See Berger's introduction and his essay "The Mutabilitie Cantos: Archaism and Evolution in Retrospect," pp. 146–76, in his edition of the Spectrum book volume *Spenser: A Collection of Critical Essays* (Englewood Cliffs, N.J.: Prentice-Hall, 1968). The similarities between the *Arcadia* and *The Faerie Queene* on the basis of my present discussion are suggestive. For instance, Isabel G. MacCaffrey in *Spenser's Allegory: The Anatomy of Imagination* (Princeton: Princeton University Press, 1976), aptly sums up Berger's argument in calling *The Faerie Queene* a "history of imagining" and asserts that "the collective mind of Renaissance Europe" is "figured in" the poem (pp. 72–73), so much so that "Fairy Land 'is' the human imagination itself, hospitable to solicitations from the world without and the world within" (p. 74). For this reason she sees *The Faerie Queene* inviting contemplation of the textual materials out of which it is composed: "The poem looks at itself and offers an eloquent argument for its own existence, commenting in the process upon how metaphors work, what is implied by various metaphorical and iconographical strategies, and how far we may trust the basic medium, language. It is often said that self-referring fictions are peculiar products of the introspective 'modern mind.' But modernity and self-consciousness are themselves recurrent historical phenomena" (pp. 9–10). James Nohrnberg, *The Analogy of the Faerie Queene* (Princeton: Princeton University Press, 1976), p. 758, similarly notes this self-reflexive dimension in Spenser's poem.

46 In this respect Sidney is remarkably like a seventeenth-century poet who was similarly fascinated with the interplay among the texts in which men have successively constructed their visions of pastoral retreat: Andrew Marvell. In some passages from *"My Ecchoing Song": Andrew Marvell's Poetry of Criticism* (Princeton: Princeton University Press, 1970), to which my present argument is indebted, Rosalie L. Colie says of Marvell's practice in "The Garden" (and in general): "[The poet assesses] in terms of his

craft, the aesthetic, moral, and spiritual possibilities of his civilization, which he has here [in "The Garden"] chosen to perceive and to present in generic literary forms. . . . the poem . . . [points] toward metaphysical and ontological meanings of which it is both indicator and screen. It points at these meanings as if to things outside itself, but it points inwards as well to those same meanings, not as symbolized by poetic elements, but as contained within the whole poem. This poem, like others but more than most, is container and thing contained, a container mirroring what is outside itself also" (p. 173). Colie here, as in her later *Resources of Kind*, comes very close to asserting the identity of human reality and the textualizations of that reality arising out of human capacity to create elaborate sign systems, which is argued by some versions of contemporary structuralism and by contemporary semiotics. For example, Julia Kristeva, *SĒMEIŌTIKĒ: Recherches pour une sémanalyse* (Paris: Éditions du Seuil, 1969), p. 146 (my translation): "every text is constructed as a mosaic of citations, every text is the absorption and transformation of another text. In place of the notion of intersubjectivity is inserted that of *intertextuality*, and poetic language is read, at least, as *double*. Thus the regulation of the word as the minimal unit of the text is confirmed as being the *mediator* which connects the structural model to the cultural environment (historical), just as [it is] the *regulator* of the change of diachrony into synchrony (in literary structure). By the same notion of regulation, the word is localized in space: it functions in three dimensions (subject-receiver-context) as an ensemble of semic elements *in dialogue* or as an ensemble of *ambivalent* elements. Consequently the task of literary semiotics will be to find the formalisms corresponding to the different types of function of words (or sequences) in the dialogical space of texts." A major desideratum, mutually beneficial to both contemporary structuralist and Renaissance studies, is an analysis of the historical links between the two.

47 A. C. Hamilton, "Sidney's *Arcadia* as Prose Fiction: Its Relation to Its Sources," *ELR: English Literary Renaissance* 2 (1972): 47, suggests as much without developing the idea: "The trial scene has revealed the potentialities of the heroic form beneath the trappings of pastoral romance and so forced an extended revision of the entire work."

48 Robert W. Parker, "Terentian Structure and Sidney's Original *Arcadia*," pp. 72ff., argues that Sidney took over the relatively loose plot organization of the Hellenic romance and imposed on it the tight relation between cause and effect indigenous to the plots of Roman comedies and their Renaissance imitations.

49 Although she believes that the two oracular predictions in the 1590 new *Arcadia* indicate Sidney's intention to conclude this version with at least some of the old *Arcadia* Books 3–5 (*The Structures of Sidney's "Arcadia"* [Toronto: University of Toronto Press, 1982], pp. 132ff.), Nancy Lindheim feels it necessary to pick and choose those episodes from the old *Arcadia* that are consistent with the new. While an advance over her previous position (in "Vision, Revision, and the 1593 Text of the *Arcadia*," *ELR: English Literary Renaissance* 2 (1972): 136–47, where she argues in a traditional manner the latter's total unsuitability), this argument remains open to question. Most important, such a position fails to grasp how the comic intrigues of old *Arcadia* Books 3–4 form a total unit and are not amenable to modular adjustments. From the perspective of my own argument, Lindheim fails also to note the complex parallels between the abductions and rescues of new *Arcadia* Book 3 and old *Arcadia* Books 3–5, parallels that go far to obviate her belief that the two are incompatible (Lindheim, *The Structures*, p. 132).

50 The 1593 version contains as an addition to Musidorus's speech the following sentence, which may or may not be authorial: "I omit our services done to Basilius in the late war with Amphialus, importing no less than his daughters' lives and his state's preservation" (Robertson, pp. 400–401). It is possible that this is not authorial, if only because Sidney probably intended to develop the ironic parallels between the Amphialus episode and the princes' own intrigue rather extensively. As it is, we have with certainty only the old *Arcadia* version, which of course contains no reference to that episode.

51 Much recent work on the *Arcadia* focuses on its political dimension. Topics include discussion of Basilius's failure as a political leader and the possible implications of the *Arcadia* for Sidney's own position vis-à-vis the political discussions and broils of his own time. Relevant in this connection are Annabel M. Patterson, " 'Under . . . Pretty Tales': Intention in Sidney's *Arcadia*," and Alan Sinfield, "Power and Ideology: An Outline Theory and Sidney's *Arcadia*," both reprinted in Arthur F. Kinney, ed., *Essential Articles for the Study of Sir Philip Sidney* (Hamden, Conn.: Archon Books, 1986), pp. 357–75 and 392–410, respectively. Kinney, *Humanist Poetics*, p. 261, cites Greville's life of Sidney to the effect that Sidney's interest in the new *Arcadia* is primarily political. Most uncompromising on this score is Martin N. Raitiere, *Faire Bitts: Sir Philip Sidney and Renaissance Political Theory* (Pittsburgh: Duquesne University Press, 1984), p. 11: "From the first page of the first version—the so-called *Old Arcadia*—the plot centers on Basilius, king of Arcadia, demonstrating the mischance

that results from his acting or rather not acting as a king must." My own approach in this book has nevertheless subordinated the very real if sporadically developed political dimensions of the new *Arcadia* to what I take to be its central concerns with heroic and erotic experiences and their interrelations. I agree with Thelma Greenfield, without accepting her limiting qualification regarding the putative focus on Philoclea, when she says that "the statecraft and warfare take place within love instead of beside it, further justifying the loved Urania as the Arcadia muse"; *The Eye of Judgment*, p. 110. Attempts to by-pass the issue of the active and the contemplative lives in the various dimensions developed in this study seem to me to apply Stillman's reaction to Pyrocles' defense at the trial—"Pyrocles' emphasis upon the love plot trivializes *The Old Arcadia*" (*Sidney's Poetic Justice*, p. 221)—to the whole work. That both new and old *Arcadia*s focus on the dialectics of heroism and eroticism seems to me prima facie, the only question being the most important of all: what sense to make of this focus? The present study is my answer to this question. It should be noted that Sidney himself provides an interpretation of the main plot that gives it a significant political twist, and a sinister one at that: Philanax's indictment of the two princes at the trial in old *Arcadia* Book 5. And Sidney's critique of this interpretation I discuss in section five.

52 On the divided reactions elicited from the reader by these matters, see Ann W. Astell, "Sidney's Didactic Method in the *Old Arcadia*," *Studies in English Literature* 24 (1984): 39–51.

53 I agree with Elizabeth Dipple in " 'Unjust Justice' in the *Old Arcadia*," *Studies in English Literature* 10 (1970): 83–101, when she calls attention to the incompleteness of Philanax's and Euarchus's knowledge of the facts and consequently of their judgments, and when she says "Sidney forces his reader into a dual realization—that the two princes are both virtuous and guilty, to be both rewarded and punished" (p. 93). I part company when she insists (pp. 97–98) on the simple irrelevance of Philanax's reading of the two princes' actions. Her insistence that the moral vision presented to the reader is "complex, subtle, and dizzily upsetting; the response forced from the reader defies any diagrammatical 'Renaissance' preconceptions" (p. 86) is directed at interpretations such as Davis ("A Map of Arcadia"), Lawry (*Sidney's Two "Arcadias"*), and Weiner (*The Poetics of Protestantism*), all of whom impose on the *Arcadia* various ethical schemata drawn from historical context that lead to the conclusion that Philanax and Euarchus are unequivocally correct in their charges and judgments.

54 William A. Ringler, Jr., in his edition of *The Poems of Sir Philip Sidney*, pp. 378–79, argues that Sidney discovered an anomaly in the old *Arcadia* when Basilius awakens and forgives the princes for crimes for which they were justly (to the reader's view) judged and condemned by Euarchus. Among these are the charges of attempting to rape the two princesses and abduction. For Basilius to abrogate the punishments for these crimes when the reader has actually seen them committed was, Ringler says, for Sidney to "completely undercut the heroic adherence of Euarchus to 'sacred Rightfullnes,' for the princes escape punishment, not by any revelation of a change in the nature of their offence, but by coming before a less impartial and less idealistic judge," i.e., Basilius. For this reason Sidney (1) removed sexual elements from the scenes between Philoclea and Pyrocles, and between Pamela and Musidorus in the forest; (2) changed the oracle to predict only the death of Basilius, so that the princes' condemnation for regicide would be obviously abrogated when Basilius revived. Ringler goes on: "But he [Sidney] must have realized that this would not solve the essential difficulty, for the princes would still be guilty of the crime of abduction." And Ringler concludes that Sidney probably intended to remove this charge as well but never lived to do so.

55 Northrop Frye, "The Argument of Comedy," reprinted in *Shakespeare: Modern Essays in Criticism*, ed. Leonard F. Dean (New York: Oxford University Press, 1967), pp. 79–89.

56 Stanley Cavell, "Pursuits of Happiness: A Reading of *The Lady Eve*," *New Literary History* 10 (1979): 587.

57 Northrop Frye, *A Natural Perspective: The Development of Shakespearean Comedy and Romance* (New York: Columbia University Press, 1965), p. 128.

Note to the Appendix

1 In n. 16 to Part Two, I cite Skretkowicz's apparent belief that Sidney intended the old *Arcadia* ending to conclude the new. He goes on to say ("Building Sidney's Reputation: Texts and Editors of the *Arcadia*," in *Sir Philip Sidney: 1586 and the Creation of a Legend*, ed. Jan Van Dorsten, Dominic Baker-Smith, and Arthur F. Kinney [Leiden: E. J. Brill/Leiden University Press, 1986], pp. 118–19) that "such a theory of the text . . . does not argue for literary unity in the 1593 text: far from it. Quite evidently the text printed in 1590 contained only that part of the manuscript which Greville saw had been thoroughly worked up into a coherent and

almost completed fragment, while the edition of 1593 reprinted with only minor adjustments that published in 1590, and added that substantial unpublished remnant of the manuscript which had undergone only a minimum of revision and obviously required a great deal more attention before it could be considered as belonging to this new version of the *Arcadia*." In this article Skretkowicz's position appears to be that Sidney intended to conclude the new *Arcadia* with the old *Arcadia* ending, and that the lack of unity between the two segments was due to Sidney's failure to revise the second one. In his edition of the new *Arcadia*, however, he states that Sidney did not intend to return to the old *Arcadia* ending.

Index

A former Guggenheim Fellow, Michael McCanles is
professor of English, Marquette University. He is the author of
Dialectical Criticism and Renaissance Literature and
The Discourse of "Il Principe."